Connecting Worlds

a memoir on art,
anthropology and activism

Connecting Worlds

a memoir on art, anthropology and activism

DANIEL BUCKLES

Buckles, Daniel. *Connecting Worlds: art, anthropology and activism.* Ottawa, Canada: Self-published, 2023.

ISBN (softcover) 978-1-7389664-0-0
ISBN (epub) 978-1-7389664-1-7
ISBN (PDF) 978-1-7389664-2-4

Published in Canada.

Cover design by Magdalene Carson, after a painting by Daniel Buckles.
Design and composition: Magdalene Carson, New Leaf Publication Design

All images by Daniel Buckles, unless otherwise noted.

Permission granted to use poem by Kusan Sunim, from *The Way of Korean Zen*, 2013, translated by Martine Batchelor, Weatherhill/Shambhala Publications.

For my first grandchild, Theo.
Never give up on the people and causes you believe in.
And remember the McRae clan motto: *Fortitudine.*

In loving memory of my parents,
Doreen (O'Grady) Ryan and Robert (McRae) Buckles.

Contents

Selected Works by Daniel Buckles

1993. *Gorras y sombreros: Caminos hacia la colaboración entre técnicos y campesinos*. D. Buckles (ed.), CIMMYT, Mexico.

1995. *A Land Without Gods: Process Theory, Maldevelopment and the Gulf Nahuas,* with J. Chevalier, Zed Books/Fernwood Books, London/Halifax.

1995. "Velvet bean: A 'New' Plant with a History," *Economic Botany,* 49:13-25.

1997. *La Reserva Especial de la Biósfera Sierra de Santa Marta: Diagnóstico y perspectiva,* with L. Paré et al. UNAM, México City.

1998. *Cover Crops in Hillside Agriculture: Farmer Innovation with Mucuna,* with B. Triomphe and G. Sain, CIMMYT/IDRC, Mexico City/Ottawa.

1999. *Cover Crops in West Africa: Contributing to Sustainable Agriculture.* D. Buckles, A. Eteka, O. Osiname, M. Galiba and G. Galiano (eds.), IDRC/IITA/Sasakawa Global 2000, Ottawa/Cotonou.

1999. *Cultivating Peace: Conflict and Collaboration in Natural Resource Management.* D. Buckles (ed.), The World Bank/IDRC, Washington D.C./Ottawa.

2007. *Food Sovereignty and Uncultivated Biodiversity in South Asia: Essays on the poverty of food policy and wealth of the social landscape,* with F. Mazhar, P.V. Satheesh, and F. Akhter. Academic Foundation/IDRC, New Delhi/Ottawa.

2008. *A Guide to Collaborative Inquiry and Social Engagement,* with J. Chevalier, SAGE Publications/IDRC, New Delhi/Ottawa.

2013. *Fighting Eviction: Katkari Land Rights and Research-in-Action,* with R. Khedkar, Cambridge University Press, New Delhi.

2014. *Tobacco Control and Tobacco Farming: Separating myth from reality.* W. Leppan, N. Lecours and D. Buckles (eds.), Anthem Press, London, UK.

2019 (Second Edition). *Participatory Action Research: Theory and Methods for Engaged Inquiry,* with J. Chevalier, Routledge, London.

PROLOGUE

< Warbler and pine needles, Temagami.

Prologue

I'm a *Star Trek* fan. For a decade Jean Luc Picard and Captain Janeway entertained and even inspired my wife and me as we started a family in the early 1990s. Later, like many people deeply concerned about human impacts on the Earth, we found solace in the idea that there might be an abundance of strange new worlds and new civilizations out there at least as interesting as ours, and hopefully wiser. We began to think that extinction of the human race might not be such a bad thing. The rest of nature would survive and possibly thrive. The scenario struck fear into our hearts as we talked about the future for our children and children's children, but also a sense of appropriateness. Extinction is a fate the human species may very well deserve.

My perspective shifted when, during the start of the COVID-19 pandemic, I read The Precipice by the English philosopher Toby Ord. His analysis of the various risks of imminent human extinction starts on a positive note, pointing to the vast expanse of time available to future generations of humanity. From what is known about the habitable lifetime of the Earth, *Homo sapiens*, a complex life form still in relative infancy, has hundreds of millions of years to get its act together, if only we don't fall off the precipice in the next 100 years. Even deeper time is possible if, somehow, we manage to go beyond our planet into the solar system and beyond. A human future on this canvas gives hope that coming generations will not only end war, poverty, nativism, injustice and disease but also truly learn to live with the rest of nature everywhere. The aggressive divisions that have marred our existence as a species, all false choices in light of our shared humanity, might fall away.

At this time scale, beyond self and kin, the stakes underlying our collective suicide seem very high to me, and the reasons to shake ourselves out of eco-despair and apathy very powerful. They prompt me to ask, besides my body and my pocketbook, what more can I offer? How can I dig deeper into myself and the challenges of the present moment?

My answer to these questions is, of course, a work in progress. I started my adult life in the 1970s Yukon as an earnest young man pursuing an artist's life. Through paintings of people in the landscape and drawings of the contours of the human body, I tried to feel the world through the senses of sight and touch. Friends guided me in the ethics of a bush lifestyle: living simply, self-provisioning what you can and providing aid to others as needed. The land connected me to rock and river even more deeply than earlier time spent in Ontario's cottage country where, as a boy, I had learned to canoe, pitch a tent and build a fire.

I eventually left the Yukon, first for Mexico and then to pursue graduate studies in anthropology. Savouring the world gave way to efforts to save it, inspired by experiences of wilderness and solidarity in the Canadian North and the culture and political art of Mexico. I was moved by the simple truth that we cannot live for ourselves alone.

Then something unexpected happened. At age 32, just before graduating with a PhD, I faced an existential threat from cancer. Melanoma had metastasized to my liver and the doctors believed that I had only months to live. I struggled with the shock, withdrawing into my fear and pending loss. Within a few weeks, however, I had a dream that created a hinge on which my life and healing turned decisively. My desire to touch and be touched, to do and to be, merged into one. I decided to bring my whole self into the task of healing, connecting intense meditation on nature—sunlight, wind, rain—with a plant-based dietary regime and mindful interaction with loving family and friends. Instead of killing me, the liver metastasis gradually shrank until it could no longer be detected.

In this book I explore the experience of connecting worlds—the inner life, nature, others, art, anthropology, activism—and what deep connection makes possible. For three decades, until my retirement from professional work in 2020, I had the opportunity to engage with remarkable people addressing fundamental challenges in unique places and diverse cultural settings: Honduran peasants inventing new agricultural technologies for hillside agriculture; landless Bangladeshi women gleaning nutrient-rich food from their surroundings; a former "criminal tribe" in Maharashtra, India facing eviction from their homes; small religious communities standing in solidarity at the centre of disaster relief efforts in the Philippines and Burkina Faso;

First Nations women in northern Canada struggling to finish high school after dropping out to care for a baby.

My role as an anthropologist was to facilitate dialogue across social divides and mobilize people and evidence in support of social and technical change. Over time, I learned how to work **with** people, supporting their own analysis and problem-solving, in contrast to doing research **on** or **for** people. This kind of engagement is the distinguishing feature of participatory action research (PAR), a research tradition with a long history and rich theoretical underpinnings developed by John Dewy, Kurt Lewin and Paulo Freire, among others.

The need for new approaches to social research is more pressing than ever. Solutions to problems designed by a few specialists are simply not up to the task in a world of ever-growing complexity and unpredictability. Adapting to the Anthropocene demands a new kind of thinking, research practice and approach to civic engagement, one which creates space for dialogue around differences, misunderstandings and competing values. It also requires that we tap into the faculties and sources of knowledge of all people, including the so-called "have nots" and "know-nothings" wrongly branded as people with little to contribute to human history. PAR is one way to advance this inclusive and transformative agenda.

My research practice included using art, movement and simple measurements to connect different aspects of experience and to focus attention on the things that matter most to people. The outcomes were often powerful, although in this book I don't hide the tensions, limitations, dilemmas and struggles of social research or my own mistakes and contradictions. Nor do I pretend to "empower" people with neat and tidy accounts of their situations and the research enterprise, or to speak "on behalf" of vulnerable or marginalized communities as though they have no voice of their own. I have tried to write an account of learning to do participatory and transformative research, free from artifice and claims to truth other than my own.

Some twenty years ago my friend Farhad Mazhar, a Bangladeshi poet, peasant and political activist, introduced me to the songs of Lalon Shah, a 19th century Fakir and philosopher of Bengal who rejected all distinctions of caste, class and creed that divide communities and foster violence. At a time when nationalist, anti-colonial movements were forming in South Asia, Lalon mocked hierarchical, religious and racist perspectives on society emerging in the new nations of the region. He called on people to be mindful of our fundamental unity with all of nature, and with each other as human beings.

"The fool," says a character in one of his songs, "divides the world into parts, and by so doing never learns to put it back together. The wise person may also examine things part by part, but the purpose is not to disintegrate or fragment a given reality but rather to understand the beauty of the unity."

This book is an exploration of the potential for connection and unity in what we do and who we are. It suggests that the creative tension between self, others and nature leads us inevitably to the realization that there is no separation between the parts of life. Like milk from our mother's breast, the experience of becoming, being and belonging connects us directly to our senses and to the world in and around us. What we chose to do with the gift, day-to-day and over the course of a lifetime, is the path, whether foolish or wise.

PART ONE

BECOMING

< My brother Casey, en route to the headwaters of the Klondike River, Yukon.

1

The Spell of the Yukon

The summer of 1973, when I was seventeen, I hitch-hiked from Ottawa to Long Beach on Vancouver Island and back, by way of Dawson City, Yukon. The journey of 13,703 kilometres took me thirty-two days, cost me fifty dollars and filled me with stories.

Pierre Elliott Trudeau, Canada's celebrity prime minister, had by then both inspired and divided Canadians. Swept into office in 1968 on a wave of Trudeaumania, he led Canada into new territory by embracing social liberalism and economic nationalism while also fostering a pan-Canadian identity. He legalized homosexuality and abortion and met in Montreal with John Lennon and Yoko Ono on their 1969 "tour for world peace." Less than a year later, Trudeau invoked the War Measures Act to confront a threat to the state from the *Front de Libération du Québec* (FLQ). When asked how far he would go with the suspension of civil liberties on the streets of Montreal and Quebec City he replied, "Just watch me."

Dancers on parade at the Palace Grand, Dawson City, Yukon.

My father, a veteran of the Second World War and an Air Force pilot, was in a love-hate relationship with our political leader. He supported Trudeau's red lines establishing law and order domestically but objected strongly to plans to reduce Canadian military participation in the North Atlantic Treaty Organization (NATO), at the time a foil against the Soviet Union. He also looked askance at the Canadian government's openness to Fidel Castro's Cuba.

I was more interested in answering Trudeau's call on youth to get to know their country. Trudeau's government had set up temporary youth hostels from coast-to-coast along the Trans-Canada Highway, charging one dollar for a night on a cot and fifty cents for a scrambled-egg breakfast.

I put my thumb out on the road west. Whenever I got stuck between hostels—the Wawa to Thunder Bay stretch or along the highway from Portage la Prarie to Russel, Manitoba—I pitched a makeshift tent fashioned from a rain poncho just beyond the ditch on the side of the road. I hitched through Saskatoon, North Battleford and Edmonton to Jasper National Park then south to Banff and west to Vancouver before taking a ferry to Vancouver Island and on to Long Beach. For years afterwards, I could remember the faces and names of the many people who gave me rides, bought me lunch, served me eggs fried in olive oil, read my horoscope and interpreted the meaning of things I could see in cloud formations over the great, open prairie skies.

At Long Beach I left an imprint in the sand under the poncho tent, then hitched up the interior of British Columbia. My older brother Steve was working at Mile 160 on the Dempster Highway in the Yukon, or at least he had been when last I heard. By luck, we met at Liard Hot Springs along the Alaska Highway in northern British Colombia as he was headed south. He had earned the money he needed to go to Mexico's Baja California and pursue a dream of sand, surf and endless sun. Four years older than me, Steve was having the time of his life before he eventually settled down and became a helicopter pilot. He encouraged me to continue to Dawson City and gave me the name of a few friends he had made there. "Go see the sights of the Klondike," he said.

After a few days in the historic city of 900 people I started the journey back to Ottawa to begin my final year of high school. A hippie in a van just outside of Whitehorse took me all the way to Sudbury, Ontario, some 4,816 km in a single ride.

When I arrived home I told my father, "Maybe Trudeau was right about at least a few things." I also announced that I wanted to study art when I finished high school. He thought it was a temporary delusion and did not stand in my way.

The summer spent discovering my country started a relationship with the people and the landscape of the Yukon that subsequently carried me through three winters and six summers. Trips to what Yukoners call "the Outside" were simply time away from my Dawson home. I acquired so many stories I could entertain interested Outside friends for hours. Eventually, the stories no longer seemed so close to me and fell away like the pairs of brown corduroy pants I wore exclusively for almost a decade. Now, some can be recalled while I explore and share the arc of my professional life from artist to activist anthropologist, and ways of becoming, being and belonging in the world.

Danny, the artist

Something I like about my name is that it has three forms: Dan, Danny and Daniel. Daniel was a prophet for Jews, Christians and Muslims alike, an indication of the unity in religions that today are often pitted against each other. My mother called me Dan but her sisters, all of Irish ancestry, called me Danny. So too did my friends in Dawson City.

I returned to the Yukon in the summer of 1975, this time via the Chilkoot Pass of Gold Rush fame and down the Yukon River in a canoe from Whitehorse, through Lake Lebarge where Robert Service's poem *The Cremation of Sam McGee* was set, and on to Dawson City. I sketched along the way, keen to use the art skills I had developed in my first year of a Fine Arts program at Sir George Williams University (now Concordia) in Montreal.

Traversing the length of the river alone was not difficult for me as I had grown up paddling canoes on lakes and rivers in Ontario with my father and brothers. Camping on the river shore, I cooked lentils and boiled tea in a battered pot. On the river, I occasionally rested in the canoe, taking in the landscape as it drifted with the

Weldon Farr mending a fishing net in front of his home.

steady current. Eventually, I arrived in Dawson some 740 kilometres downstream from my launch point.

There I met Weldon Farr, a man in his fifties known in Dawson by the nickname Windy thanks to his penchant for verbosity. He loaned me an old-fashioned pushcart with large wooden wheels that I fashioned into a mobile art gallery loaded with pictures. The cart was one of the many artefacts that sat beside the large frame house he lived in with his wife Eliza, an Indigenous woman, and their children.

Every afternoon that summer I pushed the cart loaded with artwork to Robert Services' Cabin where tourists gathered at four p.m. to hear his famous poems recited by an acting student—*The Spell of the Yukon; the Shooting of Dan McGrew; The Cremation of Sam McGee.* They were familiar stories, not only because I read them in grade school but also because both my brothers knew several by heart and recited them in tandem at family gatherings. They were carrying on an oral tradition learned from our father, who re-enacted with his three sons epic poems of the British Navy, staged in our backyard with roughly hewn ships.

By 7:30 p.m., with the sun still high in the sky, I waited in front of the Palace Grand Theatre for the tourists to exit for the intermission. Period dramas and comedies, with Can Can Dancers, Honkey Tonk Piano players and nineteenth century folk songs, entertained tourists from Omaha, Calgary and Berlin. I had a captive audience for fifteen minutes between Acts as they tumbled out of the theatre, buoyed by the music and anticipating an unfolding Klondike story. Some would gather round my cart and pepper me with questions about the landscape paintings and small portraits. "Did you paint this? What is your name? How much does it cost?" Eventually, someone would say, "I'll buy that one," and next thing I knew I would sell three for 25 dollars each.

After the show finished I would make my way to Diamond Tooth Gerties, at the time Canada's only legal gambling casino. There I poured liquor from behind the bar for these same Omaha, Calgary and Berlin couples. Gerties was a pleasure spot and employer for dozens of Canadian youth from across the country taking a turn at dealing Blackjack, serving drinks and, for those with the skills, dancing and singing on stage.

I had a bird's eye view of everything till 1:00 a.m. when the doors closed and dealers and dancers lined up at the bar for their nightcap. Calls for a generous shot of Kahlua, vodka or whatever else they fancied taught me the names of dozens of popular drinks of the day. Looking into the faces of each dealer and each dancer I could see their nightly story: Some tired from being on their feet; Others energized by the prospect of their own party-time around campfires.

The muted glow of the midnight sun—Dawson sits just a few hundred kilometres south of the Arctic Circle—gave way to a bright morning light at 2:00 a.m. By 11:00 a.m. I would be making paintings to replace the ones sold the day before. With that special gift of youthful energy, I could complete a few paintings, make my rounds with the mobile gallery and tend bar at Gerties every day all summer long. Occasionally, I partied.

At the end of my second year of art studies in Montreal I returned to Dawson for the summer and rented a shack tucked between Ruby's

Place (a former bordello) and The Westminster Hotel (a drinking establishment of local fame). It was owned by Margaret Vera Dorval, a.k.a. Bombay Peggy. She had lived in Shanghai before the Second World War, served in the Australian women's army corps and ran a bordello in the Yukon mining towns of Keno and Elsa during the 1950s. She had also owned a Dawson hotel where she rented rooms to clients one hour at a time.

The shack had little charm and was set back from the road so I built a boardwalk using slabs from the local saw mill to convey tourists over the muddy terrain. Slabs on the inside of the shack made it look like a log cabin. Cheechako Cache, I called it, a reference to the Gold Rush term for newcomers. I learned years later from my friend Eleanor Millard, who had worked as a social worker in Dawson, that Peggy died in Vancouver's Chinatown but arranged to spread her ashes in the Dawson graveyard on the hill.

When late summer came I decided to stay in town rather than return to Montreal to complete my Fine Arts degree. I figured that if I wanted to be an artist then I needed to make art, not study it. By staying in Dawson, I could dedicate myself to painting. A pale blue one room cabin attached to the Flora Dora Hotel served as my home and studio for the winter, stocked as well with root vegetables, flour for bannock, frozen meat and a new parka.

The riches of my life did not include a girlfriend, although I did manage to convince a number of women to sit for me as models. The drawings, in black Conté on paper, explored the shapes and shadows of the human body, patterns on cloth and glimpses of the outdoors, a motif borrowed from the scenes of everyday life in seventeenth century Holland.

My art was also influenced by the quiet sensibility of Japanese visual arts. I discovered through mail-orders the beauty of Japanese brushes stuffed with goat and wolf hair in the centre and pony or sable outer hairs. Appreciation of the aesthetic had roots in art school in Montreal where I had soaked in the paradoxical thinking and meditative qualities of Akira Kurosawa films such as *Rashoman* and *Dodes'ka-den*, shown regularly in 1970s film repertory houses alongside Ingmar Bergman and Luis Buñuel. I still use the bamboo mat I purchased then to protect the brushes, and the same stone mortar to slowly grind Sumi ink for painting.

Tara pouring tea.

Shelley, a cancan dancer.

Guns and Ammunition Shop, Dawson.

I drew and painted what was in front of me, and framed the pictures with weathered windows and doors, battered gilded frames from Gold Rush days and ornate mirrors. Mary Tcurchinski, an elderly Polish woman, was my supplier of bric-a-brac and all things old and interesting. She lived on the corner across from the leaning Guns and Ammunition Shop, the most photographed of Dawson buildings. Her yard and house were a treasure trove of "found objects" I converted into functional frames, a fusion of utility and meaning that became central themes in my later life as an anthropologist.

In the spring of 1977 these drawings and paintings of life in Dawson and the surrounding landscape made their way into the Whitehorse Public Art Gallery for my first one-person show. The centrepiece was an ambitious oil painting of Greg, a man of quiet self-confidence clothed in a winter jacket and wool hat. In the scene he is looking straight at the viewer as he pulls on heavy mitts before stepping outside. The back side of the panel showed the scene Greg was looking at—a yard covered in snow, stacked wood and an axe stuck in a chopping block. The whole panel was mounted in a rough-hewn wooden door with narrow strips of blue stained glass installed along each side of the panel to allow light through. Hinges and an old door knob completed the "picture frame," suspended in the middle of the gallery ready for a buyer's door jam.

Detail from "Getting ready."

Looking back, the art I made that winter was the most vital and original I ever did as a painter. It even prompted the most famous of Yukon artists, Ted Harrison, to purchase one of the drawings and to tell reporters that Danny Buckles was the most interesting up-and-coming artist on the Yukon scene. My decision to leave art school in favour of making art felt as comfortable as my brown corduroy pants.

The long winter nights allowed for other artistic pursuits. Lambert's house down the street was a hotspot for listening to the latest pop music—Fleetwood Mac, Carly Simon, Linda Ronstadt—and for friends to gather to make music of our own. I had played the snare drum as a Sea Cadet in a marching band, setting the pace with a steady beat, drum roll and paradiddle for Remembrance Day parades in Belleville, Ontario. The experience translated well to bongos, the harmonica and a penny whistle to accompany John Finley, the only real musician in the room, in renditions of the Eagles songs. In the dead of winter, we played a few gigs at the Chief Isaac Memorial Hall, raking in 100 dollars each.

My musical education was stretched in an entirely different direction by Grant Dowdell, a man of talent, grit and few words. He was my first mentor as an adult, teaching me to listen deeply to Bach's *The Art of the Fugue* and *The Easter Oratorio.* He also introduced me to *Walden, or Life in the Woods.* Grant lived the life only dabbled in for one summer by Henry David Thoreau.

Grant was one of the first of the 70s wave of young people that changed the character of Dawson and set a new standard for living off the land. He arrived from Toronto in 1970, renting a cabin in the middle of town, saving money to buy land and learning the skills he would need to farm.

When I met Grant during the winter of 1976 he was the janitor at Dawson's only school. He had recently met Karen, a school teacher from central British Columbia with a bright smile and passion for farming. They married that winter in their tiny cabin, a private ceremony I witnessed, along with the Justice of the Peace.

Soon after, Grant began to clear land on an island upriver from Dawson and build a two-story, eight-sided log home. While there were easier places to build, this location offered remarkably rich and deep silt-based soils, good for farming vegetable crops, which became their specialty. For more than forty years, the land produced ten tons of vegetables annually, feeding the people of Dawson healthy and varied local food. As with anything worthwhile, many hands made this magic possible.

Grant, Daniel, Karen and Jonathan, with their 1949 Ford 4N tractor.

Rocky, the rooster.

I visited them often on the island, in summer and in winter. In the morning, they served strong coffee creamed with fresh goat's milk that I would pull from the animal's teats. In the evening, Grant played guitar or read, often with a cat on his lap. Karen played piano, knitted or sewed. I would rework sketches from the day, including portraits of animals in the barn. A painting of Rocky, their first rooster, hung in their home for decades.

Karen named their first son Jonathan, after a mutual friend. Grant named their second son, Daniel, after me. I never met their third child, a daughter, but my wife Debra and I met Jonathan as an adult when we visited Dawson in 2008, just after he had built his first major log home across the river from Dawson. He and his family now spend the summer months there. In the winter they tend a remote trapline on the Chandindu River.

Grant died in 2022 surrounded by his children and supported by his second wife. Multiple Sclerosis had forced him to town. He told them and friends that spoke with him in his last days that he loved every moment of his life on the island, and would change nothing.

The most important thing I learned from Grant's friendship—what I hold most dear—is an appreciation for the power and beauty of enough. His choices, and similar choices made today by his son Jonathan and his family, show that high levels of material consumption and external distractions—key expressions of the current world—are not important to having a happy and high-quality life. Our task is to appreciate the fullness of life, instead of forever craving for what we lack.

My motto at the time was "earn as little money as possible and let everything else adjust." While a half joke, it expressed my firm rejection of the pursuit of more as a priority in life.

Danny, the outdoorsman

The mid 1970s was the height of the "back-to-the-land" movement when young men and women from as far away as Hamburg, New York and Montreal arrived in the Yukon to carve out a simple life in the bush. Traplines, fishing eddies and farmland throughout the Klondike were occupied and revived after decades of laying untended or fallow. Cabins sprung up deep in the woods and along the many tributaries of the Yukon River.

Many of these "bush hippies" had been prompted to leave urban centres in search of connection to nature. They wanted to know the natural world and live lightly on it. Some were critical of capitalism and the patterns of consumption and destruction documented in Vance Packard's *The Waste Makers* (1960) and Rachel Carson's *Silent Spring* (1962). The threat of nuclear war and societal breakdown hung in the air, as did the anger of the Vietnam war.

I witnessed and participated in several years of the Yukon bush boom, accompanied on hikes and ski trips to remote places by Casey, my younger brother. He arrived in town in 1976 and took up residence for the winter in a cabin on the hill above Dawson. The cabin, chinked with moss and roofed with sod, was half-buried in the slope. It had an overhanging porch, tiny door and only one window. The hobbit house, Casey called it.

Outside was an oval porcelain soaking tub that today would be a popular amenity in a luxury bathroom. As there was no running water, the tub was for summer use only when water could be delivered by truck. That first year, my place in town served as his winter pit stop and weekly shower facility.

It seemed Casey lived off trapped rabbits and Graham Crackers. The food must have suited him because he was strong and agile. Whenever he went into town he would carry a heavy staff to use as a rudder when sliding down a very steep path towards Dawson. Trees helped slow his descent, with one favourite tree helping him turn sharply right towards his job as a bartender in Hank Dubois' Sourdough Saloon or sharply left towards the Klondike River.

He also worked for a time as a stock boy at Fred Caley's General Store, the main outlet in town since 1923 for everything from food to shovels and axe handles. Few items had price tags on them. I heard that on the rare occasion when Fred was not at the counter and his daughter would call out to inquire about the cost of an item, he would shout back, "Who is it?" He was generous with those in need.

When stocking store shelves Casey would occasionally come across merchandise in the warehouse that seemed as old as the Klondike Gold Rush itself: glass bottles of concentrated "camp" coffee, tins of spices and mysterious metal boxes with faded labels. Caley's General Store was the only place in the Yukon where you could find round-toed rubber covers to fit over Inuit mukluks for use in the wet spring.

One day Casey woke up to find a wolverine in the vestibule of his cabin gnawing on a rabbit he had left hanging there frozen. The outer door to the vestibule had swung shut, trapping the wolverine inside with its meal. Casey was in the cabin, with no other exit.

If you haven't seen a live and cornered wolverine you need only imagine the terror produced by Hugh Jackman's portrayal of the character Wolverine in the *X-Men* film series. Eventually, Casey used a broom handle to pry the outer door open and let the beast escape.

Mountain Man would not have been a misplaced moniker for my younger brother, although he was sociable and liked enough that a young couple in town named one of their sons Casey. He, like I, felt good to be connected and remembered that way.

Casey helped me learn to live with discomfort. That winter we skied 160 kilometres down the Yukon River to visit John at his trapline. It was tough. After two nights on the trail in minus twenty degree Celsius temperatures, we arrived unannounced at John's cabin and were greeted with a grunt of surprise. "Damn", he said, "Now I have to wash the dishes!"

John's hospitality was genuine. He used an axe to chop a roast from the hind quarter of a moose and put it in a pot to boil. John hadn't had visitors for many weeks, time he spent checking his traps and illustrating stories raging against the military-industrial complex. I still have Issue #1 of his illustrated booklet *Yukon Komix*, a scathing story about human addiction to oil and gas and the crony capitalism behind the McKenzie Valley oil pipeline proposal of the

time. Prescient, raw and thoughtful, the comic is a remarkable and fantastically illustrated example of 1970s counterculture.

Grant told me recently that "John is the most original person I've ever met," and I would agree. When Casey and I left his cabin a few days later for our return trip to Dawson, John rustled up a breakfast of rolled oats fried in lard and peanut butter, which we washed down with boiled coffee. We didn't need to stop for lunch that day.

A few years later a life-changing event pulled John out of the bush life. He told me that in the early evening of Good Friday he had been reading a book called *Basic Christianity* by the light of a tiny window in his undersized cabin. He used decades-old kerosene in his lamp from an abandoned drum he had found on the Forty Mile River, so the globe blackened easily. A tall, thin man normally quite content with his own thoughts, he had two options for an Easter social gathering. He could travel upriver to visit with Tim and James, who had cabins and traplines of their own at Coal Creek on the east side of the Yukon River. John knew that he would be welcome there and enjoy a few drinks and some home grown pot.

Alternatively, he could go twenty kilometres downriver to Eagle, Alaska, where he could participate in a Christian Easter service. Eagle was a tiny town, populated at the time by a close-knit Christian community, some First Nations and a few back-to-the-land devotees.

John struggled intensely with his thoughts through the night, finding himself desiring to become a Christian but still not willing to give up the solitary bush life. Early the next morning, something drew him powerfully into making a commitment. "When God calls you, you don't

Casey skiing on the frozen Yukon River.

turn Him down—and you can't," John wrote to me. "Instantly upon my commitment, He took away all my desire to remain in the bush."

After breakfast John hitched up the dogs and mushed downriver to attend Easter Sunday church in Eagle, returning a number of times over the following weeks to receive instruction and be in the fellowship necessary for a Christian life. After spring breakup he moved to Dawson and joined the Pentecostal church where John has remained a central figure for four decades.

The Yukon is often referred to as "God's Country," evoking a richness in the outdoor air brighter than gold. Living there for a time opened me up to the experience of Creation and connected me to nature and an inner life I have rarely forgotten since. The Creator, however, is an experience that remains beyond my personal comprehension. The who behind the Creation we all witness directly through our senses and are a part of is a mystery I live with, comfortably for now.

When John and I saw each other last, in 2008, I took a photo of him in his tiny studio outside of the cabin I once lived in. He had returned to painting, making colourful landscapes of his own. I could see in him the joy, inner peace, hope and purpose he receives from a personal relationship with the Creator. It is beautiful. Recently, he wrote to me to say, "What I have comes from Him, and without Him I'd probably still be in the bush, spiritually blind and dead as before—or else in town, blind and spiritually dead as I soaked up beers in the Pit (the nickname for a local bar)." Kindness also shines in his eyes.

A hike into the Tombstone Mountains in the late summer of 1977, after the Dawson tourist season and work at Gerties had finished, was

John in his studio, 2008.

another highlight for Casey and me. We made a great outdoors team, buoyed by the deep trust of brothers very close in age. Our fisticuffs as teenagers were long past, mainly because he could now whoop me.

To get to the mountain range we hitched a ride up the Dempster Highway to a place overlooking Tombstone Valley, now one of Canada's most spectacular wilderness parks. The North Klondike River drains the valley and connects to the main trunk of the Klondike River and many tributaries. In 1896 the discovery of gold on one of these, Bonanza Creek, launched a human stampede that shook the economies of San Francisco and London.

The fall colours of the valley are spectacular, with black spruce, alders and willows combining with mosses and muskeg, creating a palette like no other. On the horizon, Mount Monolith stands like an inverted canine tooth forming a jagged ridge against the sky. These are signs of what the poet Robert Service was seeing when he wrote *The Spell of the Yukon.*

When Casey and I started out on our hike there were no human-made trails into the valley. An English couple, Rick and Louise, had

Casey hiking in the Tombstone Mountains.

been to a point on the highway the previous winter where they ran their sled dogs up and down the snow-covered hillside as training for the famous Iditarod race from Anchorage to Nome, Alaska. Their trail-blazing didn't help us much once the snow melted. The valley was a thick briar of alder and willows tall enough to block our passage and our view.

We quickly learned, however, to think like a moose, following what Casey dubbed "the magical, meandering moose track." It was a trail created by centuries of animals moving up and down the valley carving a very narrow track six or more inches deep in the damp moss.

We followed these animal pathways only to have them peter out suddenly and for no humanly perceivable reason. Eventually, thinking like a moose would help us pick up the trail again, an act of transhumanism we got good at as we approached Summit Lake and the base of Mount Monolith. Along the way, we marvelled at the colour of the blueberry pies—scat—deposited here and there by grizzly bears. While we had no rifle and bear spray was not common in those days, we did put dents in our pots making noise as we slowly made our way along.

Several days deep into the mountains we saw a furl of smoke rising ahead and could smell fish cooking. Casey remembers it as grayling,

Casey (left) and me at Summit Lake.

perhaps from the upper reaches of the Tombstone River or Talus Lake, but I recall it as hard-smoked salmon strips. A woman was alone at the campfire. Sitting somewhat nervously on a small bolder, Bryson told us that her companions, Tim and James, were off for the day to climb part of Mount Monolith.

She gave us some of her fish to supplement our own meagre rations, which were running low at that point. We needed the fat energy desperately and managed to turn the good fortune of meeting her into several more days of hiking down the Tombstone River before returning to the Dempster and eventually Dawson. A wooden cross on one of the hills, still there today, reminded us of the dangers of being so poorly prepared so far into the wild.

Tim later played a central role in defining the boundaries of Tombstone Territorial Park, working as one of two negotiators for the Council of Yukon Indians. When I knew him, however, Tim was a trapper, fisherman and dog musher living at Coal Creek on the Yukon River, not far from John's trapline. He had arrived in Dawson from the States in the mid 1970s when draft dodging and getting back-to-the-land was a political stance for many young Americans.

In the following years I periodically visited Tim, his partner Andrée and their son, Spruce, named after the trees surrounding their cabin. Their home, set in a small clearing, was a functional work of art with a bear proof tower next to it for food storage. Built from the largest

Cross on the horizon, overlooking Tombstone Valley.

black spruce available on the surrounding landscape, the walls and roof of the cabin created a building envelope tight enough to heat with a modest fire and roomy enough for their growing family.

To make muffins in the morning Tim would grind flour with a hand mill and mix it with sourdough starter remaining from the previous day. Doing this every day gave him powerful arms, although this didn't stop him from asking guests expecting breakfast to do the honours.

Tim mushing on the frozen Yukon River near Coal Creek.

Danny on a driftwood raft pulled up on the shore at Dawson.

He also made plain for me the distinction between ethics and legality. "Just because something is legal," referring to the draft and the Vietnam War, "doesn't make it ethical."

I mimicked the bush skills I saw in the lifestyles of Grant, John and Tim by devising my own method for gathering the wood supply I needed to heat my cabin on the edge of town. I had noticed massive piles of driftwood along the shoreline when boating up river to Grant's island farm. I borrowed a chain saw, cut logs into five metre lengths and stacked them on the shore edge to make a raft. Once it was several layers deep and tied together in a few places, I levered the raft into the Yukon River and rode it like a bearded king down to the waterfront at Dawson. The sand on the logs was hell on the chain saw but it made excellent firewood to stuff into a heavy steel barrel stove.

The cabin belonged to John, empty for the winter when he was at his trapline. The eight-sided structure had one room and a root cellar beneath a trap door in the middle. That fall, I filled the root cellar with carrots, potatoes and parsnips from Grant's farm, along with bags of rice, beans and other grains.

I knew that to be active outdoors during the winter I would also need energy from animal fat. Eating plant-based food only, as I had during my university days in Montreal, was simply not compatible with temperatures often below minus thirty degrees and sometimes dipping to minus fifty. I resolved that if I were prepared to eat an animal I should also be prepared to take its life.

An opportunity came when two school teachers keen to hunt for caribou invited me to join them on a drive up the Dempster Highway. The Porcupine and Forty Mile Barren Ground Caribou cross the road on their migration route to calving grounds at the Beaufort Sea. At 2,400 kilometres, it is the longest migration of any land mammal on earth.

We had stopped on the side of the road, looking across a nearby stretch of frozen river when a small herd suddenly emerged from the bush and out onto the frozen river. A couple of females were followed by a male with a prominent rack of horns. Eight or nine other younger animals leaped into view as well.

Our rifles made so much noise we attracted hunters from up and down the highway. By the time they arrived the herd had fled. The male with the rack of horns lay panting and then died on the blood-stained snow. A wounded female that had fallen leapt up and ran into the woods as we approached. We waited for it to stop running and then tried to track it. Soon, we lost any sign of blood or hoof prints and could do nothing but return to our first kill. I've long been troubled by the thought of the animal dying in the woods, separated from the rest of the herd.

We agreed to share the caribou meat equally between the three of us, and eventually butchered the animal using the bandsaw in the school shop. To broaden my diet, I traded some caribou meat for moose and black bear meat. While I have now been a vegetarian for more than forty years, taking an animal's life to feed people that both need and appreciate the food is not an ethical dilemma I'm concerned about. What counts, in my view, is knowing where food comes from and contributing what one can to provisioning it.

The bush skills I acquired that year added to what was already a high level of comfort with the outdoors built up during my childhood. My father would take his three sons into the woods of Ontario to hunt for partridge and rabbits with a single gauge shot gun. We walked slowly along dirt roads and across open scrublands looking for clumps of juniper where rabbits might hide. We only shot when it was safe and we had a very good chance of succeeding.

My father was frugal, having grown up during the Great Depression, and tried to make the most of what presented itself. On one

A friend's sled outside my cabin.

outing he spotted an animal killed at the side of the road. It was a raccoon with a long fluffy tail and soft fur. He skinned it and I spent hours fleshing the skin to make a Davy Crocket hat. As an eight or nine-year-old, I was excited by the prospect of going into the bush with my father sporting the best hat ever. The hide didn't tan well, however, and had to be tossed out when the hair started to fall out and my mother complained about the smell.

Our father taught other bush skills at our family cottage on a remote part of Lake Temagami, a celebrated near-north wilderness environment. We fished, practiced target shooting with a small calibre rifle and split firewood. He, and my mother, also encouraged their sons to think carefully about what is right and wrong and to stand by our convictions. Whenever we broke a household rule or were caught in a lie, our father gave us the choice between speaking the truth and taking the punishment (a hard smack on an open hand with a wooden paddle) or keeping quiet in our room. All of us learned to take the paddle.

When the owners of an eco-tourism start-up in Dawson needed someone to guide a group of four New York lawyers down the Stewart River and then along the Yukon River to Dawson, they asked me. It didn't seem to matter that I had never been on the Stewart, although I had traversed the Yukon River from Whitehorse to Dawson.

A few days after we set out we came to Bob and Rosemary's cabin at Rosebud Creek about sixty kilometres upriver from the mouth of the Stewart. These Brooklyn natives, with a half dozen winters living in the Yukon bush, invited us to pitch our tents in their yard for the night and welcomed us inside.

I asked Bob about the Grizzly bear pelt staked to an interior wall. He told me that he had seen the bear near their boat launch rolling away one of his forty-five-gallon drums of fuel. After Bob shot at it, the bear took off wounded into the thick willows. Bob was tracking it in the bush, a very foolish thing to do, when suddenly the bear leapt up in front of him. He only had time to lift his rifle halfway up and get off another shot. The bear bit Bob on the arm, and died on top of him.

Rosemary recounted that from the cabin she could hear Bob's screams during this encounter. After extricating himself from under the bear, he fired off a few more shots to be sure and then went with Rosemary to Dawson, many hours away by boat, to have his wound tended. No one ever knew what the bear planned to do with the drum of fuel.

Bush stories gone wrong were inevitable in a context where young people were arriving from all over the world, most with less savvy than Bob and Rosemary. A German man told me about a problem he was having with noise inside the cabin he had built in the fall. It was constructed in a hurry with green logs, spurred on by a fast approaching winter. He didn't bother to strip the bark off the trunks before putting up the walls and roof, although he chinked the imperfect joints with moss. Come the middle of winter, bark beetles were enjoying the heated space enough to keep themselves busy day and night gnawing away at the wood cellulose. The man could hardly sleep for the noise.

He also lost his truck to a fire. With no electricity to warm the motor oil in the deep cold, he built a tiny fire underneath the oil pan. It got away when residual oil on the chassis ignited. No truck and a noisy cabin at minus thirty degrees did not seem to dampen his spirits, however. I remember him as a man with good humour in the face of difficulties. In fact, he was having the time of his life. Germans were the biggest source of tourists in Dawson, after the Americans, thanks in part to the mythological status in post-war Germany of Jack London, Indians and the wilds of Canada. Escaping to a place where the nuclear holocaust might be survived offered something unique and attracted both the skilled and the hapless.

Most eventually moved on. According to the author Dan O'Neil, by the late 1990s the land along the Yukon River from Whitehorse past Dawson City and into Alaska had few people left to care for it. This meant a loss of local knowledge as the creeks, ridges, mountain slopes and creatures all along this great river were separated from caring human eyes and gentle uses. He called his account of the decline *A Land Gone Lonesome.*

Long after living in the Yukon, when working at the International Development Research Centre (IDRC) in the late 1990s and early 2000s, I developed a professional interest in the issues underlying O'Neil's observations. While working there, I helped develop an approach to nature conservation that argued against the separation of parks and people. A better response to the challenge, we said, was to support the sustainable use of nature by local people. Use can act as an incentive for conservation not only of the land but also of the local knowledge associated with it. Without people, there is a knowledge and vigilance gap likely to erode the abundance that remains.

Grant, in one of our last conversations, wryly commented that today there are still lots of young men in Dawson with unruly beards, but few who know what lies beyond the town's edge.

Danny, the townie

The 1970s was a time when new blood from the south invigorated Dawson with novel ideas, entrepreneurship and creative professionalism virtually unseen in the town since 1953 when it lost out to Whitehorse as the capital of the Yukon. Some young people took over small gold mining operations from "sourdoughs"—earlier pioneers who had endured many winters and fluctuating gold prices. Others brought an international sophistication to the town's growing tourism industry, buoyed by steady investment from Parks Canada and early signs of today's booming interest in eco-tourism. The two economies—active placer mining and both historical and outdoor tourism—mingled and merged even as the people involved stayed largely apart from each other.

Debauchery was also part and parcel of town life. People could drink on the street without breaking any municipal by-laws. Off-sales of beer at the Westminster Hotel, a.k.a. The Pit, started at 9:00 a.m., followed at 11:00 a.m. by jugs of beer and other alcoholic drinks. A clan of town hippies known as "The Slugs" set a low standard, sleeping on the wooden boardwalks or wherever they found themselves when the doors to The Pit were closed.

Scabies, a contagious skin infestation caused by a species of mite, swept through their extended family of men, women and children one summer. Town folk were scandalized. Weekends of non-stop drinking, "Slug Fests" organized by their Irish leader, brought little to the economic life of the town and may very well have ruined a few lives.

Music eventually became the biggest contributor to an emerging Dawson culture beyond the gold rush and counterculture pattern. In 1979 a handful of local musicians organized the first Dawson City Music Festival, described on the official website as "an intimate, two-day affair among friends, comprising a jam session on a West Dawson farm and a dance at Diamond Tooth Gerties." Vancouver's *Georgia Straight* magazine calls it "Canada's tiny, perfect Festival." The musical event, known among musicians across North America, has displaced Klondike Discovery Days as the time and place to be in Dawson.

John Steins, one of the founders of the festival, was my window into the craft of music making. We spent hours together at his cabin. He drank coffee, hot or cold, with a dollop of condensed milk from a can. We talked about the latest news and politics brought to us across the airwaves every morning by CBC's most loved broadcaster, Peter Gzowski. Then he would play twelve-string guitar riffs over and over again, polishing them until they made their way into an amazing album called *Midnight Light*, produced by the folk music icon David Essig. It was a unique experience of music, different from the wildness of my drumming at Lambert's house or listening to other-worldly fugues and choral music at Grant's farmhouse.

Creativity hooked up with entrepreneurship when John, his partner Paula and I opened an arts and crafts store—the Gaslight Gallery—in a Dawson City Museum and Historical Society building near the

Palace Grand Theatre. For two summers the gallery was a home for painters and print makers, a silver smith, trappers with furs to sell and Indigenous craft women.

John's visual art, including the linocut that graced his album cover, had a simplicity and harmony different from my more detailed aesthetic. He beat me handily in an open competition to create a special edition poster for the Dawson Tourism Office celebrating eighty years since the discovery of gold at Bonanza creek. I had gone for a traditional image of the gold pan used by prospectors, jazzed up, I thought, with jubilee diamonds instead of gold nuggets. John's design was more original, using a profile of the classic sternwheeler S.S. Keno that stood on Dawson's Front Street to create an image of a giant eightieth birthday cake.

Years later John gained artistic notoriety for a political series of linocuts. He created them as a protest against George Bush's 2003 invasion of Iraq and a challenge to the playing cards developed by the U.S. Defence Intelligence Agency to help troops identify the most-wanted members of Saddam Hussein's government, dubbed the Axis of Evil.

John's deck of cards included the American propagandists of the unethical and disastrous war, including Donald Rumsfeld, Paul Wolfowitz and President Bush. The print series, dubbed the Axis of

Bush-Ace of Clubs, Axis of Weasels Series, Linocut, 2003, by John Steins.

Lake Bennett, after a Gold Rush photograph.

Weasels, sold briskly by mail to the States but also got John banned from eBay, at least until his fans managed to overturn the ruling. John's prowess as an artist and musician, cheerful personality and sharp political views helped him to become Dawson's mayor in the 2000s.

My art took on a more commercial character after my first critical success in Whitehorse. I drew on turn-of-the-century photographs and my own experience climbing the Chilkoot Pass to retell the historic journey, selling more than a hundred small paintings every summer. I also painted the remnants of the golden era, including scenes of stern wheelers abandoned along the riverside and machinery in the bush.

I dabbled in the food business. For the Klondike Discovery Days long weekend, celebrating the discovery of gold in 1896, I sold smoked salmon sandwiches on rye bread for two dollars. A freshly painted wagon I rented from the El Dorado Hotel served as my food truck. Meanwhile, down the street, Tim and James sold salmon salad sandwiches on white bread for one dollar out of the back of their station wagon. While I had the better ambience, I had to reduce my prices dramatically. Clients were more interested in creating a base for drinking than enjoying fine cuisine. Even at a lower price, I lost most of the rye bread to mold. Such is venture capitalism.

While new arrivals such as John Steins and myself thrived during the 1970s, the Dawson that I knew was a difficult place for the Hän Indians. By then, families had moved into North Dawson from the

Bush truck.

downriver Indigenous village of Moosehide. Life in the village, initially a place isolated from the madness of Dawson, was also marked by the same kinds of abuses faced by Indigenous peoples elsewhere in Canada—the minister who ran the school in Moosehide was forced to leave after reports of sexual abuse.

In town, youth and adults of the Indigenous community were swept up in the boisterous and raucous drinking culture of Dawson. Housing was in disarray and the Indigenous language was under severe pressure. The dissonance of a shifting culture, poverty and disorientation from alcohol ended lives.

It wasn't until the late 1980s that a new life began to emerge among the Hän, renamed by their leaders as the Tr'ondëk Hwëch'in First Nation. Eventually, a land claim settlement, self-government and a series of local initiatives connected them to the economic life of Dawson and the Indigenous revival movement that swept across Canada in the 1990s. Today, they are thriving.

I saw some of the turmoil but also the love and respect for the land. Joe and Annie Henry, elders of the Indigenous community, had a cabin on the Dempster Highway I visited with my friend Eleanor Millard. Eleanor had been the youngest-ever Member of the Yukon Territorial Legislative Assembly, representing Old Crow in the far

Abandoned schoolhouse in Moosehide.

north of the Yukon. We helped Annie and Joe collect grasses and roots for use in medicines and ceremony. Joe, a famous snow-shoe maker, hunted and trapped to an advanced age.

Casey and I developed a friendship with Ray Titus, a Tr'ondëk Hwëch'in man who worked as an electrician in town. He invited us to his home for dinner with his wife and two boys, one of whom joined a gymnastics class Casey ran after hours at the school. Ray commissioned me to make a small landscape painting for the anniversary of his dad's death, which he mounted on the grave marker in the town cemetery up the hill. I protected the painting as best I could with layers of shellac but was chagrined to realize a year or so later that the watercolour had faded away completely. Only an ink outline of mountain ridges and shoreline rocks remained to represent the land.

The darkness of the North was difficult for many. In December, the sun would barely streak the sky at 10:00 a.m. Night would fall by late afternoon. This drove the northern experience of cabin fever.

A young White man I knew took his own life during my second winter in Dawson. He was part of a family with a long history of placer mining and had been working his own claim on a remote creek. Front end loaders were a big part of the operation and he was a capable mechanic. The last time I saw him alive he had come into town with grease from working on the machines smeared away from his face but still covering his neck, ears and hairline.

Joe and Annie Henry, and a daughter, at a fish camp on the Yukon River.

I balanced the darkness by making the most of the daylight hours to paint, chop wood and walk to the Post Office. I skied in the dark. The snow reflected enough light from the intense Yukon winter sky to guide my way even when the Northern Lights were not dancing.

Long spells of minus thirty degrees could be punctuated by a drop to minus forty-five degrees or lower for a few days, only to rise again to minus thirty degrees. Those rising temperatures prompted townspeople to come out of their homes with their jackets unzipped and hats off to enjoy the clement weather.

One day in December, 1977 I received a parcel from my parents including a colourful brochure describing an art school in San Miguel de Allende, Mexico. They suggested I continue the studies I'd started in Montreal and offered me a plane ticket home for Christmas, en route to Mexico.

I still had plenty of winter provisions and was happy enough painting, playing music and being in the outdoors but Mexico sounded like an adventure. I gave away my remaining caribou meat, bags of parsnips and bushel of short-grain brown rice and set off in pursuit of an artist's life under the Mexican sun.

2

Mexican Magic

On the plane to Mexico City from Montreal I happened to sit beside Lilia, a young woman who had been part of Mexico's Olympic gymnastics team during the 1976 Montreal Olympics the previous year. She was returning home to Mexico City after visiting friends she had made in Montreal.

I had been a gymnast in high school, giving me an opening to conversation with an attractive Olympian of my age. Short in stature and with compact muscles, both our body types were well suited to the sport. Lilia had been guided into gymnastics by her parents, school teachers in Mexico's public school system and avid proponents of a well-rounded life and education. Gymnastics has everything: grace, strength, fearlessness. As the only daughter and youngest in the family, she had followed a path of physicality while her two brothers became musicians and instrument makers.

Temple #33, Yaxchilán, Mexico.

Photograph of Robert Buckles, taken by his captors, rests on the cover of his wartime log surrounded by memorabilia.

My interest in gymnastics had been encouraged by my father's athleticism. He had been a champion javelin thrower and top pitcher at Parkdale High School in Toronto, a skill he honed in the prisoner of war camp he was stuck in as a twenty-year old during World War II. A Spitfire pilot, he had been shot down over France and spent nineteen months in "the can." Every time I see Steve McQueen in the classic film *The Great Escape* I think of my father, who was in the camp where the escape occurred. McQueen took a baseball with him into the "clink," solitary confinement for having stepped out of line, bouncing it against the wall as he waited out his punishment.

My father didn't like the cavalier attitude of the character McQueen portrayed in the film. It was too American for a story mostly about Brits, Canadians and Aussies. His own account of the camp included many references to the ball games he played, the friendships he made, and a few close calls. He stepped over the trip wire defining the no-go zone of the camp perimeter one day to pick up a baseball that had rolled a metre or so too far. The tower guards turned their rifles on him and were about to shoot when another prisoner shouted out "Halt!" In perfect German, he pleaded the case as a careless mistake. My father returned to the safe side of the line, baseball in hand.

Most of his war stories had a humorous touch, lightening the personal suffering and losses. Self-discipline was his first rule, something that served us well with the demanding sport of gymnastics. My brother Casey did giant swings on the high bar. I did an iron cross on the rings, although it was more a slow descent through the skill than the requisite two second hold. Still, it was enough to win us the City of Ottawa high school gymnastics trophy.

Before we touched down in Mexico City, Lilia invited me to her parents' home for New Year's Eve dinner and a Mexican ritual: eating twelve grapes and making wishes while counting down to midnight. The experience, and an ongoing friendship with the family, introduced me to Mexican hospitality. It also launched a period of intense exploration of taste, colour, sound, texture and other delights of the senses. It seemed like I had emerged from the quiet Yukon world of black, white and subtle greys into a peopled kaleidoscope.

Connecting to the senses

That night I stayed at the Gran Hotel Ciudad de México on Mexico City's famous main square, the Zócalo. My parents had treated me to two nights in this five-star establishment to cement my pledge to re-engage with the world outside of Dawson City. They were afraid Casey and I would become stuck in the Yukon, a place they considered too isolated and lonely. I did not share their worry but I loved the grandeur of the Zócalo, which houses in the National Palace the mural by Diego Rivera called *The History of Mexico.*

A few days later I was in San Miguel de Allende north of Mexico City where I would study art for the next nineteen months. To start, I took a three-month Spanish language course for four hours every morning. Afternoons were spent at the local market eating Aztec soup and trying to figure out what people were saying. I learned about *epazote,* a herb routinely added to beans to relieve flatulence and stomach cramps. *Flor de jamaica* (red hibiscus) iced tea, Dos Equis beer, and *elotes,* a grilled corn on the cob dipped in salt water and flavoured with lemon and *chili* powder were added to my palate and vocabulary.

Pulquero, after dropping off a load of "honey water."

A small *pulque* bar on the edge of town offered a place to hang around peasants and small-scale vendors over a fermented drink from the ubiquitous maguey plant. The fresh sap delivered in the morning is called "honey water" and is mixed with *pulque* from the previous day. The older batch acts much like the sourdough starter used for breads in the Yukon by kick starting fermentation. By late afternoon the mix is about eight percent alcohol.

Patrons, arriving by donkey or foot across the dry landscape, played a curious version of crokinole while drinking. Men would toss a coin onto a small wooden plate with a hole in the middle, and win if it found the centre.

Narrow cobble stone streets on the outer edges of town presented other unexpected delights: women washing clothes at a public fountain; kites made from bits of plastic and cloth stranded by the wind in the hydro lines; devotional nooks with small statues and burning candles.

At the bus station I would stand listening, entranced by the performance of ticket-takers calling out destinations near and far. "Celaya, Celaya!" A neighbouring town. "Querétaro, Querétaro!" A place further away. The code from bus conductor to bus driver—banging out

Street broom, San Miguel de Allende, Mexico.

one, two, or a rapid trill on the side of the bus—signalled stop, go and back up slowly.

The centre of town offered a different perspective, especially as the sun began to set. Birds returned in large numbers to roost in trees on the central square while teenagers strolled around in an evening ritual. Girls, arm in arm, moved clockwise while boys, also arm in arm, walked counterclockwise. Each chatted and joked within their own cluster and smiled at others when it suited them. The town jail, which occasionally housed an errant youth, was nestled within the Municipal Palace a stone's throw from the square.

Castillos, castle-like structures of fireworks set up in front of the Gothic *parroquia* or church, gyrated, popped loudly and spun wildly into the air and across the main square in celebration of birthdays of saints and national heroes. Occasionally, a spinning section of the *castillo* would bounce off the street, a possibility that frightened some and thrilled others.

The corner bar, a bare space of stone and simple tables and chairs called La Cucaracha (cockroach), hosted people interested in serious drinking. A few American men of local renown as painters were fixtures there, it seemed since the end of Second World War when the GI Bill gave veterans a new start in life. They had chosen to move to San Miguel, supplementing their modest wartime pension with sales of art and marriage to hard working Mexican women.

One painter taught me how to use shapes, patterns and the picture edge to draw the eye's attention from one place to another on a canvass. "Composition," he insisted, "is a skill to be learned by studying how the eyes want to move around the image." He also taught me how to drink shots of tequila, chased with salt and lemon. The shots eventually became too much for me, stopping my visits to the bar and to his studio.

The sites and wonders of San Miguel, some quiet and some outrageous, combined with formal classes to bring the Spanish language alive for me. Curious, and blessed with a young brain, after three months I could speak Spanish well. By six months my command and accent were good enough to create the impression that I might be a fair-skinned and blue-eyed *compadre* from Chihuahua or other northern state. I began to inhabit the language and the place, not only with my body and mind but also my voice.

The art institute in San Miguel, founded in 1950, was well connected to the intellectual and political life of central Mexico. While it catered primarily to American and other foreign students, it offered a degree from the University of Guanajuato. It could also occasionally offer unique programs.

A few months after I arrived, ten students and faculty were invited to spend three months working as illustrators for Mexican archeologists in Yaxchilán, a Mayan archaeological site on the border between Mexico and Guatemala. It was in the heart of the Lacandon jungle.

To get there, we gathered first at the Central Train Station in Mexico City, loaded down with supplies for our stay. The gear was too much for the baggage handler so half was left with me, the most fluent Spanish speaker in the group, while everyone else boarded the train.

Twenty minutes later the baggage handler returned. He was agitated as he loaded the remaining bags on his cart. I remained calm. We went down the platform towards the baggage car. The train began to move. The baggage handler tried to match its movement. I responded too. The train slowly gained speed. It departed the station without me or the baggage.

This was the first train I ever missed, a scene repeated many years later when I tried to board a train in Mumbai, India, only to find that I could not squeeze myself into the coach door while also hanging onto my luggage.

The next day I boarded the train for the same twenty-four-hour journey to Tenosique in the south west corner of the State of Tobasco. I was greeted with great fanfare on the platform by faculty and students desperate for their bags and supplies. I was an instant hero, having saved the entire expedition. The next day we were all ferried on a small plane into a grass airfield at one of Mexico's most remote archaeological sites.

Life at Yaxchilán involved a level of discomfort not dissimilar to camping out in the Tombstone Mountains in the Yukon. We slept in hammocks strung between the posts of a large palm roof. Rice and beans were the stuff of every meal. We dug our own outhouse, closing it in and starting over every week.

One morning, I picked up the shoes I left on the ground below my hammock and out popped a black shelled scorpion. Mexico has the highest biodiversity of scorpions in the world. At least 300 people die from encounters with them every year. I took the risk in stride by developing a shoe-tapping ritual every time I rolled out of the hammock.

The tall ceiba trees and other tropical vegetation protected us from the direct rays of the sun but the intense heat and humidity drove us every afternoon into the Usumacinta River for relief. We lay in the water on the narrow beach to cool off.

Guatemala was just across the river. I knew nothing of the country's violent politics but soon learned of a headless body spotted floating down the river the previous year. We also learned to keep a watchful eye on what might be moving through the water after a heavy rainfall. Snakes are flushed out by the rising waters and into the current to drift downstream.

The Usumacinta River was also the point of access for thieves attempting to steal ancient artifacts. One incident, a few years after my time at Yaxchilán, ended in a shootout and one dead attendant. An article in *National Geographic* about Ian Graham, an American illustrator from the Peabody Museum at Harvard University, describes the incident.

I had met Ian at the site, and watched him do illustrations of hieroglyphs decorating a recently discovered circular stone altar more than a metre in diameter. He worked in the early morning hours then returned at night with a flashlight to cast shadows on the fine details and adjust his drawing. The altar was later re-buried to preserve it from the heavy rains, and thieves.

Learning the craft of technical illustration took me in a completely different direction from the water colour landscapes and conte figure drawings of Dawson days. Attention to detail was a must, but also to the overall coherence of the subject. When a pen and ink drawing of temple #23 I had been working on for days became muddled, I was told to sit down and redo it in a single session. A successful product emerged from the hints of visible corners and stairways of a building otherwise covered with vegetation.

Temple #23, Yaxchilán, Mexico, pen and ink.

Not long afterwards, Roberto Garcia Mol, the head archaeologist, invited me to help him with an important excavation, an experience recorded at the time in my journal:

> ***April 20, 1978.*** *I went with Roberto today to draw a burial at temple 33. The bones lay between the building and a three-metre stalagmite that had been removed from a cave centuries ago and erected like an obelisk far above the main plaza. Roberto cleaned the dirt from around the bones with a small paint brush, an ice pick and a pointed trowel, revealing the cranium, the vertebrae, the humerus and other bones to make the position of the body clear for photographs and my drawing. We sweated, both exposed to the hot sun.*

Roberto said that the buried man was probably low in the social hierarchy of the Maya and may have been sacrificed when backfilling what he believed was a tomb below. "More information about the Maya can be gained from two or three burials than the great building before us." After the drawing was done, Roberto slowly collected all the bones to be inspected for signs of trauma. The body we excavated may have been a ritual sacrifice.

April 30, 1978. *Digging over the last few days has revealed an unexpected stuccoed wall, suggesting that the current building is built on an older structure. A few days ago, the archaeologists removed the remains of several other burials, some with a large ceramic plate covering the head and others with small ceramic heads representing the nine Maya Gods of the night.*

Ernesto, Roberto's senior assistant, was in charge when the workers, themselves Maya from the distant town of Oxkutzcab in the Yucatán, broke through to a cavity in the ground. He got down on his hands and knees and peered into the hole with a flashlight. There, spread out in an open chamber, were the bones of a ruler. Gold figurines and hundreds of jade beads were

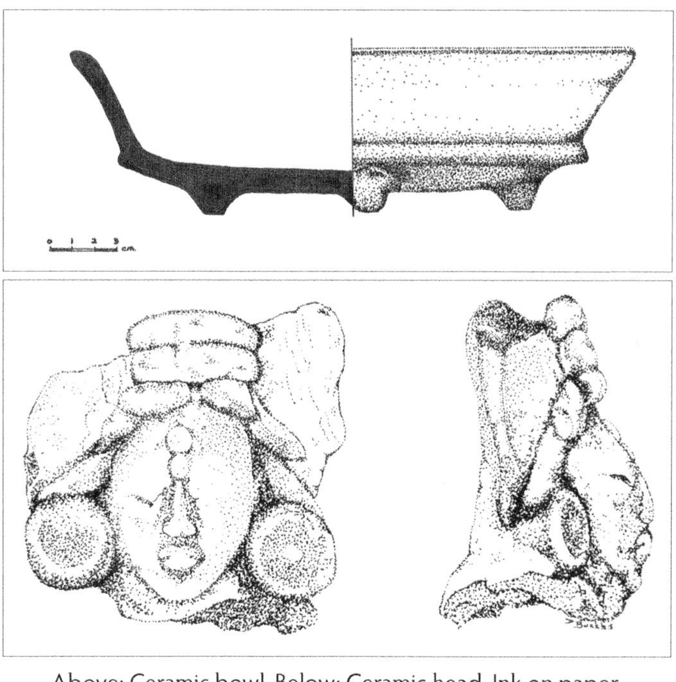

Above: Ceramic bowl. Below: Ceramic head. Ink on paper.

scattered about. A large obsidian blade lay across the chest and another between the legs.

It was nearly 2:00 p.m. when Ernesto stood up. It was quitting time during the heat of the summer months so he covered the opening with a stone and returned to camp, announcing to Roberto, "I've found the tomb of Shield Jaguar." The ruler, and his son Bird Jaguar, were prominent figures in hieroglyphs dated between 708 and 790 A.D. That night, Roberto brought out a bottle of wine from a secret stash.

I was invited the next day to look into the grave of an ancient ruler, hidden from human eyes for more than a thousand years. It was an adventurer's moment I have never forgotten.

A few months after returning to San Miguel from Yaxchilán I set out on a journey to get to know other parts of my new-found country, en route to Guatemala. I purchased second-class bus tickets for towns or cities a day's ride away. Often, I wouldn't get far, instead jumping off the bus with my backpack when it stopped somewhere that looked interesting from the bus window. After visiting a local market or hanging out in the main square, I would purchase another ticket to continue the day's journey on a later bus. Even on an art student's savings I could afford to do this without hesitation, allowing me to touch and taste the offerings of many small communities and overlooked places along the byways of central and southern Mexico.

One village square I visited in Oaxaca had a small crowd of people gathered around a busker telling stories and performing magic tricks with a large and menacing iguana at his feet. He would announce once in a while that the iguana was also a magician and that it would soon perform a trick. I stood nearby, waiting and enjoying the man's performance as people came, dropped coins in his hat, and moved on. After more than an hour watching I realized that the iguana was not going to do a trick of its own at all. It was a bystander to the main act, just like me. Whenever the man mentioned the upcoming trick, however, the crowd murmured interest, dropped money in the hat and watched as long as their schedules would permit. I imagine I was the only one to wait very long, like Vladimir and Estragon in Becket's play *Waiting for Godot*, thinking the trick was imminent. It never appeared.

Slight-of-hand took on a different form in the market stalls, restaurants and bus stops on my way south. Vendors held up two fingers in a pinching gesture to ask for patience; a hissing sound escaped from the lips of a patron calling for attention from servers; bus drivers showed the back of their bent wrist and coxed elbow to express displeasure with a troublesome passenger.

From a rancher I learned how to indicate the height of a beast using the side of the open hand, the height of plants using the palm face down and the height of a man using the index finger and thumb pointed to the sky. The language of Mexico involved the whole body, expressed crudely at times, though often joyfully and always laced with ironic humour.

Eventually I crossed the border to villages in the highlands above Huehuetenango in Guatemala. I met a Swiss woman on the bus making its way up the twisting road, and invited her to share a bed with me in the tiny hostel available in the village. She agreed, even though she could easily afford her own bed. It cost the equivalent of twenty-five cents, even less than the hostels I had stayed at on my cross-country journey of Canada a few years earlier.

We witnessed a procession through the village that stopped for a few minutes at each house to share the blessing of a religious statue carried on a wooden litter. A young priest in the village engaged us in conversation when he realized I spoke Spanish well enough for him to recounted how the military was disappearing people.

I later came to know that this period was the beginning of a systematic campaign of terror against the highland Maya, which lasted through to 1996. It reached its peak under Presidents Ríos Mont and Lucas Garcia, both of whom received lavish support from the United States. The strange mix of quiet resignation and resolve in the priest's voice in the face of clear and present danger shook me. For years afterwards, I wondered what became of him.

My companion and I returned to the lowlands through Chichicastenango and on to Lake Atitlán. To explore the villages around the shore of the lake, I rented a dugout canoe, heavy compared to a Canadian craft but stable in the wind. It took us three days to circumnavigate the lake, marvelling at the diversity of products in each village. Some cultivated *nanche* and *pitahaya*, small tropical fruits native to Central America. Others grew sisal from which they made rope and satchels. Green onions were a speciality in another village. All villages had small fields of corn, squash and beans, the "three sisters" of Indigenous cuisine.

View of Lake Atitlán. Brush, ink and lithography crayon on paper.

We learned that sellers from each village gathered once a week in the market at Panajachel, each distinguished not only by their wares but also by distinctive clothing. In one village, the men wore red and white striped pants cut-off below the knee like pirate attire while the women wore a solid colour skirt and precisely patterned heavy cotton blouse cinched tight with a waist band. Each village was different, and each villager dressed the same by gender, boy or man, woman or girl.

A fisherman, surprised to see gringos piloting a canoe around the lake, observed when he heard of our plan, "Ah, you are going around the world." We laughed together as I realized it was a world of human and natural diversity far beyond my own home range.

My Swiss companion and I spent our last night together in San Pedro, a village that in 1979 was a prime destination for young people backpacking their way through Guatemala. In the late afternoon a small group of young tourists stripped naked at a point of land along the shore and jumped into the lake. A fisherman in his canoe was livid at the sight and shouted at them until they returned to shore and donned their clothes.

Later I spoke with him, hearing his words of anger at the deep disrespect shown to his community. The bathers were perplexed by the ruckus. Were they not in a land where people are close to the earth, native and natural in every way, including their experience of the body? I reflected on their arrogance and insensitivity to a place and people with an ancient history and traditions of their own.

Steve, an American man with a PhD in psychology and a penchant for eating peyote, taught me a different lesson about cultural difference and respect. He lived with a highland farm family for a week, he said, helping out in the fields. Every morning the farmer would sit down to a breakfast of beans and tortillas. His daughter brought them a lunch for mid-day comprised of beans with fresh tortillas wrapped in an embroidered cloth. Dinner was the same.

After a few days of this routine, met with gusto by the farmer at every meal, Steve couldn't help but remark on his own culinary practice at home in Phoenix, Arizona. There, Steve said, he found all kinds of foods from many different countries. East Asian dishes, Indian curries, Italian pasta, German *weinerschnitzel* and British fish and chips were all at hand. Steve's host listened carefully. He then

Child in a doorway, San Miguel de Allende.

El Brujo (Wizard).

used a scrap of tortilla to collect the dark bean sauce in the bottom of the bowl and asked, "Haven't you found something you like yet?"

As my brothers will attest, after living in Mexico for years I came to love tortillas and beans, and for a change, beans and tortillas. I had found something I liked.

In San Miguel, I discovered the art and technical pleasures of photography, inspired by George Kraus, an accomplished American photographer teaching at the Institute. He introduced me to the possibility of constructed drama in photography, a genre similar to the thespian intensity of the Mexican muralist David Alfaro Sigueiros. This stood in sharp contrast to the documentary style of photographers I had studied in Montreal such as Robert Frank or Manuel Álvarez Bravo, Mexico's most acclaimed photographer. Rather than revealing what is found in nature, Kraus and Sigueiros used imagination to create fantastical scenes.

I experimented with his approach and learned to savour the magic of darkroom photography. Every print on paper became a performance, using my hands to block small fragments of projected light or to deepen shadows with more.

A trip to San Cristóbal de las Casas in Chiapas forced me to learn how to go beyond the constraints of my equipment as well. While on the bus I put a container of yogurt in the bag that also held my camera. Predictably, it leaked. The camera still took pictures but the mirror that permits the photographer to see through the lens directly was stuck. I could point and shoot, but could never be sure of what was in and what was outside of the frame. The situation prompted me to compose photographs with an ample background, stepping back further than the subject seemed to require and setting the focus to infinity. Understanding context became part of my photographic repertoire and personal journey.

When I arrived in San Miguel I had traded my Yukon plaid bush shirt for a white Mexican peasant pleated top, still paired with brown corduroy pants and a thick leather belt. I introduced myself as a Canadian from Dawson City, Yukon. While not entirely truthful—I had grown up in many different Canadian towns and lived for two years with my military family in a small German village—the Yukon identification was true enough and proved attractive. San Miguel, with

Self-portrait, Mexico.

its large expatriate community, two art schools and many language institutes serving travelling youth, was a vibrant playground, replete with the kinds of fun loving you might expect from the young, free and curious. The AIDS crisis had not yet started and the ethos of the town still echoed with the closing years of the sexual revolution that had begun in the 1960s.

By the time my parents came to visit for Christmas, a year after my arrival in Mexico, I had lost most of my earlier shyness. I found satisfaction in discovering the world through my senses. At twenty-three, I was in no hurry to find a different purpose.

My parents, however, were on a mission. They wanted to draw Casey out of the Yukon and the bush hippie lifestyle as they had with me. A ticket to Mexico and family gathering around a hotel pool in Oaxaca offered an opportunity to probe his interests. Steve, the eldest, was by then a licensed helicopter pilot. He arrived with his wife in their Westphalia Volkswagon camper van and dog, Carbón.

We had all learned from our parents to be self-reliant and courageous, my father from his life and my mother, Doreen, from hers. She

Doreen Ryan, A Nurse Graduate From St. Michael's Hospital, Toronto, Canada. Photographer Unknown.

had left Englehart, a tiny railroad town in northern Ontario, to study nursing at a time of war. One of ten children, her parents believed in launching their children safely but boldly into the world. While in training she fell sick with tuberculosis and convalesced for a year, unsure of making a full recovery. At a ballgame she met my father, a veteran visiting the small community with a local POW friend.

She was, as my father put it, a stunner. Thick, curly red hair, blue eyes and broad smile made her the talk of the town. The young men there wooed her doggedly until my father, smitten, convinced her to go out with him when she returned to Toronto to complete her studies. They eventually married. Throughout her married life, surrounded by three wild boys, she developed her own interests—popular music and dance, making her own clothes, entertaining friends with fine food. My interest in art connected us as kindred spirits.

Casey's challenge in Oaxaca was to find purpose. He did, soon after becoming a helicopter pilot with a gift for using a "long line" to expertly place heavy loads in tight spaces. He retired decades later from the Canadian Coast Guard, where Steve also worked as a helicopter pilot and manager until his retirement.

A political turn

Experiences in Mexico awakened all my senses but initially provided me with no sense of direction. Two friends prompted a political turn I haven't wavered from since.

Gerald was the history teacher at the art school and only a few years my senior. A Mexican born of English parents who had settled in Mexico after the Second World War, he became a Trotskyite when he went to study in London.

Trotsky was assassinated in Mexico in 1939 while exiled from Russia and living in the home of Diego Rivera and Frida Kahlo. Gerald turned to Trotskyism at university in the mid-1970s, by then among the geekiest of leftist ideologies. He and other Trotskyites regularly went toe-to-toe on the streets of London against far-right skinheads over their use of racist and anti-Semitic symbols. A small, skinny man with curly brown hair and fair complexion, he put skin in the game even at great personal risk.

Jail in the Municipal Palace,
San Miguel de Allende, Mexico.

Policeman, San Miguel de
Allende, Mexico.

The two contrasting political sub-cultures also clashed over the direction of the working class movement. Skinheads, many of whom were from working class families, focused on feelings of social alienation. By contrast, Trotskyites claimed they were building a culture of working class solidarity across racial and religious lines. Decades later, only the skinheads have any public profile although unity in diversity is now a mainstream concept.

Gerald's willingness to stand up and be counted helped me launch an art project on jails in Mexico. The family of a young man who had been arrested and jailed for a minor offence asked me if I would visit him in jail, if only to show that his treatment there was being watched. I went several times, taking photographs and making lithographs inspired by the famous skelleton graphics of José Guadalupe Posada, Mexico's most influential artists of the pre-revolutionary period. Late at night, I plastered several posters on the walls of the Municipal Palace. I was nervous and did such a poor job of it that they had fallen to the ground by the next morning.

By the time Gerald and I rented a house together his own days of political activism had begun to sink into a fog. An alcoholic and not yet thirty, he meticulously planned each evening's drinking session at Mama Mía, San Miguel's most frequented live music and restaurant venue. To stave off dehydration, he set out a tall glass of water next to his bed before heading out. He also laid out the clothes he would wear the following morning. I used these tips myself on a few occasions, until some years later I quit drinking alcohol altogether.

When my wife, Debra, met him on a visit to San Miguel in the 1990s, his most valuable possessions had just been taken by a collection agency, including several paintings by a well-known American artist. One painting remained. It was one of various brush and ink scenes I'd made from the shores of Lake Atitlán in Guatemala. The collection agency knew nothing of me, an art student painting in many different styles and producing competent images but no work worthy of name recognition. They had left it behind. Gerald was broke, but still happy with a glass of wine in his hand.

Money was a constraint I managed with periodic small loans from my parents, and fees I collected posing nude for the school's life drawing class. I could hold athletic pose's for a long time, giving the students a chance to render details of muscles bulging under strain.

I jumped at an offer from Eleanor, my Dawson friend, to accompany her to Cuba as her translator. She had been the Minister of Education in the Yukon Government for a term and after leaving politics specialized in adult education. She wanted to learn about the 1961 Literacy Campaign that helped lift Cuban literacy rates to among the highest in the world and laid the foundation for Cuba's many health and educational achievements in the years that followed.

Our two weeks in Cuba began in Havana on New Year's Eve, the anniversary of the Cuban revolution. We watched Fidel Castro's long speech on the hotel TV while sipping rum. Soon after, we went to the Isla de Joventud, the second-largest Cuban island. It hosted residential colleges for youth from Angola, Namibia and Mozambique. Cuba's ties to African socialist movements had begun a decade earlier and involved sending thousands of troops to the region. Cuba had a strategic influence too on Namibian struggles against apartheid policies imposed there by South Africa.

One of the schools had been a jail for political dissidents in Batista's time. The Africans, however, came to Cuba voluntarily for a high school and university education. They were expected to work in Cuba for some time before returning home after their education. This might mean ten years away.

A student committee ran the residence, with their own rules and methods for enforcement. Up at 6:00 a.m., they would work in the gardens and orchards around the school and study through the afternoon. This was democracy, they said: Contribute by working and through self-organization, not simply by voting in elections.

Years later, my colleague Jacques told me of his experience evaluating the Cuban component of a Canada World Youth program on civic and community engagement. The Canadians involved defined their civic engagement primarily in relation to individual lifestyle choices like recycling, volunteering and voting. Contributions to the collective good were scheduled for weekends and evenings. By contrast, the Cubans focused on the professional choices they made, including entering teaching and helping professions such as medicine and social work. Civic engagement was part and parcel of their livelihood predilections.

The two notions of politics and civic engagement, expressed by Cuban and Canadian youth, reflect my own experience with the African youth on Isla de Juventud and their perspective on democracy and the rights and responsibilities of citizens. It was an early part of my own turn to the politics of free will and right livelihood.

Melville's wisdom

Just before leaving Mexico to return to the Yukon I received a postcard from Steve, the American psychologist. He told me he was back in the States learning to become a small engine mechanic. He set himself the task, he said, in the spirit of the Russian mystic George Gurdjieff, who gave his followers unexpected and difficult instructions to help them wake up to the world. He also thought he could use the skill to support himself travelling anywhere in the world.

The card included a quote attributed to Herman Melville: "We cannot live only for ourselves. A thousand fibres connect us; and among those fibres, as sympathetic threads, our actions run as causes, and they come back to us as effects."

I had just received news of a grant from the Canada Council for the Arts to support my return to Dawson. My proposal to paint and photograph life in the Yukon included references to the American assemblage artist Joseph Cornell and Pop art icon Robert Rauschenberg. Both of these modern artists blurred the distinctions between painting and sculpture, found objects and constructed realities, form and function, the theme of my first art show in Whitehorse several years earlier. I also wrote in the proposal that, "I have many friends who are trappers, miners, farmers, bird watchers, craftspeople, businessmen and hippies in search of alternative lifestyles. I will be greatly assisted by these people."

I arrived in Dawson a few months after the Great Flood of 1979. An ice jam on the Yukon River had forced water over the riverbank during the spring break up and back through the sewer system into the town. Buildings that had stood on the shifting permafrost since the Gold Rush were unsettled further and board sidewalks scattered about by the flood waters like jumbled matchsticks.

The paintings I had stored in a riverfront shack during my time in Mexico were destroyed—watercolours, drawings, oil paintings, antique frames and other bric-a-brac I planned to use in my new art—all stained and warped beyond repair, or turned to mush.

I had little time to grieve. My journey from San Miguel to Dawson had been aided by Carole King (no relation to the singer-songwriter).

Carole in her Mexican poncho looking out over the Tombstone Valley, early winter.

She offered me a ride in her early 1970s Chevy Impala to her home town in Chicago. A romance bloomed. After a stopover in Albuquerque, New Mexico to visit some of the world's best printmaking studios, we parted ways in front of the Chicago Art Gallery with a plan to meet up again in Dawson.

I had to prepare for winter and her arrival: wood to cut, bulk food supplies to buy, a long extension cord to bring electric light into the cabin I had rented from John while he was at his trapline. The loss of my art to the flood had to be set aside.

Carole had a lot of adjusting to do as well. She struggled with the lack of running water or indoor toilet while I didn't mind sponge baths and occasionally shitting in a paper bag when it was too cold to go to the outhouse. She was truly frightened, however, by a touch of frostbite during an outing on the frozen river. After that, she said that she wanted to return to Chicago for Christmas and get a break from the cold weather. A long soak in a bath at her parent's house prompted her to write to me to say goodbye, wishing me luck with my efforts to document the life of people and landscapes of the North.

Early in the new year a stray cat arrived at my doorstep, and stayed till spring. I think of that winter, my last in the Yukon, as a change in life direction by stealth and by revelation. After the heartbreak came the soul searching. I joined a Bible Study group offered by an evangelical minister new in town, closely reading Paul's "Epistle to the Romans."

The Bible was a book I had only leafed through before, despite the Scottish Presbyterian roots of my father and my mother's Irish Roman Catholic heritage. The contrast in their religious upbringing was so severe they had to elope to marry. As a gesture of reconciliation, they announced to their parents that they would raise their children in the Anglican Church.

Scholars of religion will find satisfaction in this choice because Anglicanism, the religion launched by Henry VIII when he couldn't get the Pope to allow him to divorce, is the closest Protestants can get to the rituals of Catholicism and "the ancient church." This choice of church was acceptable to both their parents as a place to teach the fear and love of God to the grandchildren. I sang as a choir boy, and occasionally carried the burning incense through the church.

Paul's words, dated 55 to 57 A.D., intrigued me. The epistle is much loved by evangelical Christians because it offers salvation through the gospel of Jesus Christ. The core debate about interpretation is the distinction between salvation through faith and salvation through righteous actions. Protestants tend to focus strictly on faith while Catholics balance the two paths, at least in theory.

By the time we finished the reading I came to respect the minister's intellectual rigour but did not experience Christ as he had. As a young man living alone through the Dawson winter, Paul the Apostle's core question about the path of faith and the path of deeds weighed on me. I don't remember any details now that give a hint of how conscious I was of tension in my own life between connection to self and connection to others, another underlying theme of the epistle. I do know, however, that I was unhappy and uncertain about my life purpose. Surely art is for something?

Finally came the leap of faith. In the spring of 1980, I bought a Dodge van outfitted as a camper. It became my home, allowing me to explore parts of the Yukon I had never visited, as promised in my proposal to the Canada Council. Gravel roads took me to the mining town of Faro to attend a folk festival, the Burien family cattle farm on the Klondike River and the Schmidt goat farm on the Stewart River. I put together an exhibition of photographs and drawings, often with the same subject rendered in different mediums, hung that summer at the Edmonton Public Library.

Stray cat, minus thirty degrees.

Stray cat and cabin interior, minus thirty degrees.

By late summer I went south again from Whitehorse to Carcross where I picked up a friend who wanted a lift to Atlin in northern British Columbia. We drove the long, dead-end road to this isolated community and spent a few nights in a tepee on the outskirts of town. Our host, a woman, had recently given birth. In the tepee.

The three of us lounged around a spring that bubbled up at the camp. A male moose emerged suddenly from the nearby woods. Its large upper body and full spread of horns balanced improbably on long, spindly legs as it approached the baby sleeping on a blanket. It stopped a few paces short, surveying the human child from high

Self-portrait, Coal Creek, Yukon.

above. Time seemed to stand still. Then, the mother slowly but resolutely moved towards her child. The moose turned and loped away.

I came to a crossroads after returning from Atlin to the Alaska Highway. Turn north and I would head back to Dawson, a place with friends but also isolated from the wide world. Turn south and I could head towards Ottawa, my home town, with two universities and a thriving artistic community.

My decision was not one of religious inspiration like the one my trapper friend had experienced standing on the Yukon River shoreline. It emerged more as a search for connection to others. I'd experienced the wonder of intense cold and striking winter night skies, the pleasure in learning my craft and discovery of the human body, mine and others. I'd seen something dramatic and beautiful in the Mexican people and in the tactile details of their lives and history. The idea of commitment to others and the politics of life had also broken through my relative self-reliance in the Yukon. I wanted to make art that might make a difference but had no idea what for, who for or how to do it. I needed a bridge between the worlds of art and anthropology.

3
The Eddy

The Yukon River is full of silt. It makes a hissing sound as it brushes the shore at a brisk six kilometres per hour, traversing the length of Yukon and Alaska some 2,000 kilometres to the Bering Sea. The silt comes from the Saint Elias Range and Canada's tallest peak, Mount Logan. Sharp rock cliffs bank the river in many places while other parts of the river are wide floodplains characterized by thickets of willow and alder and dense stands of spruce. Near the sea, the river is over 800 metres wide, frequently braided by sand bars and islands. On the whole, it is neither a placid river nor a raging one but rather grand, calm and relentless. The volume of water it carries to the sea

An eddy on the Yukon River.

drains an area approximately 850,000 square kilometres, the fifth largest in North America.

All five species of Pacific salmon are found in the Yukon River but only the king (a.k.a. chinook or spring salmon) and chum (a.k.a. dog salmon) penetrate into Canadian territory on their migration from the sea to spawn in the river's freshwater streams. Salmon stop eating as they start the migration, converting stored fats into energy. Sexually mature king salmon become very red-skinned and in males the snout becomes enlarged and hooked. Not a pretty fish at that point but still firm and good to eat. Chum salmon are considered excellent dog food. Both species die after spawning. Like the river, they are relentless until the end.

P.V. Satheesh, a friend in India and a man steeped in the complexity and beauty of dry land agriculture, once asked me, "How is this battle by salmon going up rivers to spawn even possible?" The answer, I learned from work with my fisher friends in the Yukon, is "the eddy." Shoreline cliffs create slack water areas on the downstream side and temporary respite for migrating fish. This is where people catch them, using surface gill nets in locations scattered along the length of the river.

Spawning ground

I arrived in Dawson in the spring of 1982 after two years in Ottawa making connections between nature, art and anthropology. The transformation began with qualifying courses to get into a master's program in Canadian Studies at Carleton University. The pitch I made to the Director was to examine northern Canadian views on the environment, and to make art of my own as part of the process.

He pointed me to courses where I could learn about contemporary forces transforming the Canadian North and offered me a teaching assistant position with George Swinton, an art historian of Austrian origin specialized in the sculptures of the ancient Dorset people of the Arctic. My job was to organize his mammoth collection of slides, carefully coding each, slipping them into plastic sleeves and preparing a paper record. Dr. Swinton was putting his life's work in order, a task being repeated now with my own life as I sift through decades of memories and images.

My original thesis started with a critique of Albrecht Dürer's 1504 engraving of Adam and Eve. With its mix of domestic livestock and wildlife, it told the story of deforestation to make way for open pastures, sheep and cattle. The mouse at the feet of Adam, wild and yet closely associated with domestic life, seems to signal the inevitability of things to come: dominion over the earth. Bush life in the Yukon, I suggested, pointed in a different direction, a different future. I wanted to study that.

When I returned to the Yukon after a year of graduate studies the idea of challenging Dürer's religiously inspired vision of nature felt effervescent and untameable for someone with no training in social theory and philosophy. It also felt useless.

Questions about the utility of research came in part from course work with John Cove, a specialist at Carleton in the people of the salmon on British Columbia's West Coast. After classes, we drank beer at the university pub and talked about fishing and photography, our respective passions.

One night he gave me a book called *Malay Fisherman: Their Peasant Economy* by the New Zealand anthropologist Raymond Firth. Firth's contribution, I learned, was to the development of the field of economic anthropology—the study of human economic behaviour using a historical, geographic and cultural lens. Firth had a concern for improving the economic conditions of peasant communities, a perspective that informs much of what became "international development studies" and the core of my later work at the International Development Research Centre.

John Cove passed away a decade ago so I cannot ask him again why he gave me Firth's book. Reflecting on it now brings several things to mind. First, it is a richly detailed study of virtually every dimension of fishing livelihood one can think of. It is also extensively illustrated with straightforward photographs of people, places and activities. I admired this attention to detail and simple gaze. Second, it provokes in modern readers a critical understanding of the colonial thinking of the time and implications for the ethics of research.

John, an academic personally involved in Canadian Indigenous politics of the 1980s, was acutely aware of the risk that anthropologists might become government informants, knowingly or not. Firth was aware of the risk too and the attention given to solving so-called "administrative problems" of the British Empire. In his Preface, Firth takes great pains to situate his book between disciplinary concerns (curiosity-driven science) and a genuine preoccupation with the improvement of livelihoods (action-oriented assessments).

He got it in the neck from all sides—by theoreticians for being "merely practical" and by politically aware researchers for being "naive" about the use of anthropology to advance the interests of Western colonial powers.

The ethical challenges of useful learning, and who the learning is for, have a long history in the social sciences. Eric Wolf, the eminent American anthropologist and author of *Peasant Wars of the Twentieth Century*, spent the last years of his career fighting against the Vietnam War. He and others forced the American Anthropological Association to re-write its code of ethics to prevent anthropological data from knowingly being used in military campaigns.

More recently, Canada's Tri-Council of research funders, while focusing on the familiar ethical principles of respect for people, protection of privacy and fairness, acknowledges the possibility of alternative codes of conduct where research is in collaboration with the subjects involved. Benefits for communities are a primary consideration in this framework, a perspective on ethics reflected in my own later research life.

As a young anthropology student, the question of who research is for, whose values it promotes and how it might be used was just beginning to form in my mind. After a summer job in Whitehorse with the Yukon government's Department of Natural Resources, I learned of plans by the Council for Yukon Indians and the Dawson Indian Band to support construction of a commercial fish processing plant. The transition from subsistence to commercial fishing and questions about who might benefit seemed like a reputable topic for anthropological study. I was still part of the bush community in Dawson with an insider's perspective on living on the land. My teachers approved and I got a grant from the Northern and Native Studies program at Carleton to fund the research.

The experience of nature and the outdoors while doing the research was one of the most pleasurable in my life. For an entire summer I travelled up and down the Yukon River, stopping at fish camps, taking photographs and taking notes on everything I saw. The federal

Dried chum salmon to feed sled dogs during the winter months.

Department of Fisheries and Oceans had loaned me a sixteen-foot flat bottom boat, thirty horsepower motor and drum of gas from their stores in Whitehorse, delivered to Dawson at the beginning of the summer. In exchange, I counted fishing eddies, sixty in all, along 200 kilometres of the Yukon River upstream and downstream from Dawson City.

Sometimes, when travelling down river, I would turn off the motor and drift, taking in the landscape and listening to the hiss of the silt on the aluminum boat hull. Stopovers at a fish camp usually involved spending the night, sleeping in a small tent and drinking tea with my "informants" until it came out of every pore.

Along the way, I came to understand the true meaning of hay-wiring, an art perfected by the isolated fishermen and occasional fisher-woman who managed to keep their own motors running by adapting parts from one model year or another and fixing broken pieces with things on hand. Most preferred the older machines—Envinrude and

Marcy and Mel at their fish camp on the Yukon River.

Johnston motors from the 1950s and 1960s—because these had fewer electronic parts that once broken could not be fixed.

My own good sense was tested on occasion. When motoring upstream to a camp I pulled the drain plug to let the forward movement of the boat expel the rainwater that had collected in the bottom, rather than taking the time to bail it out by hand. It is an effective and not unheard-of technique in a small boat but usually requires that the plug be put back in when stopped. I pulled up to the camp and joined the lone fisher for tea. The two of us leaped into action a few minutes later when he noticed the rear end of the boat sinking in the water, almost taking the motor down with it.

When I was not on the river I spent days among local Indigenous youth cleaning and washing fish in a brand-new processing plant. It had been converted from what was once the Ladue Sawmill and then the Band Hall by First Nations hands and specialist tradesmen from Vancouver. A few years earlier, in this same sturdy frame structure, I had played congas and a penny whistle late into the night as part of a dance band.

The Hän fisheries plant was a source of pride for those who participated in its construction. Equipped with a state-of-the-art flash

Opening day at the Hän Fishery, 1981.

freezer and stainless-steel fish cutting trays and benches, it had the capacity to process 200,000 pounds of fish per season. Less than half of that amount was caught that first year but the red chinook carcasses, flash frozen and shipped in freezer trucks, eventually made their way to New York where they were transformed into smoked salmon delicacies for the kosher market. It demonstrated that the commercial potential was there.

One local Indigenous leader told me that "the fishery is like an early realization of a land claim dream." After decades of exclusion from the economic life of Dawson, the fishery brought jobs and hope. The Dawson Band would have to wait, however, more than ten years more before a land claim was actually settled, one of the first of the modern treaties between Indigenous peoples and the Crown.

Pull of the current

I still had feet in two worlds, with a notebook in one hand and a large format camera at my side. While studying at Carleton I had enrolled in a photography course at the University of Ottawa with Robert Bourdeau, one of Canada's premier large format photographers and former student of Minor White and Paul Strand, influential American photographers. I learned to use several unusual cameras, including one that produced a four by four inch negative and required a black cape to block out light as I focused on the glass screen. It was a Klondike style camera which offered an image sharper than anything I had produced to date.

My art production also combined the visual and the narrative in the form of small sets of images bound together into hand-made books. I wanted the intimacy of the relationship between the artist, the work and the audience that a book format could attain, so learned the craft of bookbinding. Several old and damaged volumes from my father's book collection, including an edition of the Complete Works of Guy de Maupassant, provided scope for practice.

While I was a competent artist, my work did not stand out on the Ottawa scene, dominated at the time by conceptual and performance art with little in the way of tactile craft. The art getting accolades was intellectual and urban—an artist living in a hidden corner of the gallery for a week, producing evocative notes and video for visitors to read and view. The art left me feeling unmoved and anachronistic. I was also now a small fish in a big pond, no longer a student or valued Dawson artist but rather competing with other talent in a creative pool with the historical scope of centuries and continents.

Tim, James and Andreé cleaning fish, Coal Creek, Yukon.

My photographs from the summer on the Yukon River are telling. They do not depict nature as serene and tameable as Dürer had shown during the Renaissance. Nor do they evoke the constructed drama I'd imagined I might produce for the Canada Council. My photographs were straight forward and plain in their observation of people and nature. This seems right for the time and place: witnessing an early foray by the First Nations in Dawson into local economic development that, although unsuccessful, marked the beginning of a new era.

My writing, by contrast, said little of the social life I was witnessing. A first draft, which waxed poetic about the landscape and personalities of fisherman friends, was soundly rejected by my future colleague Jacques, who sat on the committee. No structure, he said, and too descriptive to be a thesis.

I pivoted quickly, presenting the Yukon fishery story in the language of contemporary sociology, including quotes from Karl Marx about the labour process. Wally Clement, my lead supervisor, was an icon of Canadian political economy, having turned his master's thesis, *The Canadian Corporate Elite,* into one of the most widely read works in Canadian sociology at the time. Both advisors were looking out for me, ensuring that I demonstrated the understanding required of a thesis in a discipline still new to me. Artistic expression, and unfocused description, simply wouldn't cut it or could wait for another time. I took the advice. The final thesis received the honour of distinction.

My fisher friends were also satisfied, mostly. They told me that I had correctly described the fish, the eddies, the fishing tools and techniques, the income earned and the history of prior and current efforts to start up a commercial operation. I had told the truth. Copies made it into the local library, the Department of Natural Resources in Whitehorse, the Council for Yukon Indians and the First Nation Band Office. Later, I learned that a consultant hired to find new funding for the fishery lifted without citation three pages of verbatim text from my thesis to set the scene for the proposal. I was glad the thesis was useful, but also demanded an apology, which I received from the Council for Yukon Indians.

One person expressed disappointment in the thesis. Tim, a fisher and Dawson friend from hikes into the mountains near the Tombstone, said that he had expected the thesis to be more political. Despite the sympathetic portrait of the plans and motivations of the First Nations and non-Indigenous fishers involved, and Marxist argument that capitalism would likely subjugate and undermine the future success of this nascent local industry, the thesis had missed the most consequential story. Why, after years of resisting local initiatives, had the federal and territorial governments decided to approve a major investment in a commercial fishery on the Yukon River? Why had the Department of Fisheries and Oceans loaned me, a student with a background in art, a valuable boat, motor and a forty-five-gallon drum of gas?

The explanation, only partially addressed in my thesis, points to international politics and competing claims on the ownership of the fish. Pacific salmon are heavily fished by Japanese and U.S. factory ships during their adult life in the open ocean and as they congregate at the mouth of the Yukon River in preparation for the long struggle against the current to spawning grounds. They are also fished along the many kilometres of the Yukon River in Alaska, in numbers vastly greater than in the Yukon. This extended gauntlet means that fish returning to specific creeks at the Canadian end of the watershed have suffered predation at many stages in their life cycle and at numerous downstream locations. Yukon fishers are the last in line and a final hit on fragile fish stocks.

For several years before my study Canada and the United States had been in negotiations regarding the allocation of Yukon River salmon between fishers in each country. The Americans played hardball, enjoying the *de facto* advantage of a well-developed industrial fleet in the Bering Sea and hundreds of inshore and river fishers with a long history of taking large numbers of fish. I interviewed some of these officials in Fairbanks and a few Alaskan fishers in places on the river like Eagle, just across the Yukon border. However, I do not recall asking any hard questions or being even remotely belligerent about the unfairness of the situation. Fully one third of the watershed is in the Yukon, which might mean that Yukon fishers had rights to one third of the entire catch.

Only later did I realize that a shift in Canadian policy to allow for a Yukon fish plant, and my boat gas, was an attempt by Canada to leverage concessions from the Americans. The investment in the plant showed that the fish and the fishing capacity existed in Canada.

A traditional fish wheel on the shoreline at Dawson,
run by Weldon Farr and his son.

The government strategy worked, more or less, because Canada did eventually get acknowledgement from the Americans of a theoretical share. Deal-making, however, was immediately followed by the sudden and long term collapse of the entire Yukon River salmon population. While the causal linkages were coincidental—over-fishing for decades by the Japanese and American industrial fleets had gradually ground down the fish population—the fish plant was a major threat to the spawning fish that made it up the long Yukon River. It was shut down after only a few years of operation. The freezers rusted and the collector boat was sold. Fishing around Dawson returned to a minor subsistence practice of a handful of First Nations and non-Indigenous fishers living on the land. Meanwhile, industrial fishing continues unabated on the high seas.

The complexity of the situation and the naivety of my research enterprise—doing the work of solving the administrative problems of the Canadian and American empire—was largely invisible to me and even to smart university professors with only indirect and partial pictures of the world I was studying. My supervisors were, understandably, mainly concerned about guiding a student through the requirements of a university degree. This was in keeping with the linear approach to learning typical of universities where disciplinary building blocks are put together in a measured and orderly fashion and transmitted from professor to student.

My experiences during Master's studies confronted a few of the limitations of university learning and hinted at new pedagogical strategies that later became important to my professional development. In later years, Jacques, who became my friend and close professional colleague, was clearer and more vocal in his criticism of the university experience. He began to promote at Carleton the idea of student engagement with the real world at all levels, including undergraduate studies. Complexity, and the messiness of research with human subjects, could be a crucible, he argued, for a grounded and strategic approach to student learning. Our later work together in Mexico proved to be the prompt and testing ground for this pedagogical shift.

In the meantime, however, with a B.F.A. and an M.A. under my belt, and stories to tell from the Yukon and Mexico, I was resting in the ease and flow of a creative and engaged life. I could savour the world and dream of saving it, without a real care in the world. Everything seemed possible.

Even today, as I immerse myself in the memories, I can feel the steady pulse of the river and hiss of the silt.

4

A Land Without Gods

Grey beaches along the Gulf of Mexico, dotted with blue and white fishing boats, carried me through a "gap year" after completing a master's degree in Canadian Studies. I would rise before dawn and join the four-person crew of a twenty-five-foot open fibreglass *lancha* making its way out to sea to check nets and baited long-lines that had been set the evening before. Depending on the catch, the crew might decide to stay out for several hours more and still-fish for red snapper, a more lucrative species than the small sharks, grouper, flounder, rays and other fish they might find on the end of their night hooks.

Anchored above a shoal a mile from shore we would fish under the morning sun with several baited hooks on a single nylon line wrapped around a tin can, and joke using the vulgar and sexually charged idiom made famous throughout Mexico by the fishers of Veracruz. I had to learn to protect myself from the verbal barbs while leaning

Fishing for Red Snapper on the Gulf of Mexico near Chachalacas, Veracruz.

over the edge of a small boat to pull in a fish. Relief from the macho word play would come when the crew decided the fishing was done and make haste for the shore and a late breakfast. By the time we headed back to shore my pale skin, inherited from my red-headed and freckled mother, was often burned to a crisp.

Happenstance took me to the coast of Veracruz in the summer of 1983, after winning an internship in a Canada-Mexico exchange program organized by the Canadian government's Department of External Affairs. A small number of recent Canadian graduates, and a similar number of Mexicans, were provided with one-year grants and letters of introduction allowing them to offer their skills and services, free of charge, to prospective employers. It was a paid internship with an international twist. After graduating, I had no reason—partner or financial need—to simply get a job and settle down. Nor did I want to enter a doctoral degree program without some idea of what I might have to say or contribute. Chance, and an eye for things Mexican, meant that on campus I saw a poster for the exchange program, applied successfully and away I went.

Roots and wings

Mexican culture gives a great deal of attention to chance events in life and in death. My friend Lilia told me that people play games of chance on the graves of their ancestors during *The Day of the Dead*. First they pull weeds and clean up the site. Then they lay out food for their ancestors. While waiting for the spirits to come, they play games with dice, pick-up-jax and cards. This pastime is a reminder that family roots mix with good fortune to create a path in life.

My own family tradition emphasized a related but more privileged perspective, summed up in the words of Henry Ward Beecher, an American clergyman best known for his opposition to slavery. The verse hung on the wall at our cottage for decades: "There are two lasting bequests we can give our children. Roots and wings." My access to higher education provided lift that many Mexicans didn't have.

I found a place to use my good fortune in Jalapa, the capital of the state of Veracruz. It had a good university, a thriving arts scene and a world class museum of anthropology only an hour from the Gulf of Mexico. The head of the museum agreed to host my internship focused on the anthropology of fishing.

In Jalapa, I found a room to rent in the home of Doña Teresa Blanco Rosas, a short, round woman with twinkling eyes and a reluctant smile. Her husband, long dead, had been a leader of the 1930s Veracruz agrarian reform movement. By the 1940s, the movement had been crushed by "the Black Hand," a violent network of thugs at the service of large landowners and supported by national political leaders. When they married in the late 1950s, Doña Teresa was a young woman while he was already an old man. She bore two children and inherited from her husband a tall, sturdy building in the middle of the city which she converted into a home for herself and her children, and rooms for rent. I stayed in the roof-top room and ate breakfast and the traditional early afternoon main meal in her small dining room.

An amazing cook, Doña Teresa was well versed in the medicinal properties and uses of food. I adopted her recipe for treating and preventing Moctezuma's revenge: a daily concoction of garlic cloves crushed with lemon juice and knocked back on an empty stomach. "Start with three," she said, "and increase to ten for the complete treatment." Because of her advice, I had a healthy belly but no steady girlfriend.

After learning how to defend myself on a Veracruz fishing boat, I met Yvan Breton, a university of Laval anthropology professor doing fisheries research in Veracruz and the state of Campeche. I heard about him through a mutual friend and tracked him down at the sprawling Mocambo Hotel outside the port of Veracruz. The salt air had pitted the walls and archways of the hotel, giving it the same rundown look of most buildings near the sea.

There we drank *mescal*, Mexico's true hard liquor, and ate seafood soup sharply spiced with *chili*. We talked about the culture, politics and economics of coastal fishing. When his wife and two kids arrived for a visit, we played cards late into the night. Later, he asked me to work with him in the Port of Alvarado, the heart of the fishing culture of Veracruz.

The port had everything in the world of commercial fishing: independent *lancha* fishers like the ones I first worked with, fleets of shrimp boats organized into cooperatives and large corporate tuna fishing boats equipped with freezers and plans to ply the Gulf for

Shrimp vessel in Alvarado, preparing to go to sea.

several weeks at a stretch. Artisanal fishers trapped crabs and fished for the native species of tilapia from dugout canoes in the nearby lagoon and mangrove-lined estuary.

Yvan was a delight to work with and provided me with a great example of how to be incisive, humble and practical as a researcher. He paid particular attention to producing meticulous field notes and to publishing initial findings in the local language as quickly as possible. This commitment to sharing early results in local languages was not a common concern in the anthropology of the time but became a routine practice for me as well.

From Yvan I learned other elements of the trade that also stuck with me. I thought of him as the epitome of the character "Columbo," the homicide detective with the Los Angeles Police Department played by Peter Falk. Yvan's jet-black hair, deep gentle voice and calm wit was disarming and completely authentic. Like Columbo, he could draw anyone into a conversation that revealed much more than they initially wanted to. When necessary, he would validate the information with a striking summary. There was no malicious intent in Yvan's art, except perhaps when dealing with the fish market kingpins or nefarious characters leading some of the Alvarado fishing cooperatives. His work was not naïve. He was intent on defending the interests of small and vulnerable fishing communities and workers.

He also knew how to open doors into worlds blocked to overly earnest researchers such as myself. A personal connection to Quebec's diplomatic representative in Mexico, who lived next to the Mexico City home of the governor of the state of Veracruz, translated into an introduction to the fishing union power bosses. Like wind beneath my wings, the connection sent me directly onto the shrimp vessels plying the night waters in the Gulf of Mexico. I took copious notes, got sea sick far from shore and had a close call with a poisonous water snake while checking crab traps in the lagoon. Like Columbo, I observed and looked for clues of what was going on below the surface.

In search of the fourth world

Yvan and I remained good friends for decades but did not work together again after publishing the results of our Alvarado research. Part way through my internship at the Museum of Anthropology, Jacques, a member of my master's thesis committee at Carleton University, contacted me in search of a project for his first sabbatical. Only six years my senior, he was the youngest professor in the history of the Department of Sociology and Anthropology and a rising star.

His PhD thesis, converted into a critically acclaimed book called *Capital, Kin and Cult in Eastern Peru*, challenged many assumptions of Marxist anthropology about the relationship between Indigenous cultures and capitalism. Ernesto Laclau, the Argentinean philosopher who is often credited with inventing post-Marxist political theory, applauded the innovation and wrote the forward to the book. The period marked a decisive shift in left-wing critical theory, distancing itself from the fascist practices of Stalinism. It tried to retain the sharp Marxian insight into the historical development of capitalism without taking on the political project of a proletarian revolution, a tension the left has still not fully resolved.

In the fall of 1983 Jacques turned his attention away from teaching and administrative duties to consider new anthropological research. Mexico was an option for him to do field work relatively close to home. I provided him with local knowledge. We met up in Jalapa, spending several days in Doña Teresa's house discussing ways to combine my interest in fisheries with his interest in studies of Indigenous Peoples. While neither of us could have known it at the time, his initial phone call from Canada and our subsequent meeting launched a working relationship and friendship now three decades on and counting.

Resolving our two interests initially took time. I knew that despite the long coastlines of Mexico, few Indigenous groups specialized in fishing. Most are agrarian cultures, with maize as the common story of where they originated as a people. The Seris of coastal Sonora are one exception, having integrated a remarkably detailed knowledge of the sea and its resources into their culture. The Lacandon Maya located near Yaxchilán, Chiapas, where I had worked as an archaeological illustrator, are also an exception to the agrarian rule. However, they take their cultural cues from the Lacandon jungle, not the sea. Even the Maya of the Yucatan among whom Yvan conducted fisheries related research are farmers first and foremost. Fishing is a supplementary livelihood only partly connected to core cultural stories and livelihoods.

Faced with few options to combine fishing with the study of Indigenous culture, we turned first to Catemaco, Veracruz, a place known for its sorcerers and located beside a large inland lake. We set out in search of the Indigenous "fourth world," only to find that Catemaco was a pleasant tourist destination of little interest anthropologically. Only a handful of people made their living from fishing and the Indigenous sorcerers were mostly oriented toward entertaining Mexican tourists.

We moved on, approaching the region from the coastal side where we knew the Indigenous language *Nahuatl* was still spoken. James Stewart, an American anthropologist, had researched their subsistence economy for his own 1978 PhD study. We followed his path to Peña Hermosa, a tiny hamlet on the coast in the shadow of the San Martín volcano. We only stayed a few days but the journey there and back on horseback provided several lasting impressions.

The first is a story Jacques tells anthropology students to illustrate three approaches to the study of myths. One approach is to examine the functions myths serve in society. Another is to explore the underlying cultural meaning of myths. A third is to determine what truth there really is behind a myth.

"The Nahua tell of powerful serpent spirits protecting the secrets of a cave," Jacques would say to his students. "Daniel and I went to see the cave during our stay in the hamlet, but without having

Jacques on horseback, in search of the fourth world.

performed the Nahua cleansing rituals. On our way back, Daniel noticed a venomous coral snake at my feet and shouted a warning. I jumped away, just in time."

"Now," he would ask his students, "is the serpent legend guarding against unclean entry true or false?"

The second impression from our journey to Peña Hermosa is a pair of photographs showing each of us on horseback, hats set jauntily on our heads and windswept views of the Gulf of Mexico behind. Tales of Indiana Jones had only recently swept the world with the release in 1981 of Raiders of the Lost Ark. For Jacques' children, the photo of a tall man wearing a Planter's hat and a thin beard on a white horse conveyed an image no father could resist, prompting Jacques to later frame the photo for his office wall.

What the photo doesn't show is that Jacques is allergic to horse hair and suffered greatly from the reaction throughout the trip. I sat comfortably enough on my horse, an animal I had learned not to fear, but soon developed intense irritation in my groin. Cattle Ticks had worked their way into my pants. It is hard to imagine Indiana Jones dealing with the same indignities.

Much is made in anthropological lore of Bronislaw Malinowski, the Austro-Hungarian who pioneered participant observation in the

Trobriand Islands of Melanesia where he stayed for several years studying the Indigenous culture. The method, unique to the anthropological perspective, involves becoming part of a community as much as possible by engaging in the rituals and activities of everyday life.

While long periods of time in the "field" are key requirements of participant observation, John Cove, one of my teachers at Carleton University, was fond of pointing out that Malinowski did this pivotal field work during the First World War. A citizen of the Austro-Hungarian empire, he was in fact trapped on the islands by the impossibility of travelling home through British and Australian territory. It was unsafe to leave, so he stayed.

John's punch line for this story was that when Malinowski settled in England after the war and launched a career as an anthropologist at the London School of Economics, he made every anthropology student since spend much more time in remote places than they really needed to accomplish the task at hand.

Jacques and I did not quibble over the need to spend time with the Nahua and learn from them by participating in their daily activities. Still, we decided not to stay in Peña Hermosa because it was simply too small and too isolated from other Nahua communities to provide new insights, beyond what Stewart had already documented. Instead, we went to Jicacal, a *Nahuatl* speaking hamlet on the shores of the

Grilling fish on the beach at Jicacal, Veracruz, Mexico.

nearby Laguna del Ostión. Mangrove trees lined the shore of the lagoon and most inhabitants lived off fishing, collecting oysters and growing watermelons on the sandy beach soils. Oil refinery workers and other working people from Coatzacoalcos and Minatitlán sometimes made their way by boat across the mouth of the lagoon for a weekend beach and dining experience under small palm huts on the beach.

We stayed in Jicacal for three months, sharing a corrugated tin shack with two cots and a rough table. While not as comfortable as Catemaco or as isolated as Peña Hermosa, Jicacal proved to be the perfect location for us to do what anthropologists are supposed to do: participate in the life of the community and listen for the stories of people living lives rooted in non-western traditions challenged by encounters with dominant outside cultures.

For me, this included collecting oysters growing on mangrove roots and learning how to cast a net while standing in a dugout canoe. I was fascinated with fishing techniques and in awe of the spear fishermen searching for northern red snapper, the common snook and other fish hiding in ocean reefs a few hundred yards from shore.

Spear fishing in the ocean was impossible for me, not least because of my fear of deep water. As a toddler I had fallen off a dock at the family cottage, unnoticed during a party that neighbours were hosting. My mother spied me at the bottom of the lake and shouted for my father to snatch me out. I was unharmed and later learned to swim, but never felt comfortable in the open water.

I could, however, manage swimming in a shallow lagoon. Fishermen had created micro-environments by anchoring large branches cut from the shoreline mangrove forest on the sandy bottom. Fish would congregate there, as though it were a natural reef.

Once or twice a day we came to the fishing spot and surrounded it with a net weighted to the bottom with lead and held at the surface by floats. I would then slip out of the canoe and into the water, making my way with a short wire spear into the middle of the encircled area. Fish scattered as I entered the water, encountered the net barrier and then slowly returned to see what new creature had come to their shelter.

My task was to hold still at an anchoring branch until a fish came close enough. When the fish satisfied its own curiosity it usually

Two Nahua fishers in the mangroves of Jicacal, Veracruz, Mexico.

turned to show its broadside, my cue to release the elastic on the spear, pierce the flesh and thrust the point into the sand until the fish no longer struggled to break free.

My successes were rare but at least enough to be able to describe the activity to the standard expected by what is now known as the British tradition of social anthropology.

Jacques did much the same, although in a different field from mine. He established a relationship with a neighbouring village *curandero*, or healer, which required him to show he was worthy of the knowledge to be acquired. I remember him returning to our shack one day to report that he may have made a major mistake by performing for the *curandero* a parlour trick involving a disappearing coin. We were both fans of simple magic tricks and entertained children and adults in Jicacal, which had no electricity and plenty of idle moments. The trick backfired, however, when the *curandero*, who was similar in age to Jacques, became spooked by Jacques' power and decided not to continue the teaching.

Grandmother and grandchild collect wood from the slopes of the volcano San Martín Pajapan, Veracruz, Mexico.

We even received *Nahuatl* nicknames: *totol texis* (turkey egg) to refer to my freckled skin and *ikstak chagalin* (white shrimp) to remark on how Jacques' pale skin turned red under the hot sun.

One day, near the end of our time in Jicacal, I took a hike to the top of the San Martín volcano some 1,500 metres above sea level. I wanted to reconnoitre the landscape, including the communal lands of Pajapan, the municipal centre for Jicacal, Peña Hermosa and other small Nahua communities along the coast.

By then we had realized that many of the families in Jicacal had been forced off community lands near Pajapan where they had grown maize and other crops. With few options for a livelihood, they turned to even more marginal livelihoods such as fishing and petty trade.

A man from Jicacal accompanied me, carrying a packed lunch for both of us and a small calibre rifle in case we encountered a jaguar at the peak. Still shrouded in thick cloud forest, the peak is where an ancient Olmec statue of a god grinding maize, *El Señor del Cerro* (the Elder on the Hill), once sat, protected, according to local lore, by animal spirits. In 1962, the state government had removed the statue and sent it to the Museum of Anthropology in Jalapa.

The removal happened at a time when the maize fields and secondary forests of the area were rapidly being converted into large cattle ranches. Communal land tenure characteristic of Indigenous communities in Mexico made it easy for the locally powerful to graze their animals everywhere, and impossible for others to protect agricultural fields and fallowing lands. Deforestation and displacement, first framed by the British environmentalist Norman Myers as "the hamburger connection," was all around us. "These *caciques* (local bosses)," my guide said, "are ignorant and selfish. Instead of thanking God for what they have received, they let their cattle move into and eat the forest."

Just short of the peak we saw something large dart by us as we struggled through thick forest. A jaguar? It was gone immediately and no fatal shot was fired.

"The gods are gone," explained a Pajapan healer Jacques worked with, referring to the stolen statue. The worst possible mythical scenario had come true, with the *chaneques* (legendary creatures in Mexican folklore) hiding themselves and the animals under their protection in the underworld, *Talogan*.

El Señor del Cerro (the Elder on the Hill).

We realized then that our search for the "fourth world" had come full circle. If we were to understand life in Jicacal we needed to turn our attention to Pajapan, the largest and least isolated of the Nahua communities, where traditions were strongest and also most at risk from the machinations of a "glocal" world.

The shift in locale took us, over a period of another few years, into a much more complicated world, where cattle, corn and the oil industry of southern Veracruz came into conflict. Eventually, we wrote a book called *A Land Without Gods*. The fronticepiece is a drawing I made of the statue at the museum of anthropology in Jalapa, surrounded by jungle vegetation on fire.

The initial experience in Jicacal and later exposure to the broader challenges facing the Nahua helped me clarify the question that had been holding me back from entering a PhD program: did I have anything to say about what I was witnessing? I needed a compelling reason to commit to a long period of study and a path different from the creative and pleasure seeking life I had made for myself until then.

Paradoxically, if I was to find a fulsome answer to the question I first needed to comply with the university requirement to study anthropology before actually doing it as I had been. The decision to return to university led me inexorably to other questions and responses grounded in the impulses that had taken me from art and beauty as an end in and of itself to a broader quest for a better world. Does the future offer that prospect, one created through human effort, or is what we see and live simply an immutable gift from gods that in this new age have fled into holes in the earth while forests burn?

Theory and practice

As with many sociology and anthropology departments around the world, post-Marxism was the dominant theoretical orientation at Carleton in the early 1980s, reflected in Wally Clement's approach to political economy and Jacques' own anthropological take on peasant societies. The prominent Marxist scholar Leo Panitch worked one level down in the Department of Political Science.

Fortunately for me, Mexican social sciences were at the leading edge of critical thinking on land, conflict and agrarian struggles that were central to my experience in Jicacal and Pajapan. My fluency in Spanish meant that I could offer Carleton faculty access to the dense theory and rich contextual analysis of Mexican authors such as Gustavo Esteva, Rodolfo Stavenhagen, Roger Bartra and Luisa Paré.

After completing various qualifying courses at Carleton, I moved to Mexico to read the Mexican Marxists in context, settling into the tourist village of Tepotzlán near Cuernavaca, Malcolm Lowry's home when doing his alcohol soaked research for the classic novel *Under the Volcano.*

Away from the main square, the village was a quiet place of cobbled stone streets and a mix of modest local homes and weekend retreats for families from Mexico City. A good location, I thought, for reading Mexican anthropology without distractions.

For a year I travelled back and forth between Tepoztlán and Pajapan, where my research, and Jacques', were now centred. On one trip, I visited the home of an elderly member of the *Comisariado de Bienes Communales* of Pajapan, the local land administration body. He was responsible for protecting the archives of the community stored in a large wooden box. Every three years, when elections occurred, the box would be taken around the village from home to home, much like religious statues were when celebrating the day of particular saints. Inside the box were copies made in the mid-1880s

Smoke in the kitchen protects seed corn, Pajapan, Veracruz, Mexico.

of Pajapan's primordial land titles. Many documents had been lost, he said, or simply fell apart with humidity and age.

The experience inspired me to travel to Mexico City and spend days in the Lands Branch of the National Archives looking for additional evidence of Pajapan's earliest recorded history. I felt like a detective on the trail of something thrilling and jumped at every small discovery in ancient books. Eventually, I found something remarkable in Volume 3030: a copy of a map of Pajapan from 1611 and references from 1605 to agreements with colonial powers.

Coming to understand the dynamics of land tenure in Mexico was for me the study of myth, both its truth and its falsehood. The *bienes comunales* of Pajapan are a form of land tenure different from and much rarer than the better known and widespread *ejido* system. *Ejidos*, created by the Mexican state after the Mexican Revolution, have vestiges of the pre-conquest Aztec *calpulli* and the medieval Spanish *ejido* but their function in contemporary society is to distribute individual parcels of land owned collectively. *Ejidos* also serve as a means for government administrative control of peasant communities. By contrast, *bienes comunales* are only found in a handful of Indigenous communities in Mexico with documented land title going back to the Spanish colonial period. They are like the earliest treaties of Canadian First Nations, recognizing immutable land rights.

The legal distinction proved to be useful to Indigenous cattle entrepreneurs, the *caciques* or local bosses of Pajapan. With no assigned individual parcels, they could claim that all lands were open to all members all the time. Peasant crops were conveniently at the mercy of free-range cattle. So too were the *acahuales*, fallow fields gradually recovering the vegetative biomass needed to restore soil fertility in a shifting cultivation system. With cattle everywhere, farmers could no longer confidently protect their own parcels or plan for future crops.

By the late 1970s, forty Indigenous *caciques* effectively controlled half of the arable land in Pajapan, more than 9,000 hectares in all. They also occupied many of the political and religious positions of authority in the municipality, including the mayor's office, the *Comisariado de Bienes Comunales* and sponsorship of festivals for important saints such as San Martín, the patron saint of the community.

The merging of authority in political and religious spheres helped a few individuals convert one kind of power into another—political control over communal land and religious titles used to expand wealth in cattle. It also helped the locally powerful keep external arbitrators out by asserting the independence and autonomy of Indigenous institutions and decision-making.

Jacques and I witnessed the process directly, sometimes getting drunk as an extension of our participant observation. I recall funeral rites sponsored by an aspiring Indigenous cattle rancher who had switched from his Protestant congregation to the more popular Catholic church in order to capture a religious post. He told us his plan unabashedly as we drank mescal with him and other mourners, eventually collapsing into our cots in the shack we rented nearby.

I felt anger in the morning and refused to engage with him again. The poverty of artisanal fishers in Jicacal, and their palm huts, dugout canoes and bow and arrow fishing technologies, took on a less quaint aspect. The grave situation of the fishers was an effect of the greed and raw power being exercised by the few over the life and livelihoods of the many.

Gustavo casting a fishing net in the Laguna del Ostión, Jicacal, Veracruz, Mexico.

The nefarious use of Indigenous institutions and traditions was an unexpected discovery for us, mixing with other "glocal" dynamics also central to our research. The locally and regionally powerful cattle ranchers were at the time in a David and Goliath battle with PEMEX, Mexico's national oil company. The nearby refinery town of Minatitlán processed sixteen percent of Mexico's crude oil, shipped out from the port of Coatzacoalcos.

PEMEX wanted to make use of Pajapan's coastal lagoon where Jicacal was located to build a new port. It expropriated a third of the communal lands of Pajapan, setting off several years of resistance, protest and negotiations detailed in our book and in a master's thesis by another of Jacques' students, Dominique Caouette.

The Indigenous *caciques* used their control over local Indigenous institutions to protest against the expropriation, mobilizing support from state officials and framing the conflict in ethnic and geopolitical terms: the native people of Pajapan versus the government of Mexico.

The strategy worked for a while but could only distract the vastly more powerful interests of PEMEX. The ensuing negotiations pushed the port project ahead while also lifting the veil covering inequity and local exploitation by large scale ranching. The dispossessed Indigenous peasant farmers of Pajapan also fought back, mobilizing thousands and eventually gaining support from PEMEX for their cause. Expropriation payments were made to landless farmers and the remaining territory converted into a conventional *ejido* with individual parcels of land. Peasants won land back but with the extinguishment of their original title also irredeemably lost pre-hispanic institutions.

The two stories—Indigenous ranchers using local institutions to expel Indigenous farmers from the land, and national oil industry interests brushing aside locally powerful ranchers—illustrated the complexity of Mexican society. The realities of life in Pajapan did not fall neatly into theoretical definitions of exploiters and exploited, a discovery that reinforced the theoretical position we eventually adopted to explain the two-way influence of Indigenous and Western capitalist societies. Hybridity, not purity, was the norm, as we put it in our book published after I graduated.

One day, near the end of my field studies in Pajapan, I was detained by the Mexican navy patrolling the expropriated area. I had been taking pictures of the early stages of port construction, including

A view of refineries in Minatitlán, Veracruz, Mexico.

scenes with burning oil fires in the background. The officer in charge questioned me for over an hour, called higher ranking officers and took the film canisters from my camera and camera bag. Fortunately, I was not arrested and kicked out of the country.

Life in Jicacal, and later in Pajapan, was a unique experience. Nevertheless, in later years neither Jacques nor I returned to this way of working, which is grounded in the British tradition of Malinowski and other proponents of curiosity-based research driven by disciplinary and personal considerations alone. Instead, we came to focus on doing research to address pressing topics of interest to the people directly involved, the hallmark of participatory action research.

We also shifted from taking a lot of time to learn as much as we could about local ways to being strategic with time and timing. We came to understand that experiential learning, the underlying spirit of participant observation, can be a lot more efficient when action oriented and tied to an analysis of priorities by those affected. A shift away from doing monumental monographs towards strategic and action-oriented study gradually became central to my professional development. It was more in keeping with an ethics of social research that places the relevance and usefulness of research ahead of knowledge creation for its own sake.

Before I could start this journey, however, I had to learn about myself in a way that resulted in a change in myself. My life circumstances at that time differed little from earlier experiences of ease and flow, financial and otherwise. I did not have much money, but enough from grants and odd jobs to pay rent and eat rice and beans. In addition to study, I practised Aikido at the university, becoming reasonably adept with the *jo*, a short wooden staff effective as a weapon. I learned to do Shiatsu massage, practicing on my parents and brothers when they were at home. I also experimented with different photographic and visual art styles, and continued to explore relationships. I had an open heart but felt no compelling call to commit. I remained happily carefree in a student life. Becoming an engaged researcher required a random component.

5

Under the Volcano

My life pivoted suddenly around random and fixed elements in life in November of 1986, the month of my thirty-second birthday. I was visiting a *temazcal* or mud bath near Popocatapetl, Mexico's most famous volcano. I went there with a few friends from Tepotzlán where I was studying the Mexican Marxists and falling in love with Rosa Maria, a medical doctor with a specialization in paediatrics.

At the bath, we rubbed mud on our skin to draw out toxins, improve blood flow and exfoliate. Rosa Maria noticed a lump in the middle of my back, out of my sight, and suggested I have it looked at by a specialist.

A few weeks later I returned to Ottawa for Christmas and visited a dermatologist who excised the lump. The laboratory analysis came back showing a Clark's Level V malignant melanoma, which comes with a ninety percent probability of death within five years. The news,

Children playing ball on the rail tracks in Minatitlán, Veracruz, Mexico.

delivered gently by the dermatologist as we stood in his office, took the legs out from under me.

The tests that followed brought even worse news. An ultrasound and biopsy showed that a metastatic melanoma had already formed on my liver. The oncologist called me on the phone as soon as he got the result rather than waiting for a face-to-face appointment. I needed to put my life in order, he told me, because I might have only three to four months to live. Metastatic melanoma is a very aggressive cancer with no known cure.

The news took my breath away and shocked and frightened my parents, brothers and friends. What followed was an experience that distinguished my life to that moment from everything else that had gone before. At the same time, the earlier life experiences gave me an orientation to living that remained unshaken even as I struggled to find my feet.

The likely cause of the cancer was simple enough to explain, sparing me from the anguish of casting about for reasons "on high" or in the sins of my youth. Sun exposures early in life and hours as an adult in an open fishing boat on the Gulf of Mexico were not a good idea for the son of a freckled, red-headed mother of Irish descent.

I did, however, fall directly into despair. As a fit young man the prospect of dying within months from an illness I still could not see or feel was incomprehensible.

I resolved the dissonance in part by sleeping on the floor and subjecting myself to other small gestures of bodily mortification. I stopped talking for a time, ate sparingly and walked around my parent's house barefoot.

The people around me did not immediately launch into promises that everything would be alright. My father fell apart in his own way, crying softly while driving me to one appointment or another. My mother was paralyzed with fear. Neither denied the gravity of the moment. Friends and other family didn't try to pull me out of the negativity of the experience I was living either. Rather, they simply remained present.

I realized later that sinking deeply into the emotional terror was actually the best thing for me. It forced me to be fully present with my fear, anger and anguish. I felt it deeply. There is always wisdom in holding true to what is, including pain and suffering. Staying with the experience of now, rather than wildly rushing on to somewhere else, is all we really have and perhaps the true face of love for ourselves and for others.

Several weeks into the storm I had a dream. I could see, in opposite corners of a room, a black alligator threatening to attack a baby next to a green alligator. There was only one small window to the world outside. The moment was filled with the fight or flight choice I had to make. Then, just as I was waking up, I became the green alligator and moved decisively to protect the baby.

Upon awaking, I knew what I had to do. I no longer felt the need to make my emotional pain the centre of my life and instead embraced the situation. I left behind the funk and despair of the previous weeks and resolved to use my body and my mind to heal.

I started with a daily meditation practice. A university professor of anthropology steeped in the Thai tradition of Theravada Buddhism gave me a tiny statue of the Buddha encased in a globe of plastic. He taught me to rest attention on the breath going in and out of my nostrils as I held the object in the palm of my hands. Quickly, my meditation deepened and lengthened to a consistent practice of four hours over the course of a day. A metaphor I heard years later describes the level of intensity the practice of meditation involves as getting to the temperature needed in an oven to bake bread.

I combined the meditation with a deeply personal visualization practice inspired by Bernie Siegal's book *Love, Medicine and Miracles.* The book had just been published, breaking new ground in popular culture regarding the role the mind plays in fighting disease. The meditation and visualization practices became, in my imagination, a sharp instrument to excise the tumour on my liver and sweep aside any other rogue cells floating around in my bloodstream and lymphatic system.

Imagery from other dreams—Aztec warriors, white butterflies—and experiences from my daily life became metaphors for visualizing my body's own immune system at work. As I showered, I imagined the water inside me washing away cancer cells. When I walked, I imagined the wind blowing through me like a cleansing force. Butterflies emerged from my thymus gland in the centre of my chest and carried away what was not needed. Sunlight coming through a window or noticed out of the corner of my eye connected me in my mind to the energy of all things—the sun, stars and the space in between.

A medical doctor, trained in hypnosis, supported the visualization practice with a holding environment of her own, carefully protecting the light she said she could see radiating from within me. Other friends made similar observations about the deep peace I seemed to have found so quickly.

By the time various ultrasounds determined that the growth on my liver was shrinking rather than growing as the doctors expected, I took the good news as no great surprise. Of course, I thought, my mind is a healing force.

This bold interpretation of the practical outcome—the tumour slowly shrank and then disappeared four months after the initial diagnosis—eventually gave way to a more subtle understanding of the forces at play. I realized that there was agency, but not control of the outcome: I had created favourable conditions (meditation, visualization, healthy food, large doses of Vitamin C, light exercise) for my body's own immune system to distinguish the cancer cells from healthy tissue and act accordingly. This was an explanation that did not require me to believe that I had cured myself entirely through an act of mental will. The body is wise, I concluded, beyond human understanding. It need only be free of the turmoil of the mind to find healing and to embrace it fiercely, without attachment.

Talk therapy

Some six months after my initial diagnosis ultrasounds could no longer detect signs of a tumour on my internal organs. I was dropped from an experimental treatment protocol the oncologist had been pursuing, leaving me with the original diagnosis of a ninety percent probability of death within five years. Monitoring continued but I was free to turn my attention to what was now before me.

The diagnosis had thrown my plans for marriage to Rosa Maria into question. When could I return to Mexico to complete my dissertation and what would I do about the ongoing risks of living the rest of my life under the Mexican sun? An ardent nationalist rooted in her own culture, she doubted my commitment to staying in Mexico and broke off the engagement. I had come out from under the dark cloud of melanoma only to fall into heartbreak.

Help came this time from a psychiatrist available through the medical services of Carleton University, a bearded man in his forties with a gentle smile and curly hair. He offered to listen to my story. We talked, putting both traumas into a perspective that was manageable.

It helped that a year earlier I had experienced close-up the abrupt end to Jacques' marriage. I had observed the pain and the joy of love complicated by life's entanglements. Jacques and his new partner, Michelle, had set up a home with me in a ski chalet out of town. I got to know his young children, and hers, when they visited on weekends, and listened intently to the children's stories of friends at school even though my command of French was rudimentary. It was a painful time for all of them, but also the logical outcome of adults discovering soul mates.

In talk therapy, my own heartbreak and the shock of a near-death experience mixed with another unresolved question in my life: What am I to do about the baby in my dream?

Sisters playing and working outside their home, Pajapan, Veracruz, Mexico.

When Jacques and I lived in Jicacal two years earlier, I had met Amelia, a working woman from the oil refinery town of Minatitlán. She was on a day-trip to the beach with her cousin. We chatted over a drink and later dated, dancing in Minatitlán and walking along the waterfront in the commercial port city of Coatzacoalcos, named after the Aztec "plumed serpent" god.

A romance bloomed. She was not a native encountered during field work, a relationship forbidden by the mores of anthropology. Rather, it was a romance with someone outside the culture I was studying but not of my own. We were different but attracted to each other. Within a few months, Amelia got pregnant and decided immediately that having a child was exactly what she wanted. Six years my senior, her biological clock was also at work.

I was not committed to the relationship and struggled with how I could meet my responsibilities to the child I had fathered. This became the central question I was left with in sessions with the psychiatrist, after working through my recovery from a cancer threat and break up of a relationship. Eventually, I arrived at a resolution I felt comfortable with: I would stay connected to my son so he would know who I was and have access to me if he wanted it. This was the opposite of what a lawyer friend had advised me—you can't know what demands this may place on you in the future, he said.

Keeping the connection alive felt entirely correct to me, a decision I made with conviction and have never regretted. Over the years, we corresponded and I visited periodically. Amelia made no demands on me and respected my later marriage. It wasn't until my son came from Mexico to Canada at age eighteen and started to study here that I really got to know him. Soon after, he followed in the footsteps of my father and helicopter pilot brothers by becoming a helicopter engineer. Today, he is an important part of my life.

Holding rightness and awe

Months after the health crisis was over and my mind and body were no longer conflicted, I moved into a cottage a few miles from Ottawa overlooking the Gatineau River and hills beyond. I said to my new landlady that I was writing a book and needed the peace and quiet of living close to nature to get it done.

Me, at Gleneagle, 1989.

I spent a year there, watching the seasons change as the leaves turned red and yellow, the river froze and broke up again and the summer days brought out the blue forget-me-nots in the garden. I made slow but steady progress with the dissertation. Wally, one of my supervisors, advised me, "Just do it. Everyday, all day, until it is done". Jacques had similar advice. It took a woman, however, to actually make it happen.

In the spring of 1988 I met Debra, the woman I married and have lived with for thirty-four years. Soon after we met, she shared with me the story of her last name, Huron. It was a name she had chosen instead of the name of her father or mother. It honoured her Ojibway Anishinaabeg great grandmother and her family connection to Manitoulin Island and Lake Huron. I was captivated by her feminist perspective, her rootedness and the snake earrings she wore on our first date.

I introduced Debra to my mother in the final days of summer at an outdoor patio in Ottawa's downtown. We had lunch, talked about Debra's family in Sudbury and my mother's own connections to northern Ontario. Little did we know when eating and chatting together that my mother's lungs were already heavily laden with a cancer that killed her five months later. She was only sixty-four, younger than I am today, and had just started the phase in life that for people with financial security offers time to explore and to dance. My father was two years older and had been retired for less than a year when she died.

In a conversation Debra and I had with my mother as she was dying, she gave her blessing to the marriage we planned and made a gift of a diamond earring later fashioned into a wedding ring. One of the last times I sat with my mother alone I gently took her hands and placed them on my face and on my head, crying quietly. She wondered how my father would fare after she passed. It was the evening of his birthday and she had valiantly clapped with her frail hands to join in the celebratory birthday song.

As we sat together she looked at me and offered another gift, saying that she and I were kindred spirits. The truth of this overwhelmed me. Sobs racked my body as I continued to hold her hands to my face. A few days later, she died in her bed, surrounded by her three sons, husband and two sisters reciting the Lord's Prayer as she took her last breath and grew still.

My parent's deaths—my father died several decades later at ninety-three—showed me two views of passing from life, both graceful and full of family love. When my mother died, the wisdom that says we live on in the memories and actions of others seemed true and right. Her love of beauty and her empathy for others have been guiding lights for me in all my days before and since.

My father also passed away at home, cared for by his second wife and his three sons. Casey slept in his bed with him for a week so that he could be on hand to help our father go to the bathroom and get back safely. When he died in the dead of the night I was alone with him, listening to his breath become more laboured and somehow softer as well. His last breath was a complete letting go, a deep exhale followed by stillness. I called to Casey and he roused Steve and my father's wife Eleanor to join us in the moment.

Before they arrived, as I sat holding my father's cooling hand, I both felt and saw with my eyes a wispy light lift slowly from his body, hover for a moment and then move decisively up and away. This experience suggested another interpretation of life after death, as a time when we start another journey, a soul journey.

Both fountains of wisdom imply movement in death, forwards to another existence or resting in the memories and kindred spirits we leave behind. Death, however, is also the antithesis of movement. It is stillness. Perhaps nothingness. I am unable to fully resolve these views so I simply hold them both gently, waiting for the unarguable truth that will come with my own death.

What stays with me from the threat of a shortened life, struggles and joys of relationships and death of loved ones is what the experiences taught me about change itself. I came to realize that any wisdom I managed to wrest from the opportunities and difficulties presented to me was fragile, subject to the ebb and flow of time, new circumstances and new challenges. Powerful experiences, whether blessings or curses, are not truly distinguishable from less powerful ones in that the lessons they teach us still need to be reaffirmed and reworked day-by-day and moment-by-moment. I may have changed fundamentally in some ways but I was also the same, habituated by a lifetime of experiences. Only a new act of will, with mindfulness and resolve, can cut through the fog of these delusions.

The same can be said of efforts to change the world. Ongoing struggles to improve situations and solve problems facing people and societies that are marginalized from the mainstream or exploited by others never end. They are ongoing and invite constant engagement, independently of the outcome.

A Rumi poem expresses the mystery I felt at the time and still feel today: "You must have shadow and light source both. Listen, and lay your head under the tree of awe." I remain in awe and deeply thankful that I did not die from cancer within months or even within the expected five year probability window. I also remain deeply thankful for the choices I made and the paths that were closed by others. As for the experience of healing and renewal, I can call on the memory, an internal point of reference. Sunlight in the corner of my eye is all I need to transmute again, if only for a moment. Becoming, rather

Debra, with the Yukon River behind, 2008.

than arriving, is always available, perhaps the only permanent state of being.

Entering the world

Completing a doctoral dissertation is inevitably a slog. Some seventy percent of students entering Canadian doctoral programs in the social sciences drop out after courses and exams. Those that do not, average seven years to completion. Many are mired in endless literature reviews, immobilized by the fiction of writing the *Magnum Opus* or rushed into the practical demands of making ends meet.

A practical person, Debra did not want a lingering PhD project hanging over our married life so she made getting it done a condition of the marriage agreement. Finish, or no marriage. I obliged, just barely, by submitting the final version of the dissertation to my committee twenty-four hours before we got married. While not yet defended, this was good enough for her.

My efficient path to graduation was due in part to Debra's practical wisdom but also the approach to study encouraged by Jacques, my lead supervisor. He directed me to use empirical analyses from the field as raw material for course work and to write comprehensive exams as draft chapters for the dissertation. It was an early sign of our later work together, which combines learning with strategic action.

Finding a job after completing my PhD proved to be difficult, although not because of gaps in my training. I was not a good candidate for the few university positions available in Canada during the late 1980s. Most universities were well stocked with white, male faculty and hard-pressed by declining budgets and stagnant student numbers. Women were almost the only graduates getting interviews for entry level university positions. This made sense to me, of course, and I was not so committed to an academic life that I would not consider another livelihood.

As an Ottawa resident, reaching out to the Federal Government was simple enough but here too I met with resistance. I knocked on a lot of doors and was greeted with polite indifference to my doctoral degree. One official at the Canadian International Development Agency (CIDA) remarked after listening to my pitch, "We only hire people that have worked for us before."

I was caught between two images of professional development, neither of which really applied to me. I was not committed to the theoretical orientation of academics passionate about the latest literature or key ideas and debates in their field. Nor was I a researcher with my head in the clouds, devoid of practical goals and experience.

In response to the prospect of unemployment, I set out to create my own job, writing a grant proposal that included a modest salary for me and the prospect of moving to Mexico with Debra. I invited Jacques and Luisa Paré, a Québécoise and professor at the National Autonomous University of Mexico (UNAM) in Mexico City I had met the previous year, to co-sponsor the project.

We met at a patio restaurant in Gatineau, across the river from Ottawa, when Luisa was visiting family. There we hatched a plan to write a proposal for an action-oriented research project in the Sierra de Santa Marta, Veracruz, organized around new and emerging concepts of sustainable development and community engagement.

Our book on the Nahua, still in draft form at the time, provided the background for the proposal, giving our ideas a depth that must have impressed the International Development Research Centre (IDRC). They funded a joint project between UNAM and Carleton University.

As tenured professors, Luisa and Jacques were excited by the prospect of research that could make a difference for Indigenous peoples in a sensitive tropical environment. From my perspective, it was an opportunity to launch my professional life as a married man.

Moving to Mexico was a reasonable adventure for me, with my Spanish language skills and good knowledge of Mexico's geography and people. For Debra, it was a leap of faith. She was willing to put her own career as a journalist and editor on hold. She was also pregnant, adding a whole other level of courage to her decision. Her explanation now is that youth, and nine months she had spent a few years earlier in Botswana working on an anti-apartheid campaign, made her think she was invincible. "People disappeared in the middle of the night there," she said of the situation in South Africa and Botswana during apartheid. "Mexico would be tame in comparison." She also felt excited about the prospect of starting our life together with an adventure far from the conventional lifestyle of most Canadians of her age and professional situation.

So we moved to Mexico, although as it turned out not to pick up coordination of the project as planned in the IDRC proposal. The grant application was successful and the research project laid the foundations for creating a non-governmental organization, the Proyecto Sierra de Santa Marta (PSSM), that thrived for more than twenty-five years. The organization in turn played a critical role in establishing the region as a UNESCO Biosphere Reserve and supported many livelihood initiatives with the Nahua people we had studied. It did so, however, mainly under Luisa's leadership. A different dream job in Mexico unexpectedly came my way.

PART TWO

BEING

< Moonlight, Temagami.

6

Cowardly Land Becomes Brave Again

My first real job as an anthropologist began with Cajun blackened fish and Louisiana mud pie at an upscale restaurant in downtown Manhattan. Debra and I were guests of the Rockefeller Foundation and their program to bring PhD graduates of the social sciences into the highly technical world of plant breeding and agronomy in developing countries.

The Foundation, working with the Mexican government, was the early architect of the Green Revolution, a period between 1950 and the late 1960s when new crop varieties dramatically increased wheat and rice production worldwide. The successes eventually prompted the establishment of crop-based agricultural research centres in various parts of the world: maize and wheat in Mexico, rice in the Philippines, potatoes in Peru and dryland crops like sorghum and millet in India and Syria. The United Nations, The World Bank and many national governments, including Canada, funded the research. At its height in

Farm family, Atlántida, Honduras.

the early 1990s, the global network included eighteen centres, each with a mandate for a specific crop, a major ecosystem or a strategic food and agriculture issue.

The productivity gains that had launched the Green Revolution were based on a novel research paradigm from the Midwest of the United States. The paradigm involved a wholesale rejection of traditional agriculture's reliance on animal traction, human labour and crop biodiversity. These inputs were replaced with artificial fertilizers, chemical pesticides, machinery and crop varieties selected to perform well in a highly modified field environment. Instead of working with nature, as farmers had for millennia, the Green Revolution technologies invited farmers to remake their fields into a radically different landscape where a single variety of a single plant could thrive. Monocultures produced a dramatic bump in harvested grain and were appealing to scientists, governments and farmers alike. As Dorothy from the Wizard of Oz might have said of the radically transformed landscapes, "We're not in Kansas anymore."

By the early 1970s, problems began to emerge with trying to remake diverse developing country landscapes into versions of the new Kansas and Iowa. The cost of the suite of technologies, and who was able to make use of it, was one problem but environmental harm from chemicals and impacts on the overall biological diversity of farming systems had also become apparent.

Founders of the Green Revolution such as the Rockefeller Foundation responded by broadening the base of science involved to include agricultural economists, anthropologists, sociologists and people trained in the emerging field of ecology to work alongside the plant breeders and soil scientists. Interdisciplinary and more socially aware research, they thought, might help resolve the problems.

One of these initiatives was a program of post-doctoral fellowships to identify talented, young and adventurous graduates in the social sciences and bring them into settings where new agricultural technology was being developed. Joyce Moock, the Associate Vice President at the Rockefeller Foundation, oversaw the program and chaired my interview in New York.

My wife Debra participated and received almost as much attention in the interview as I did. She was impressive, dressed in a bright red suit jacket and sitting calmly at my side. Wisely, Joyce knew that for most North Americans the success of an assignment to a developing country depended a lot on the happiness of the spouses involved. She later turned the program away from its focus on North American graduates towards scholars emerging from African universities. She continued to include spouses in interviews whenever possible.

The success of the post-doctoral fellowship also depended on an offer of an assignment from one of the research centres. I immediately turned down a position based in The Netherlands because the centre wanted me to live there and work with partners in South America. I calculated the hours in an airplane and determined that my body would soon feel like it was drowning somewhere in the mid-Atlantic.

Instead, I went for an interview at the International Centre for Tropical Agriculture (CIAT) in Cali, Colombia, where I was offered a position with their tropical pastures program. They needed a social scientist to work with ranchers in Brazil to study how a novel pasture variety might work in their farming systems and assess its impact on rates of deforestation. My PhD research on cattle, corn and conflict in Veracruz, Mexico, seemed like a good fit.

I remember one of the Rockefeller Foundation committee members asking me in New York if I was "willing to take the bull by the horns." This turned out to be a prescient question I only recognized as I stepped off the airplane in Cali and was greeted by two young CIAT researchers with a warning that the proposed research was not exactly as it seemed. "You won't get the full story from the pastures program," they said. At some risk to their careers for snitching, they wanted me to know of early evidence they had collected showing strongly negative environmental and social impacts from the new pasture technology.

I appreciated their concern and candour but remember being more unsettled by the apparent dispute within the organization than anything else. I also had doubts about life in Cali. By 1989, the "Cali Cartel" had successfully broken away from Pablo Escobar and the Medellín group to establish a second Colombian node of drug-related crime. While CIAT staff assured me that their campus was safe—there had only been "a few" incidents affecting staff and families—the prospect of leaving my pregnant wife in Cali while I travelled for long periods of time to the Brazilian Amazon was worrisome.

On my way back to Ottawa from Colombia I made a side trip to Mexico and arrived unannounced at the International Maize and Wheat Improvement Centre (known as CIMMYT, the Spanish acronym). It was located a few kilometres from Chapingo, Mexico's premier agricultural university outside of Mexico City.

The organization is the direct outcome of Norman Borlaug's work on the Green Revolution, a contribution to global food supply that earned him the 1970 Nobel Peace Prize. Because of his work, CIMMYT is arguably the most storied of all the international centres. With no other offer in hand, and Cali looking dicey, I needed to take my life into my own hands again if I was to make something of the good fortune I had been given. I made my way to the CIMMYT Economics Program offices and, according to Derek Byerlee, the head of the program, introduced myself and boldly asked, "Why haven't you hired me?"

Much later Derek told me the audacity got his attention. I don't recall the interview but he and his colleague Rob Tripp offered me a job. Accepting it turned out to be the most consequential decision of my working life. It drew me deeply into a fascinating world of agricultural science and helped establish a reputation for rigorous and engaged social research. Mostly, however, I was relieved to be able to return from Colombia and Mexico with a job offer my new wife might find appealing.

A year or so after I became a "Rocky-Doc" working at CIMMYT in Mexico, I found myself sitting on an airplane beside a US Army Engineer. He asked me what I was doing there. After a few unsuccessful attempts to explain, his face brightened and he said, "Ah, you are a human-factors engineer." This seemed apt enough, although I later described my work at CIMMYT as that of a translator between technical scientists and farmers, each with a deep understanding of their own world but confused by the complexity of the other.

The experience changed my world too. I became both a strong critic of the industrial agriculture paradigm underlying the Green Revolution and a proponent of a participatory and action-oriented approach to the creation of new technology and new knowledge. I learned to listen deeply to farmers and scientists, generating in me both respect for the values of science and great admiration for the power of what farmers discover on their own.

Teodoro Reyes and the fertilizer bean

While the culinary art of a fine New York restaurant marked the beginning of my journey as a professional anthropologist, Honduran farmers and an obscure bean became my primary teachers.

Teodoro Reyes, a farmer I met on a hillside near La Danta on the Caribbean coast of Honduras, was one of the first. He told me when I interviewed him on a steep slope overlooking a series of broken hillsides that, "With the fertilizer bean, cowardly land becomes brave again." He was referring to *Mucuna pruriens var. utilis* (a.k.a. velvet bean), an audacious plant with the humble purpose of protecting and improving the soil.

The farming practice is a simple crop rotation, locally called an *abonera*. It starts with clearing a field and planting the bean into the ground every metre or so using a dibble stick. After seven to eight months the plant develops into a thick tangle of soft, broad leaves, vines and seeds. It withers quickly when slashed with a machete and forms a dense layer of decomposing leaves and vines. Maize is then planted directly into the mat, which acts as a mulch.

The brilliance of the technology soon revealed itself to me and others I worked with, culminating in several books and stimulating

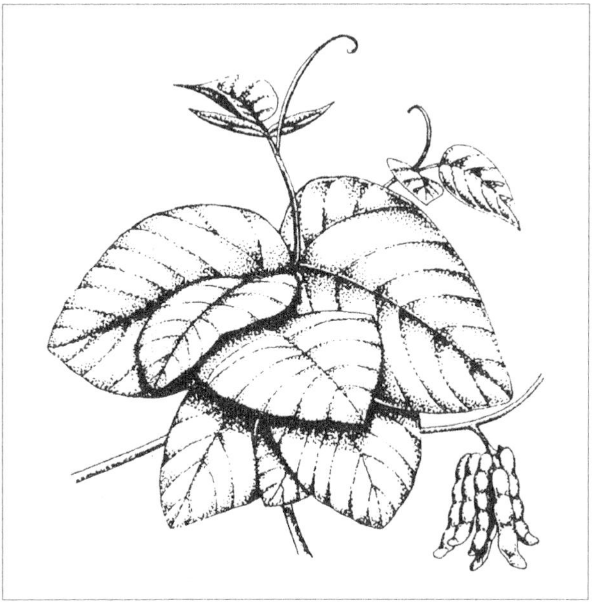

Velvet bean leaves and seed.

Maize coming up in a velvet bean mulch layer, with farmers and agronomist checking the plants.

two decades of research by dozens of agronomists and social scientists spanning the tropical regions of Mexico, Central America and West Africa. It still stands as one of the most impressive stories of farmer discovery in an era when sustainable agriculture and working with nature to grow food without costing the earth was just beginning to pull away from the technological orbit of the Green Revolution.

The aggressive vining plant easily smothers all other vegetation in the field, leaving the space virtually weed-free. There is no need to burn the field to control weeds and debris, as in the traditional slash and burn systems of Central America. By the time the maize crop is established, the bean has set its own seed. The pods burst open when dry, ejecting seeds over the field fairly evenly and eventually sprouting on their own to start another cycle of growth. They take over the field once the maize crop is harvested. Weeds are suppressed by the mulch throughout the cycle.

These features keep labour costs low compared to the alternative slash, burn and weeding operations of a traditional woody fallow field.

Farmer slashing an *abonera* field in preparation for planting maize.

The caution, farmers pointed out, is that the abundant, leafy growth provides excellent habitat for rats, and consequently for dangerous snakes. Care is needed with the hooked stick and machete used to move through and cut down the soft vines.

The thick mat of decomposing plants provides another advantage specific to the environment of northern Honduras. Like the Miskito Coast that extends into Honduras from Nicaragua, the region is wet almost all the time. Rainfall exceeds 3000 millimetres a year, with daily downpours of 100-200 millimetres. The distribution of rainfall, the key factor in any rain-fed agricultural system, is bimodal, with peaks in March and six months later from October to December. This pattern is driven not only by exposure to storms from the Caribbean Sea but also the sudden rise from sea level to 2400 metres at the peak of the Nombre de Dios mountain range. Running parallel to the coastline for over 200 kilometres, the mountains interrupt moisture laden prevailing winds, producing some rain virtually every week of the year. For farmers, this creates two growing seasons, and the possibility of harvesting winter maize when prices are at their annual peak.

A colleague at CIMMYT, a Colombian agronomist, said the best way to visualize the topography of Honduras is to crumple a piece of

Honduran hillside, desperately cleared for maize.

paper into a ball and then lightly stretch it out. The jumble of peaks, valleys and slopes of the paper could easily stand as a topographic map of the country.

The topography can also be a guide to the distribution of wealth in agricultural land. The valleys are owned by a small number of wealthy ranching families and plantation owners, leaving the hillsides to everyone else. This upside-down-world places pastures in the valleys where crops should be grown and crops on the hillsides where pastures would do better at holding soil in place. The result in most parts of the country was and remains an ecological and socioeconomic disaster, choking the rivers with precious soil and pushing the poor higher and higher up the hill until no forested peaks remain. Even in 1990, much of Honduras was deforested, vulnerable to severe land degradation, landslides and drought.

The northern coast was an exception. Hillside land was still available, but vulnerable to soil erosion. The *abonera* rotation with velvet bean solved this problem by keeping the soil covered year-round,

Two ears of corn, with velvet bean beginning to reassert itself.

conserving water in the soil profile and protecting it from direct exposure to high velocity rainfall. There are limits, however. On slopes greater than fourty-five degrees, the soft soil underneath an *abonera* field can slump suddenly, causing localized landslides.

A third advantage, reflected in the name "fertilizer bean" by which it is best known in Honduras, is perhaps the most striking. As a legume, velvet bean has the capacity for nitrogen fixation, a chemical process by which molecular nitrogen in the air is converted into ammonia and "fixed" in the soil. The roots develop nodules that feed the leaves and vines of the plant with significant quantities of nitrogen (more than one hundred kilograms per hectare) and other nutrients made available to support any succeeding crop.

Maize is a nitrogen hog compared to most grains and makes effective use of the *abonera*, doubling yields by the second year. The yield bump comes literally from the air, at no direct cost to the farmer. It also allows for the continuous cultivation of the same field, year after year, without the need to extend fallow periods or add external fertilizer. This ability to make cowardly land become brave again was unheard of in any agricultural system in the humid tropics, anywhere in the world.

My first encounter with velvet bean and the farmers growing it was in October, 1990, two months before Debra's date to deliver a child. I had negotiated an arrangement with CIMMYT that allowed us to live in Jalapa, Veracruz, for the duration of her pregnancy and until we could return to CIMMYT headquarters outside of Mexico City with our baby. Luisa Paré, who was living in Jalapa and managing the IDRC funded Sierra de Santa Marta Project by then, had kindly arranged for us to rent a tiny apartment on the outskirts of the state capital, overlooking a small forest. It met our needs, which were to have a secure, clean and beautiful place for a home birth, far from the polluted air of Mexico City. We knew that if we had stayed at CIMMYT our child's first breath would include unhealthy amounts of carbon monoxide, sulphur dioxide, ozone and both course and ultra-fine particulates hanging across the valley of Mexico. Jalapa was familiar territory for me and we had a kind and skilled midwife on hand to care for Debra while I was away.

I was gone for three weeks, meeting Honduran researchers at the Regional University Centre of the Atlantic Coast (CURLA) located in La Ceiba, a small, picturesque coastal city with a large Garifuna population. A national park, Pico Bonito, covered in an old growth, humid tropical rainforest, protects the city from flooding by rivers descending wildly to the sea. The islands of Roatan, famous for snorkelling, are offshore, adding to the tropical paradise vibe of La Ceiba. The third largest city in Honduras, La Ceiba had a reputation among Hondurans as distinct from the other main cities. Whereas Tegucigalpa (the capital) was where "people decide" and San Pedro Sula (the economic centre) where "people make money," La Ceiba was where "people dance."

The university faculty rarely received visits from international scientists, who were drawn to the bigger national school, Zamorano, located near Tegucigalpa. Jorge Salgado, a young professor in charge of the agronomy program at CURLA, was open to working with me, a Canadian anthropologist who spoke Spanish fluently and came from CIMMYT, the best known and one of the most prestigious agricultural research organizations in the world. We hit it off, and within days began implementing an exploratory survey to find out who, where and why farmers were planting their hillside maize crops in a layer of dead leaves and vines. At night, I danced with his friends in a local bar.

On that trip, and during many subsequent visits to Atlantic Honduras, I established a working relationship with partners new to me and to CIMMYT, planning and executing large surveys of farmers

Honduran agronomists interviewing a farmer about the advantages and disadvantages of "the fertilizer bean."

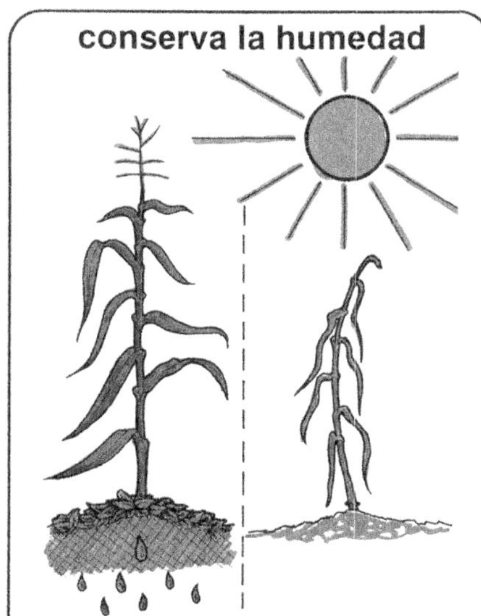

Card used to illustrate the moisture conservation advantage of velvet bean mulch.

CIMMYT

along the coast. I also developed an innovative approach to assessing farmer priorities, bringing out the detailed reasoning of mainly non-literate farmers by using coloured drawings of the advantages of the system: Labour savings, free fertilizer, weed control, erosion control, moisture conservation. The survey crew laid the laminated images in front of farmers and asked, "Of these advantages, which is the most important to you?" They then removed the selected card and asked, "Of those that remain, which is the most important to you?"

This method of questioning produced a hierarchy of priorities, an approach I integrated into many participatory tools that became the focus for my research contributions decades later.

The hierarchy, and statistical analysis that followed, showed that adopters of the *abonera* system valued specific combinations of benefits. Differences in farmer circumstances showed a statistically significant connection between reasons for using the system and the land and labour resources available in each household. In short, the land-poor prioritized land productivity criteria and the labor-poor prioritized labour productivity criteria. The disadvantages—a haven for rats and snakes, loss of access to the land for eight months of the year while the cover crop developed, landslides on very steep slopes—were also assessed and correlated to land and labour constraints of individual households.

The concept of "farmer circumstances" is one of many research innovations developed and championed by CIMMYT throughout the 1980s and into the 1990s. It refers to the constraints new technology encounters in a given situation that would need to be addressed or modified to create conditions for technology adoption. Don Winkelman, an economist and the first non-technical scientist to lead CIMMYT, pioneered the perspective and its corollary, the "recommendation domain." This referred to the unique combination of the features of an agricultural technology and the specific circumstances of farmers. The strength of the two concepts was that they provided a pathway to scale up new crop technologies systematically or incrementally.

When I returned from my first field visit to Honduras in the fall of 1990 I was thrilled. I thought I had encountered an ideal cropping practice for hillside farming, suitable for a wide range of farmer circumstances. I thought it could solve many intractable problems in tropical agriculture.

Debra was happy too, but for a different reason. I had left her pregnant and alone to go to Honduras but stayed home analyzing the survey data and writing the first report in Spanish while she and our midwife prepared to give birth to our son. To this day, I associate the launch of my professional life with Ryan's birth in Jalapa on December 26, 1990, one of the happiest days in my life. A favourite family joke (at least a favourite of mine) is to say that Ryan was *"Jalapeño, pero no pica"*, that is, he was born in Jalapa (the namesake for the hot Jalapeño *chili* pepper) but doesn't burn your mouth. For me, it meant that he was bright and good-natured, much like the fertilizer bean.

Down a rabbit hole

The study of velvet bean, a plant virtually unknown at the time to all but remote farmers and a few development organizations in Central America, offered me a unique opportunity to do a kind of anthropology well suited to my character: I was curious, focused on detail and able to think laterally. These qualities, and ease of working in Latin American cultures, were the reason CIMMYT kept me on for another three years after my two-year Rockefeller Foundation fellowship was over. The additional time allowed me to go deeper into the topic, learning everything I could about this audacious plant.

What I discovered was a world in a grain of sand. The *Mucuna* genus includes about a hundred species of annual and perennial legumes, a dozen or so cultivated species and numerous crosses and hybrids. Some of the wild types, called cowitch in English, have abundant, long stinging hairs on the pod and can cause intensely itchy dermatitis in humans. In southern Veracruz where I completed my PhD research without once coming across the plant, the wild type is known as "Pica Pica Brava" (Sting-sting-ferocious) while the cultivated type is called "Pica Pica Mansa" (Sting-sting-tame). The *brava* type was used to keep people from wandering into fields where they were not welcome. In Nigeria, it is known as the Devil's bean.

The cultivated species, *Mucuna pruriens var. utilis*, probably originated in southern China or northeastern India where reports from the eighteenth and nineteenth century indicate that the bean was eaten as a vegetable. Raw velvet bean seeds contain about twenty-seven percent protein and are rich in minerals and medicinal properties. The bean also contains chemical compounds that, in high concentrations, produce nausea and vomiting. An incident of acute psychosis in Mozambique in the 1980s was attributed to velvet bean consumption during a drought when water was not discarded as part of the food preparation process.

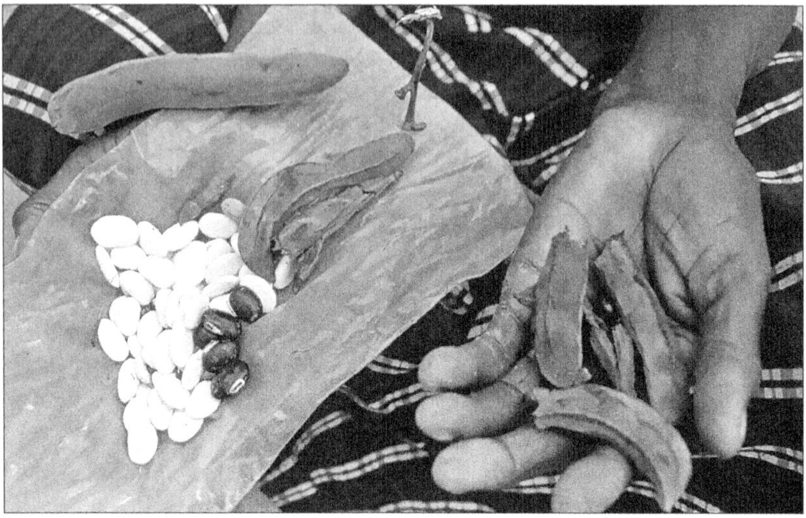

Velvet bean seed collected for making soups, Kumasi, Ghana.

A year after I joined CIMMYT I came across velvet bean in a backyard garden near Kumasi in Ghana, West Africa. The elderly Ghanaian woman tending the garden showed me her harvest and explained that she boils the seed twice and discards the water each time before grinding the seed into paste and adding it to soups as a thickener. Farmers in Mexico and Guatemala told me they grow and roast velvet bean seeds to make a coffee substitute, a use reflected in another local name for the plant: Nescafé. A decade later I also came across velvet bean in a backyard garden in Nagaland, a remote corner of northeast India. The Naga woman growing it in her yard explained to me that the seed was boiled, crushed, boiled again and then eaten like any other vegetable.

English common names for the cultivated species of *Mucuna pruriens* include velvet bean, monkey tamarind, lacuna bean and Lyon bean. It was used historically as an aphrodisiac and in Ayurvedic Indian medicine to treat nervous disorders and arthritis. One of the chemical compounds, levodopa, is extracted commercially from raw seed and combined with another compound, carbidopa, to make a safe and effective drug for the treatment of Parkinson's disease. The Parkinson's Foundation considers development of the drug and research in the 1960s on the use of related dopamines, compounds essential to the normal functioning of the central nervous system, among the most important breakthroughs in treatment of neurological disease.

Reconstructing the story of how velvet bean got from China and India to the Honduran hillside, and converted from a minor vegetable to a major agronomic crop, turned me into a plant detective. I combined archival research with fact-finding trips to remote jungle rivers in Guatemala and Indigenous fields in southern Veracruz, as well as West Africa. Even my father pitched in. When I learned that velvet bean was at one time a prominent crop in the southern United States, he sought out professors at universities in Florida where he was spending his winters in retirement. He copied articles for me from the archives of small research stations across the state.

According to the files, velvet bean arrived in Florida during the 1870s from islands in the Caribbean, where it was probably grown as a vegetable by South Asian indentured workers. Today's Indo-Caribbeans in Trinidad and Tobago, Jamaica, Martinique and other countries of the Caribbean basin are descendants of the colonial system of servitude expanded by the British, French and Dutch after abolition of slavery in the mid 1800s. They may have carried velvet bean with them from India when they were pressed into Caribbean indentured servitude.

By 1897 some 300 Florida orange producers were growing velvet bean as a cover crop to control weeds and improve soil fertility. Farmers in Georgia, Alabama and Mississippi then picked it up as a forage crop. Livestock, including pigs and cows, grazed directly in fields of velvet bean and the pods were taken to mills and crushed or ground with the hull to provide feed for cattle, horses and mules, largely replacing cottonseed meal as the protein component in animal feed.

It was also very popular in the cotton belt as a "green manure." According to many it had "no equal as a soil improver." One American researcher, publishing in 1902, said that, "velvet beans are a cheaper source of nitrogen than is any nitrogenous material which may be bought as commercial fertilizer." Another noted in 1919 that "the story of the velvet bean might be called an agricultural romance" and "the saviour of southern agriculture." From about 1915 to the early 1940s it covered more than a hundred thousand hectares in Georgia, Alabama, Mississippi and South Carolina and was grown in parts of Louisiana, Arkansas, North Carolina and Florida.

Then something changed. By 1965 velvet bean had disappeared altogether from the agricultural statistics of the United States. No one was growing it. My hypothesis for this decline, hinted at in the archives of Florida research stations, was confirmed by statistics I acquired tracking the dramatic drop in the price of commercial fertilizers immediately following the Second World War. As petrochemical sources of nitrogen became cheaper, supplying the nutrient by fallowing land with velvet bean presented farmers with an opportunity cost. They couldn't grow a paying crop while the velvet bean was building up the soil and controlling the weeds.

Soybeans, introduced to southern farmers following the Great Depression, proved to be a more versatile solution to agricultural problems, with high value as a cash food crop and a few of the agronomic benefits of velvet bean. Livestock production also changed focus at this time, shifting from grazing open fields in the American south to feedlots in the American Mid-west and new pastures in the Latin American tropics. These developments sealed the fate of velvet bean in the United States.

Retracing the velvet bean journey across the globe took on a distinctly Hollywood turn a year or so after I arrived at CIMMYT when I decided to follow up on verbal reports from Honduras that in the 1970s two Guatemalan brothers had carried the fertilizer bean with them from Guatemala to the Atlantic coast of Honduras. I went first to Puerto Barrios, Guatemala's port on the Caribbean, and then took a ferry to Livingston at the mouth of the Rio Dulce, today a UNESCO Biosphere Reserve.

Livingston is one of the largest of the Garifuna communities dotting the coast from Belize through Guatemala and Honduras to Nicaragua. The Garifuna are a mixed African and Indigenous people descended from "Black Caribs" of the islands of St. Vincent. They have a distinct language, food tradition based on yucca (a root crop) and a musical form called *punta* with a unique rhythm that moves the whole body. This cultural profile, and the thick tropical rainforest surrounding the village, made Livingston the perfect backdrop for the 1935 film *The New Adventures of Tarzan* with Herman Brix in the starring role. While not as famous a Tarzan as Johnny Weismueller, Brix was also a star athlete, winning a silver medal in shot put at the Olympic Games held in Amsterdam in 1928.

Scenes of Herman Brix going into the jungle were filmed at the mouth of the Rio Dulce next to Livingston, a route I took in a motorized canoe searching for signs of velvet bean. I found it. In the fields of several Indigenous farmers along the remote river, velvet bean was intercropped with maize.

While in Guatemala, I also interviewed elderly residents in the valley of Polochic on the shores of Lago Izabal and former banana plantation workers in Morales and Puerto Barrios. They told me that mules grazed fields of velvet bean planted by the United Fruit Company, until the animals were replaced by tractors to transport bananas to the railhead. This reflected the use of velvet bean as a forage crop in Georgia, Alabama and Mississippi, where the company had roots.

A reference my father had found of an anthropological study published in 1969 by the University of Florida provided the final piece of the puzzle. In it, the anthropologist describes *quenk mula* (mule bean) used by the Ketchi Indians of Guatemala as a crop rotation with maize. When I read the name they used for the plant, the penny dropped. I concluded that Ketchi workers had seen velvet bean used on banana plantations as a forage crop for mules and noticed that the soil underneath the residue was weed-free and moist even at the height of the dry season. From these observations they invented the rotation with hillside maize, a technology passed on to Honduran farmers by two brothers migrating from Guatemala.

I published the account in *Economic Botany,* a prestigious journal for the New York Botanical Garden "devoted to Past, Present, and Future Use of Plants by People." The article, called "Velvet Bean: A "New" Plant with a History," is my most-cited sole-authored paper and is still used as an authoritative source on velvet bean history. I started it with the cliché "Everything old is new again" but fortunately, for my own self-respect as a writer, the editor of the journal rejected the line and published the rest.

Farmer discovery

While not apparent to me or others in CIMMYT at the time, the Honduran experience with the *abonera* technology was fundamentally different from anything else the organization had worked with. Not only did it not rely on any purchased external inputs, it had been developed without the direct help of researcher science. It was a modern era act of "farmer discovery" and had spread among thousands of

Milton Flores, inspecting the velvet bean residue in a farmer's field, Honduras.

poor farmers without the aid of professional communication strategies known in the agricultural sciences as "farm extension." From a few early adopters between 1970 and 1980, by 1992, the date of our largest survey, it had reached the vast majority of hillside farmers in the region, spreading directly from farmer to farmer.

It was also a revolution in hillside farming practice in the humid tropics, one I ironically called "the Green Manure Revolution" in several articles I published in international venues. Credit for being the first to notice the invention goes to Milton Flores and Roland Bunch, two men based in Honduras. They worked tirelessly to promote cover crop rotations and intercropping practices with this and other legume species in a wide range of settings in Central America. Milton, a young man at the time with a gentle demeanour, warm smile and infectious positivity, set up and ran the International Centre for Documentation and Information on Cover Crops in Tegucigalpa. He produced a remarkable video compilation of farmer testimony on velvet bean called *What the Fertilizer Bean Has Taught Us.* Internationally acclaimed scientists in the U.K. and the United States also picked up the thread, as did researchers in West Africa and throughout Central America and Mexico. Countless experiments with velvet bean and other cover crops gave a significant boost to emerging practices of regenerative agriculture beginning to challenge the Green Revolution paradigm.

For a time, I was at the centre of the excitement, including efforts to promote cover crops in West Africa through an information clearing house and to sponsor research on potential food uses of velvet bean. Someone at CIMMYT said that velvet bean would make me famous. While this never happened, the velvet bean story quickly became an attention grabber.

Don Winkelman, the Executive Director of CIMMYT, decided to make the slide show I had created on the subject a preferred presentation for guests and dignitaries visiting to learn about CIMMYT's work. The story was interesting and showed that CIMMYT was more than a plant breeding centre and capable of engaging in research on emerging trends in sustainable agriculture. At times I felt like the dog and pony show for an organization heavily invested in the old paradigm. However, I was hooked on this plant that made poor or degraded land productive once again, and did my best to tell the story.

My approach to research publications emphasized collective impact over individual achievement: I always wrote the initial results in Spanish, creating co-authored, publishable papers in short periods of time and circulating these widely in the region. One of the first of these, *Tierra Cobarde Se Vuelve Valiente* (Cowardly Land Becomes Brave Again), made its way into virtually every research organization and many non-governmental organizations in the region. This practice, modelled by Yvan Breton in my earlier training on Mexican fisheries, became a routine, and was appreciated by Latin American researchers and activists alike.

Bernard Triomphe, a coauthor with me of one of the most frequently cited books on the topic, provided what agronomists needed to know about how the technology worked, in a language and form they could recognize: quantified measures of long-term changes in soil properties and crop productivity, painstakingly collected in the field over a period of several years. These findings credibly conveyed the power and potential of the practice. Gustavo Sain, another coauthor and Argentinian economist, worked with me on the economics of the *abonera* system. This gave weight to key observations about why a rotation crop made economic sense from both farmer and market points of view. The three of us worked well together, aided by

Gustavo's constant stream of jokes about Argentines, the Pope and the American President sitting together on an airplane (Unfortunately, I've forgotten all the punch lines).

The work we did together contributed to the internationalization of the Central American experience with cover crops. Most importantly, the origins of the technology in farmer discovery established a credible link between the living practices of the farmer world and a growing body of evidence on ecological and regenerative agriculture emerging from the scientists' world.

The linkages traced by the velvet bean story across time and space illustrate something important about the nature of scientific discovery. First, they show the social qualities of innovation and knowledge generation, whether it be by means of scientific methods or mindful observation and the application of reason and creativity in a problem-solving mode. The various uses of velvet bean, including at least five distinct agricultural technologies (food crop, cover crop, forage crop, rotation crop, intercrop), are the result of experimentation by numerous farmers spanning several centuries and at least six countries.

The lesson that innovation is a collective, transpersonal act has been demonstrated time and time again by formal histories of discovery, even though the misleading image of the lone scientist-inventor persists. The velvet bean story smashes this mindset utterly.

Second, the story reminds us of humanity's debt to women. At the base of all the *Mucuna* spp. inventions was the act of taming the wild bean in the first place, and learning to make it food through the technology of cooking. It was undoubtedly women that did this—the Naga in crimson red pressed into servitude as an indentured worker bound for British Trinidad and Tobago; the Ghanaian grandmother dressed in sapphire blue straining the soaked seed to make soup for her grandchildren. Observing and transforming the gifts of nature into food from one generation to the next is truly the mother of invention.

Finally, the journey of velvet bean from India to Mesoamerica and around the world shows that creativity and invention don't operate in a vacuum, with something appearing out of nothing as it were. Each new use of velvet bean emerged from some quality observed in its present use: food, forage, cover, weed control, fertilizer. Steven Johnson, who studies the natural history of innovation, calls this creative space "the adjacent possible," that is, the realm of possibilities available at any given moment. He describes the moment as "a kind of shadow future, hovering on the edges of the present state of things, a map of all the ways in which the present can reinvent itself."

These lessons are encouraging, even reassuring in this age of grave threats to human existence. What is required of us to survive and thrive is not some rare scientific genius or mystical intervention but rather the most common of human capabilities: the collective call to be attentive and mindful of all of our senses and faculties interacting in the present moment. From the possibility of what is, the magic of what could be emerges as an image of maize plants growing in a thick mat of velvet bean residue. This is the science of the concrete.

Postscript: the courage to listen

Use of *Mucuna* in coastal Honduras declined sharply in the 2000s. An article on the topic by Shawn Neil and David Lee suggests that the decline was due to pressure from cattle ranching and the arrival of itchgrass (*Rottboellia cochinchinensis*), an invasive weed difficult to manage. Currently, the region is reeling from many forces, including drug cartels growing coca on remote hillsides. While the *abonera* system remains a remarkable technology, unbeatable as a system for growing maize on hillsides in the humid tropics, it could not compete in this wider and vastly more complex social and economic context.

In retrospect, I believe that the efforts to document and promote the use of velvet bean and other cover crops in hillside agriculture were worthwhile, even though the successes were temporary. Today, the world is struggling to redirect agriculture from its destructive path towards a mode of production that can feed the world without costing the earth. Regenerative and ecological practices, and cooperation between scientists and farmers, remain central to this undertaking, if only we have the courage to listen to both.

7

Heart, Head and Hands

In the morning hours of March 1, 1993, I was standing in Gregorio Hernandez's maize field in southern Veracruz with a who's who of leading agricultural researchers and activists from across Latin America. Gregorio, a Nahua from the Indigenous community of Tatahuicapan, was managing a field trial of his own design. Velvet bean grew vigorously between the rows of maize as a cover crop, fixing atmospheric nitrogen. The ground was covered by a thick mat of decomposing leaves and vines from the previous season, unburned despite the long history of slash and burn agriculture typical of the region. And the maize plants looked very healthy, standing strongly upright in the hot sun and already laden with two ears of corn per plant.

I watched the faces of the scientists gathered in the field examining the leaves of the maize plants for signs of disease, and finding none. Someone asked Gregorio what prompted him to plant the velvet

Me and Gregorio in his maize and velvet bean field.

bean intercrop. "The land was tired," he told us, pointing to a nearby section of his field with pale and thin maize plants growing in bare soil. Rather than wait for the land to rest under a traditional fallow of trees and shrubs, Gregorio had decided to speed things up by letting volunteer velvet bean plants emerge as an intercrop, pruning them back when they threatened to engulf the maize. The practice was novel and offered a more intensive option than the longer rotation from Honduras everyone standing in the field was already familiar with.

Observing Gregorio's field, and learning from his experience, was the opening session for an international workshop I organized to share observations on cover crops and draw lessons on how to do research with farmers. I wanted to ground the event in farmer experience and set a farmer-centred tone for researcher discussions.

By late afternoon, the workshop shifted from the field to Catemaco, the closest town with a hotel conference room and amenities for a group of twenty-four people, including several farmers. Gregorio was invited, but declined because, like most farmers, he had more pressing things to do.

After three more days of discussion I edited the proceedings into a book with one of my favourite Spanish titles: *"Gorras y Sombreros: Caminos hacia la colaboración entre técnicos y campesinos."* It translates poorly to English ("Peasant Hats and Scientist Caps: Paths towards collaboration between scientists and peasants") but the hat reference evokes the crux of the challenge we were gathered to discuss: how to bridge the life worlds of two distinct communities.

Farmers in Latin America sport a wide range of broad-brimmed straw hats: cowboy, chupalla, sombrero Cordobés, homburg, panama, planter's, broad sombrero, Stetson, *vueltiao*. Rural markets in Mexico offer many of these choices. Technical people and scientists that work outdoors almost always wear ball caps, usually advertising an organization or an agricultural input such as a brand of pesticide.

While a scientist, I liked to wear a cowboy hat with a wide, flat brim because it protected my neck and face from the sun and was cooler than a synthetic cap. It also reflected my farmer wannabe impulse and growing preoccupation with making a difference in the world of agriculture. My hat collection today still carries the memories of these efforts in the stains on the sweat band and frayed edges of the brims and peaks.

Innovation within tradition

According to Derek Byerlee and Greg Edmeades, two colleagues at CIMMYT, the late 1980s and early 1990s marked the beginning of a move in international agricultural research from a narrow focus on seed-fertilizer technology to consideration of emerging conservation technologies, including cover crops. The trend reflected a growing awareness of the many technical problems of industrial agriculture: pollution from toxic inputs, biodiversity loss, soil erosion, and compaction from mechanization. It also followed on the development of the theoretical and practical foundations of ecological and systems perspectives on sustainable agriculture and food production, brought forward by Miguel Altieri, an influential Chilean agronomist, and others.

Miguel and other critics of the Green Revolution, such as Pat Roy Mooney, visited CIMMYT while I was there, pushing research in new directions. The work I was doing at CIMMYT fit nicely with this new agenda, including the participatory approach to developing new technologies that was just beginning to eclipse CIMMYT's on-farm research methods of the 1980s.

Researcher sharing results with a community. Cartoon by Marc Roesch.

Mark Versteeg, a Dutch agronomist with a handlebar moustache and contagious smile, had come to the conference in Catemaco from Benin, West Africa, with cartoons by Marc Roesch, a French illustrator based in Benin at the time. I included three in the workshop proceedings to draw attention to the growing pains of researchers wanting to do farmer-based research but uncertain of how to go about it. The cartoons demanded of us a shift from the conceit and overconfidence of the researcher's gaze to a posture of listening and regard for differences in world views and practical priorities.

One shows a researcher, sitting with a tall stack of papers, presenting the results of a diagnostic assessment to farmers. The farmers are scattered about, lying down and bored to the point of falling asleep.

The scene reflects a limitation found in all kinds of conventional research involving people, then and now: experts survey individuals separated from each other by randomized sample designs, spend months in the office analyzing their findings with complex statistical tests and then (at best) validate the results with formal presentations to only some of the people that provided the information.

Findings are often presented in a language that is difficult to understand, with few opportunities for people to discuss among themselves

Researcher showing off a complex experimental design. Cartoon by Marc Roesch.

or challenge the conclusions. Years later, when I began writing with my colleague Jacques about the foibles of conventional research methods, we likened the practice to that of mosquitoes sucking blood: extractive and irritatingly useless to the people involved.

Another of Marc's cartoons illustrated a different challenge. It shows a plan for a field experiment littered with "treatments" and "control plots" needed to meet the statistical requirements of experimental designs. These are presented to farmers by the agronomist as though the many plots can address the many different interests and considerations of farmers. The scene makes fun of the idea that on-farm experiments can do everything for everyone: be scientifically rigorous, sensitive to farmer perspectives and comprehensible to all.

I had fallen into this delusion myself a few months earlier with an experiment in a farmer's field in the nearby Indigenous community of Soteapan. My purpose was to see how well cover crops could control weeds, compared to treatments with herbicides and manual weeding. When my colleague Hugo Perales and I visited the field towards the end of the experiment we found to our dismay that the various control and treatment plots were indistinguishable from each other. The experiment was gone.

The farmer informed us that his wife and son had gone to the field a few days earlier when he was busy with other chores. They had weeded everything by hand, uniformly, leaving only the maize plants.

He had neglected to tell them about the details of the experiment, and we had failed to meet with them in the first place to plan and agree on the purpose of the experiment and what it would look like. The experiment was overridden by the more compelling challenge of growing the best maize crop they could, today and with the resources at hand.

The failed experiment prompted a shift in my thinking about work with farmers for whom experiments have material consequences, settling on a solution different from the complex design in Marc's cartoon. A later paper published by Hugo and me, "Innovation within Tradition," suggested that research start with farmer-led experiments aimed simply at scoping out what is of interest to them, without any pretence of creating verifiable data sets. If promising, researcher-led experiments could follow to measure effects. Our point was that the two groups could complement each other sequentially, rather than trying to merge farmer and researcher experiments into one common design.

We said that respect for and engagement with farmers did not mean simply asserting that farmers are scientists just like us, which was a position implied by Robert Chambers, a pioneer of participatory methods and his early notion of "role reversals." To ignore farmer knowledge and creativity is arrogant but to treat farmer knowledge as the only word is equally unwise and disingenuous.

"You walk a lot," one farmer had said to me, referring to my travels to many farmers fields throughout Mesoamerica. We understood this observation as an invitation to actively share the scarce and vital knowledge resources our position of privilege had allowed us to collect.

Another presenter at the Catemaco workshop made a similar point. Jeffery Bentley, a young American anthropologist working on alternatives to pesticide use for insect control in crops, shared a room with me at the hotel. Solidly built, with arms as big as stove pipes, he did a hundred push-ups every day before breakfast. His work focused on providing farmers with information on a few key features of insect biology and inviting them to invent their own pest management strategies. An example I recall is of a peasant woman who, once she understood how ants control other insects in her crops, invented several uses of Coca Cola to attract and help establish ant colonies in her field.

Of course, recognizing that answers to some problems are not readily available to farmers applies to all social groups. Much later, Jacques and I wrote that what counts is the synergy between contrasting standpoints and methods, where all knowledgeable actors contribute what they can to a workable understanding of a given reality. The challenge for researchers with specialized knowledge is to learn to listen and speak at the same time, a sensitivity Jacques playfully described as the rapport of finely tuned married couples. For many social problems, the key is to be sure that the scientist is neither the first nor the last to speak, an idea captured in Robert Chambers's later book title *Farmers First and Last.*

Hugo modelled the patience and humility of this perspective, and the spirit of a life-long commitment to working with farmers. He told me one day that his chosen path was the way of Karma Yoga, one of the classical spiritual traditions of Hinduism. It focuses on the daily

Hugo (right) with farmer and his daughter, Soteapan, Veracruz, Mexico.

practice of work and the significance of what we might call career choices. Much like the African students I had met some years earlier in Cuba (Chapter 2), the work Hugo did as an agronomist was an expression of that path. Work infused with the principle of solidarity with others, a path different from career choices that separate work from charitable acts and volunteer time.

I had made a similar life decision, dedicating myself to an action-oriented anthropology. Still, I tended to rush ahead to get things done according to my understanding of getting things right. I still struggled to listen and speak at the same time, and to temper my desire to control the fruits of my labour.

The third cartoon is more visceral. It shows a man in a straw hat saying that he would love to experiment on various types of researchers. The digging tool on his shoulder, of African origin, makes one wonder exactly how he intends to carry out his experiments. "Back off," seems to be the message hidden under the smile.

A CIMMYT agronomist I worked with strongly objected to the implied violence of the image. He also had the view that new agricultural technology should not be aggressively promoted until and unless it had been thoroughly vetted by scientific study. Too much

Farmer offering to experiment on a researcher. Cartoon by Marc Roesch.

was riding on every corner of a farmer's field to risk it with uncertain technologies.

I was more willing to see humour in the cartoon and felt confident promoting the use of cover crops in ways that were already part of farmer practice in some places and by some people. To my mind, the velvet bean experience in Honduras and experiments such as Gregorio's were clear proofs of concept for the technology. Little did I know at the time, the CIMMYT agronomist was right to be cautious. Velvet bean was not a panacea. Promoting it without attention to broader forces at play was myopic and potentially harmful.

Farmer-to-farmer

My years at CIMMYT, from the time my son Ryan was born in 1990 until he was about to turn five, were my alpha male years. I drew people to me, showed bold leadership and focused attention on advancing collective goals.

After proving myself with studies of the Honduran green manure revolution, I was a prominent researcher in the tiny tribe of regional promotors of sustainable agriculture.

I was also a key player in the Sierra de Santa Marta Project (known by its Spanish acronym, PSSM) coordinated by Luisa Paré, the Mexican Québécoise Jacques and I had developed the project with.

The role allowed me to bring the promise of cover crops to Veracruz, the region that had preoccupied me during my earlier doctoral studies and where I wanted to improve the livelihoods of people and protect the landscape and its tropical coastal rainforest. Both were important to me, cemented as well by the fact my son Daniel was born and raised in the nearby city of Minatitlán. I wanted to remain connected to him, and to give something back to the people and landscape that had made me an anthropologist.

I was convinced that cover crops could help farmers feed the soil and rebuild their farming livelihoods. The practice also meant that farmers would not need to burn the forest to clear fields for crops, linking my two objectives. All I needed to do was to figure out how to bring the solution to farmers throughout the region.

The answer I settled upon was to launch a campaign to provide farmers with cover crop seed and information on uses. I developed simple visual materials and organized training sessions for farmers, drawing on farmers we had been working with to lead the sessions and tell other farmers about their own experiences with the technology.

The sessions often took place in the local Indigenous language, either *Nahuatl* or *Popoluca* depending on the community, with me, Hugo or Lorenzo, the campaign coordinator, standing nearby. While the campaign had a narrow technology focus, and was researcher-led, it broke with conventional approaches to agricultural extension on two important fronts: the interventions were grounded in local, farmer-based inventions; farmers were the direct conveyors of the information and seed to other farmers, farmer-to-farmer.

The farmer-trainers, *promotores* in Spanish, received a modest payment for the time they spent on the campaign, which included staking out experimental plots where farmers decided to test out the technology. For many farmers, the idea of direct comparisons piqued their curiosity almost as much as the cover crop itself.

The effort also brought the farmers and *promotores* together in farmer fields and helped to build relationships. Over a period of two years (1992 and 1993) the campaign reached several thousand farmers and was formally organized into a network called the *Red de Promotores Campesino* , the farmer-trainer network.

In 1994 I learned about another hillside cropping technology developed by Mexico's national agricultural research institute (INIFAP) and tested in farmers' fields around Catemaco. It used *Glyricidia sepium*, a local, leguminous tree species to create a low hedgerow on a contour line. The technology was a variation on the ancient practice of contour farming with "living fences" planted along the contour to stabilize the soil and foster the gradual formation of terraces.

I was impressed, and convinced Luisa, the coordinator of the Santa Marta Project, to collaborate with state and federal government officials on a campaign to bring cover crops and living fences to even more farmers over a larger area. Like velvet bean, it was easy to promote by providing farmers with access to seed, training and use of a simple A-frame and plumb line to mark the field contour lines. Over the subsequent two years, more than 200 fields were marked with contour lines and planted with thousands of linear feet of hedge rows, supported by a network of fifty-six farmer-trainers in communities across both the Los Tuxtla and Santa Marta sides of the coastal mountain range.

How I managed to mobilize the people and resources needed to conduct these campaigns is still something of a mystery to me. It was a risky undertaking because the benefits of both technologies took several years to achieve and few farmers had adopted the practices without at least some kind of subsidy (free seed and technical advice, in the case of cover crops; seed, advice and paid labour in the case of living fences).

Working with the state government, dominated at the time by the PRI, Mexico's most corrupt political party, was also a stretch for Luisa, whose academic work was highly critical of government. She was also a formidable activist, respected by very sophisticated and politically engaged intellectuals throughout Mexico. By becoming a professor at UNAM, Mexico's most prestigious university, she had accomplished something very difficult in a field with strong nationalistic hiring practices that blocked most foreign-born academics from permanent university jobs. She had a lot to lose by getting too close to government.

I was less concerned and through CIMMYT's connections to government agencies brought together a wide range of technical and policy oriented people to support the initiative. They seemed committed to a common goal. Luisa was also well connected to potential allies within government. Between the two of us, we could open doors.

I was interested in getting things done by identifying and eliminating barriers to adoption on the assumption that the technologies were inherently good. I also thought that the partnership would be a clever way to co-opt government programs and resources for sustainability and empowerment-oriented activities the government wouldn't attempt otherwise.

Ironically, this thinking, with its focus on leading through technology, was the same blind spot found in the conventional work of CIMMYT and Mexican government agricultural programs I so confidently criticized. The only thing that was different was my perspective on what was good technology and a good approach to technology development and dissemination—farmer-based innovations with sustainability goals built into the practice in the first place, and farmer-to-farmer dissemination strategies. The intervention simply needed to fit this "better" supply.

I received encouragement on this path for good reasons and from many sources. When bringing the idea of a campaign to my boss, Derek, I asked if he thought I should set it up like an experiment, with controls and areas receiving some kinds of supports that others wouldn't have. "No," he said, "just do what you think will work best with the resources you have."

Without knowing it at the time, by following this advice we avoided the practical and ethical dilemmas of development interventions designed like clinical drug trials where some receive the new drug and others don't. In a sense, the approach we adopted was closer to what farmers tend to do: show indifference to precise measurements and abandon controls once convinced of benefits.

None of it would have been possible but for Lorenzo Arteaga, the campaign coordinator. Tall and lanky, Lorenzo had trained to be a priest, abandoning the vocation after a few years to marry Concha, a woman from a community near Catemaco where he grew up.

Lorenzo radiated warmth and positivity, showing genuine care for people and enthusiasm for what we had to offer and how we

Lorenzo (top left), Hugo and two farmers assessing weed control in a farmer's field, Veracruz, Mexico.

were going about it. He was a farmer himself, experienced in the commercial production of Jalapeño peppers and versed in several novel technologies for managing cattle with electric fences. He threw himself into the task, covering for me during long periods when I was working elsewhere.

While the work in Veracruz was important to me and to CIMMYT, I had many other irons in the fire, travelling some 120 days a year for almost five years. I attended conferences in Panama and Costa Rica, visited remote parts of Nicaragua and Guatemala and returned regularly to the Atlantic coast of Honduras. I also gave talks at Wye College in the U.K. and Cornell University in upstate New York, spreading the good news of farmer innovation and adoption of cover crops.

I went to Ghana in search of traditional food uses of velvet bean and to Benin where I encouraged and evaluated efforts by CIMMYT sister organizations to promote velvet bean in the fight against *Imperata cylindrica*, an invasive grass undermining maize productivity throughout West Africa. This included providing support to the Sasakawa Foundation's dissemination of velvet bean to thousands of farmers in Benin.

It was exhausting, and I would often return home sick with intestinal parasites. On one occasion I arrived at my house with a mysterious pustule in my toe full of tiny, wriggling worms.

Debra would nurse me back to health. Weeks would go by as I wrote reports, typically as the lead in co-authored publications with agronomists, economists and plant breeders, and secondary author on reports of the Santa Marta Project.

Our home was on the CIMMYT campus, a quiet green space where Debra also poured her love into raising our son, Ryan. I could walk home from the office for lunch and be thrilled by his joy at seeing me approach, shouting "Daddy, Daddy!"

Mexico was an easy country to travel in. We took many short and longer trips by car to the colonial cities of the central plateau, western and coastal communities rich in Indigenous crafts and unpopulated beaches. We also went to the tropical regions of southern and south-eastern Mexico. The violence of drug cartels, today so ubiquitous in Mexico, had not yet dominated the society.

Ryan was portable and easygoing as a child. His smile and open demeanour attracted attention in every restaurant, periodically prompting the server to ask permission to whisk him away into the kitchen. He would disappear for the longest time and return smiling and vocalizing some new word. The Mexican people love children and care for them passionately.

Near the end of our time in Mexico we went to the Sierra de Santa Marta as a family, stopping at Lorenzo's home in Catemaco. He and his wife Concha lived in a modest house on a large property full of fruit trees. She made us *chili rellenos,* a Mexican dish of mild poblano *chili* stuffed with *cotija* cheese, covered in an egg batter and lightly fried. The result is drizzled with a light tomato sauce. It was served by Concha with freshly made tortillas, strong coffee and fresh papaya harvested from their yard.

Debra and I still talk of that meal and the warm conversation. Lorenzo had a way of engaging with people I admired. Smiling, joking but always focused on what he could do to help. He experienced in his own life the anxiety and pressure that comes with trying to find a better way to make a living as a farmer, bridging the psychological distance between farmers and researchers such as myself who make a living working with farmers but not being one.

Later, Lorenzo told me the tragic circumstances of Alvaro, a handsome and bright eyed man of twenty. Alvaro put himself enthusiastically into the various tasks he was asked to do as a farmer-trainer with the *Red de Promotores Campesino*, including working with cover crops in his own fields, taking his neighbours to see what he and others were doing and helping set up a simple comparison of a cover crop with a normal practice.

He was not an ideologue or technological purist. To control weeds Alvaro routinely used the glyphosate-based herbicide Round Up, originally produced by Monsanto. This brand is still the most widely used herbicide in the United States, Canada and Mexico because it is relatively effective at killing weeds that compete with crops. It is also toxic to human beings and most other life forms.

One day Alvaro was spraying weeds in a field when he noticed that the back-pack sprayer he was using had cracked and the pesticide soaked his entire back, buttocks and legs. This was the second time he had been exposed like this, having previously spent time undergoing emergency treatment at a local hospital. This time, his body went into shock due to a reaction that wiped out his red blood platelets. Despite medical assistance, he died a painful death, leaving behind a wife and young child.

At the time, I felt outraged at the chemical companies that manufactured and promoted their products knowing full well that resource poor and non-literate farmers often used them inappropriately. I also felt empathy for Alvaro's decisions. Farmers in the Global South are like people everywhere. They have families they feel responsible for, personal ambitions that go far beyond their current circumstances and a desire for connection to something greater than themselves. While I could not be sure of Alvaro's motivations, I did recognize that my own position of privilege allowed me to walk away from risky behaviours that for farmers offered the hope of immediate gains. In real life, genuine desires and dreams mix in complex ways with technological choices not easily dismissed by ideological judgements.

My foray into organizing farmers in response to farming problems was sensitive to individual and group needs but lacked grounding in the dynamics of broader system change. I had been exposed to but, in retrospect, did not fully appreciate the significance of the kind of peasant and union organizing I had heard about from Eric Holt-Gimenez and Marcial López, two Nicaraguans at the 1993 Catemaco workshop. They had presented on the Sandinista experience of the 1980s building the capacity of farmers and farmer institutions to help themselves. Eric, like me at the early stages of his career, went on years later to write the definitive English language history of the Nicaraguan *Campesino a Campesino* movement. He now heads the organization Food First, a "people's think tank" founded in 1975 by Joseph Collins and Frances More Lappé, author of *Diet for a Small Planet.*

Lorenzo, through his connections to the Catholic Church, was also familiar with the philosophy and approach of local Jesuit groups steeped in the Latin American tradition of liberation theology. I visited a seminary in the lowlands of the Sierra de Santa Marta and was moved by their patient and caring perspective on working with local communities.

Luisa was also attracted to the progressive political agenda implicit in the religiously inspired community work of the Jesuits. She was the most politically savvy and energetic person I had ever met, a firebrand with a keen eye for how power seeks advantage and a firm resolve to bring justice to situations of injustice. Her first campaign as the director of the Sierra de Santa Marta project was to beat back an ill-conceived plan by a US-based company to establish a eucalyptus plantation on the communal lands of Pajapan where Jacques and I had worked. It brought her into conflict with the state government that supported the plantation, adding to what was already her reputation for agrarian causes. Like other activists I worked with later, she put skin in the game, taking personal risks to protect others. She was courageous.

Under our joint leadership, the *Red* survived the encounter with the state government extension campaign, including delays in resources that seriously undermined the credibility of the initiative. The network quickly became a central player in all activities of the Sierra de Santa Marta project, helping to deliver on goals but also defining what the project would work on. In response to farmer demand, Luisa and others broadened the range of livelihood strategies the *Red* addressed: honey production, cultivation and marketing of decorative palms (*Piper auritum*), tree planting to protect water sources, ecotourism in communities with intact forests, more sustainable ranching practices and techniques for improving oyster production in the Laguna del Ostión. Many of the livelihood projects suffered set-backs and limitations. Some thrived, however, at least in particular communities and for particular households.

My own involvement in the farmer network and in the Sierra de Santa Marta project ended in June, 1995 when I moved back to Canada. Our son was about to turn five and my wife and I did not want to send him to school in the polluted haze that was and still is Mexico City. Debra gave me permission to live anywhere I wanted to, so long as it started with "C" and wasn't Cambodia or Colombia.

A few weeks before our departure for Ottawa, Canada, Luisa organized a *fiesta* in the Popoluca village of Soteapan hosted by women *promotores* she had been mobilizing. Minerva, a leader of the group, presented me with a cloth tortilla-wrap embroidered with an image of velvet bean and the words *"Manshu siik Red de Promotores Campesino"* (Velvet bean farmer network). It hangs today in a frame above my basement workbench as a reminder of that day. Sitting on benches in front of Minerva's home, we ate soup, freshly ground tortillas and refried beans, washed down with a hot drink. The "Nescafe" was made from finely ground velvet bean seeds.

Postscript: means and ends

Most researchers, and all activists, dream of having a positive impact on the landscapes, people and institutions they work with and dedicate their professional lives to. The desire for impact is deeply personal, and easily coloured by preconceptions and the desire to preserve a successful, coherent and tidy image of the enterprise.

The Sierra de Santa Marta project was my first experience at the helm of a development intervention. Launched in 1990 by Luisa, Jacques and myself, it survived 28 years, finally closing in 2018. This persistence is in and of itself a significant accomplishment. Different people took on the mantle of leadership over the years and several sister organizations emerged along the way, each with a similar geographic focus but own specific character. All included among their goals the improvement of rural livelihoods and the conservation of the remaining forests of the region.

Little remains locally of the two technologies I promoted. Farmer use of living fences and cover crops began to decline a few years after the campaigns stopped. Subsidies were necessary to get over the initial costs of shifting to the new practice, something anticipated in the design of the campaign but not delivered efficiently or sustained. I recall hours of argument with government officials over delays in the delivery of seed and payments to farmers. Broader forces were also at work, much like on the Atlantic coast of Honduras where the *abonera* system also faded away.

I felt partly responsible for the failures and frustrated by the outcome. Towards the end of my time at CIMMYT, Mario Ramos, a Mexican biologist and senior manager for the Global Environment Facility (GEF), contracted me to do a study on what it would take to bridge the gap between the short term costs of the technologies and the longer term benefits of forest conservation. I did the analysis with Olaf Erenstein, a young Dutch economist with CIMMYT who later headed the CIMMYT Economics Program. We concluded that three years of subsidies was the minimum investment needed to create conditions for stable adoption.

The need to invest serious money in a transition period is true of many technologies and techniques designed to conserve and improve the soil, water and biodiversity of agricultural systems, making the switch to sustainable agriculture extremely difficult in most settings. The decision in the 2020s of the government of Sri Lanka to suddenly cut off farmer access to chemical inputs threw agriculture and national food supply in the country into a crisis, in large part because the policy failed to recognize that ecological approaches to agriculture take time to create favourable conditions. Transition strategies that respect farmer livelihoods are needed, rather than cold turkey conversion therapy (see Chapter 12 on the transition out of tobacco farming in Bangladesh).

My friend Grant, a successful farmer on an island in the Yukon River above Dawson City, put it this way: "I'm here, in one of the most remote and coldest places on earth, not to make a statement but rather to make a living." Cover crops and living fences, on their own, couldn't produce that outcome.

Other changes are more promising than the technologies of the day. The rate of deforestation in the Sierra de Santa Marta has slowed significantly. While much of the remaining forest is naturally protected by exceptionally steep and rough terrain, a key factor has been the creation of Los Tuxtlas Biosphere Reserve, recognized by Mexico in 1996 and by UNESCO in 2006. This legal entity puts pressure on all levels of government and local people to avoid damaging the remaining forests. The Sierra de Santa Marta project had more to do with this legal victory than any other player on the scene.

As with any real-life story, however, the accomplishment is tinged by lost opportunities. In a 2006 book, Luisa and a colleague document the tortured tale of conflict and competition between the state and federal governments over the creation of the biosphere reserve. Representing two different levels of government, the state and the federal agencies undermined each other at every turn, confusing communication and bungling the process of setting up the reserve.

Eventually, each government expropriated land for the reserve nucleus from communities, some of which, like Pajapan, had titles going back to the 1600s. This act of state impunity, and corrupt handling of compensation, turned the process of creating the reserve into another bitter agrarian struggle. It closed off any possibility for direct community participation in co-creation of the reserve and co-management of the buffer zone that was meant to protect the nucleus and the sources of water the communities and nearby cities depend on. Instead, there was, and remains, conflict and resistance.

The dreams we had of co-creating a biosphere reserve with the local population and facilitating the adoption of sustainable agricultural technologies were not to be. They were not well aligned with the political, economic and social realities of the region and the time. Dominion by cattle interests, government corruption and fragmentation of Indigenous and local leadership pulled in different directions.

In a recent conversation with Luisa, I reflected on these and other lessons of our work together, especially with respect to the network of farmer-trainers, our joint legacy in the Sierra de Santa Marta. While well intentioned, we had treated the *Red* as a means to an end, defined at the time as better livelihoods for farmers and reduced pressure on the remaining forests through use of meaningful and accessible technologies. This orientation was misaligned in a different sense, driving change from the outside-in, from us to them. It inevitably lost energy and direction as circumstances and individual involvement changed.

Luisa later tried to correct the gaps we had left in the network leadership structure, starting with reorganizing the *Red* as a member cooperative and encouraging individuals to take up positions in the ejidos, municipal governments and ecology commissions in their own communities. She had come to understand that self-organization was a more compelling end goal than any particular technology or even general outcomes such as better livelihoods and forest conservation. Her efforts, over a dozen years, involved constant and caring attention to people and political dynamics she had come to know well. Various people responded, in turn making a difference by contributing in small and larger ways to better local governance.

Today there is a dynamic, Indigenous-led social organization in the Sierra de Santa Marta. It forcefully articulates collective demands, raising concerns about fracking for oil and gas in their territories, threats to water sources and land policies driving young people out of the region. While there is no direct line connecting the work of the Sierra de Santa Marta project and organization to the present state, I do believe that is a hopeful sign.

I lived in Mexico for ten years, as a young man in San Miguel de Allende, doing doctoral studies, and working at CIMMYT. While I never returned to live there again, I feel *medio Mejicano,* half-mexican. After all, both my sons were born there. That too is a hopeful sign.

8

Celebrating Food, Ecology and Culture

Anthropology is a nearsighted discipline, grounded in the details of geography and community practice, place and place making. This perspective guided my master's research among fishers in the Yukon and doctoral study of the political ecology of the Nahua of southern Veracruz. Post-doctoral studies examined the details of a single plant—velvet bean in all its human and biological splendour. This focus appealed to me. I wanted to get to the bottom of things, to something concrete and useful.

In 1995 I was pulled into a different world, where research connects to policy advocacy and sometimes collides with political activism. Only a few months after arriving back in Canada from Mexico with my wife and our son, I left for Jakarta, Indonesia to participate in the

Villagers on the Deccan Plateau, India, celebrating a food and biodiversity festival.

second Conference of the Parties to the Convention on Biological Diversity (CBD), an international treaty that came into force shortly after the 1992 Rio Earth Summit. I turned forty there, excited by what lay ahead as I moved from the trenches of farming technology to the front steps of global governance institutions.

Travel to Indonesia was my first assignment after being hired by the International Development Research Centre (IDRC), a Canadian government agency dedicated to research and building research capacity in the Global South. The IDRC's role at the Conference of the Parties to the convention was to sponsor and advocate for a place at the conference table for Indigenous peoples. They earned it. Most of the world's remaining biodiversity is in the traditional territory of Indigenous peoples. Furthermore, most modern medicines also have their origins in Indigenous knowledge of the properties and uses of particular plants and other natural materials.

Many governments, however, including Canada, discriminate against the territorial rights of Indigenous peoples and embrace the perspective that people living in protected areas are the primary conservation problem rather than the basis for a solution. The use of their knowledge, typically brokered by anthropologists and botanists on behalf of pharmaceutical companies, also largely ignores or fudges questions of prior, informed consent and ethical sharing of the benefits.

IDRC sponsored six people representing Indigenous organizations from Asia, Latin America, North America and Africa, to lobby for the inclusion of Indigenous peoples in high-level discussions on the conservation of biodiversity, the sustainable use of its components and the fair and equitable sharing of the benefits of biodiversity. The arrangement had been set up by Chusa Ginés, an IDRC biologist I was replacing while she was on maternity leave.

Chusa was an elegant woman originally from Spain, with a feisty personality and sharp mind. Her knowledge of Indigenous groups and spirited advocacy of their perspectives made it possible to bring together in Indonesia an impressive and well-organized group of Indigenous leaders.

I was there to observe and, if possible, facilitate introductions to scientists and government delegations. The Indigenous leaders did not need much introduction, however. They organized their own parallel sessions and, for the first time since the Convention had been signed, established a compelling presence from the floor of the plenary hall and in back room meetings. As the conference unfolded, various government delegations, including Canada's, started to listen.

The meeting in Indonesia opened my eyes to Indigenous rights and broader ethical concerns in ways I had not previously considered. The Convention on Biological Diversity was the first legally binding treaty among the various UN environmental agreements and for a time played a key role in international debates on the intellectual property rights of nations in the Global South, Indigenous peoples and peasant societies. While eventually eclipsed by trade regimes developed through the World Trade Organization (WTO) and by the Convention on Climate Change, it provided leverage on national governments reluctant to recognize Indigenous and farmer rights.

Some activists thought the Convention could act like a Trojan horse inside other international institutions and agreements. Academics such as the American ethnobotanist Darrell Posey and international civil society organizations such as the ETC Group, led by Canadian Pat Roy Mooney, helped to place the problem of bio-piracy in the context of global governance institutions, corporate concentration of control over food and medicines and intellectual property abuses.

IDRC funded cutting edge research and policy debate on these issues for almost a decade under the banner of the Sustainable Use of Biodiversity Initiative started by Chusa. She died in a plane crash in the Andes Mountains on January 28, 2002, doing the work she loved. By then, she and others had pried open spaces for Indigenous perspectives to be advanced inside international bodies.

Today, some progress has been made, with Indigenous rights enshrined in the United Nations Declaration on the Rights of Indigenous Peoples (UNDRIP). It was a distant dream in 1996 and even now is a non-binding resolution for key governments such as the United States, Australia and, until 2021, Canada. Still, UNDRIP resonates powerfully with Indigenous peoples and may yet serve as a strategic vehicle for airing historical grievances and bringing forward the political and cultural aspirations of Indigenous peoples.

Using diversity

I worked at the IDRC from 1995 to 2005. I considered myself a "talent scout" paid handsomely to scour the world for people and organizations doing important work. When I found them, and verified the quality of their work on the ground, the IDRC team funded the organizations with grants of about $100,000 a year. These sometimes turned into phases spanning four to six years, allowing research to mature along with our relationship to the researchers.

Over a period of ten years, I travelled eighty to ninety days a year to South Asia, Latin America and occasionally Africa, directly supporting more than one hundred research projects in twenty-eight countries. It was a productive and satisfying period of my professional life. My drive to get things done fused easily with the opportunities afforded by pots of funding for research and policy advocacy.

The scope, number and range of projects I was able to support during this period still astounds me. Most explored the interaction of socio-economic and technical dimensions of agriculture, fisheries and forestry initiatives in rural and urban settings. Broader themes included conflict over natural resources, food insecurity and environmental degradation. Research partners in the Global South identified issues and discovered solutions. My job was to help enrich these findings and bring them into the light, even though they might not reach policy tables until decades later.

Six months after the conference in Indonesia, I travelled to New Delhi, India, for a meeting with leading South Asian scientists and activists, scouted by another IDRC colleague. I stayed at the India Habitat Centre, a unique facility in Central Delhi designed by Joseph Allen Stein, an American architect and pioneer of the San Francisco Bay environmental design movement. He had moved to India in 1952 and was commissioned to design several important buildings a stone's throw from the famous Red Fort commissioned by Emperor Shad Jahan in 1638. IDRC had a membership in the Centre to provide staff with access to the tiny guest rooms, extensive gardens and meeting rooms on the site.

My meeting, however, took place at the Pusa Campus of the Indian Agricultural Research Institute outside of the city centre. I wanted to ground the discussions in national and regional agricultural institutions, and unbalance traditional donor-recipient relationships. Power exercised unilaterally by funding agencies was and remains a fundamental problem on bilateral aid, distorting the priorities of those directly affected by the situations funding is meant to address.

Southern leadership was important to IDRC at the time and consistent with my own values and budding approach to funding research.

South Asian scientists and activists highly critical of Western dominance and funding largesse would not see a meeting in the India Habitat Centre, a facility catering to foreign expatriates, as a propitious start to a respectful relationship.

Dr. S.K. Singh, an eminent plant breeder, was the host at the Pusa Campus. His kind and gentle manner helped to bridge sharply differing political perspectives within the group, which included many regional stars in the world of science and activism. By the end of two days of discussion, the group agreed to manage a regional programme of small research grants to grassroots organizations and farmer groups in neglected, high biodiversity regions of South Asia.

The title of the program, "Using Diversity," reflected the idea that the best way to conserve agricultural biodiversity is to know it and to use it. I acted as the secretary for the group, crafting a mandate and focus they could all agree on: documenting research on uses of agricultural biodiversity in local languages for local purposes and under local authorship and control.

In the early evening hours after the meeting concluded, I was paid a visit at the India Habitat Centre by Farhad Mazhar and P.V. Satheesh, two members of the new steering committee. They had talked among themselves and concluded that I had potential as an ally they could take under their wing. They wanted to introduce me

Seed pots and seed types from the Deccan Plateau, India.

to the strategic agenda of a new network they were creating in the lead up to the 1996 World Food Summit in Rome.

I was lounging in the gardens of the centre nursing an intense headache and the beginning of a fever threatening to overwhelm me. I managed to listen, however, as the two outlined for me the political perspective and practical strategy they had in mind for the summit.

The 1996 World Food Summit was convened by Jacques Diouf of Senegal, the first African Director-General of the Food and Agriculture Organization (FAO). It was the first time since 1974 that governments would gather to discuss the global state of food and agriculture and aimed to rally nations around the goal of achieving "food security for all." This slogan later became the centre piece of the Rome Declaration on Food Security signed by 186 countries.

The concern raised by Farhad and Satheesh was that the means to address food insecurity being promoted by the FAO focused entirely on aid and trade. Hunger and malnutrition, they felt, were being reduced to a humanitarian and market problem for the rich countries to solve, a prospect unacceptable to societies with long and rich agrarian histories. "People are not just stomachs to be filled like holes in the ground," said Farhad. "Food in our culture is not just another commodity to be traded, like zinc and copper."

The FAO declaration gave little attention to the negative impacts on national and local agriculture of multilateral trade regimes such as the World Trade Organization (WTO) and numerous bilateral agreements between governments and private interests linking trade, aid and human security arrangements. Satheesh said plainly, "Transnational companies are trying to make independent, small-scale farming obsolete through international trade in food surpluses from industrial farming. If they succeed, farmers and whole nations will become prisoners to global food corporations."

Later that evening I took a heavy dose of acetaminophen to bring down my fever before presenting myself for check-in to a plane bound for Ottawa. Some twenty-four hours later Debra picked me up at the airport and took me directly to Emergency at the Ottawa Hospital. I had a fever of over 104 and spent several days self-isolating in our basement, waiting for a diagnosis of malaria, dengue or some other viral disease. The cause was never identified.

By the time I recovered, the die was set. I had begun to see agriculture, international agreements and corporate interests in a new light.

Poster by the Sustainable Agriculture Action Group, Pakistan, a member of SANFEC.

The network Farhad and Satheesh were bringing to life—the South Asia Network for Food, Ecology and Culture (SANFEC)—captured in its name what was missing from the FAO vision and at the same time articulated an alternative perspective embedded in specific cultures and ecosystems. Defending local sources of food and local farming practices from the universalizing tendencies of international institutions and agreements—the mission at the heart of the politics of food sovereignty—had a new global champion.

Over the following years, SANFEC members organized meetings, published proceedings and position papers and mobilized parallel sessions and protests at multi-layer gatherings of governments and international bodies such as the WTO and FAO. IDRC and the Canadian non-governmental organization InterPares were active supporters. The network inspired a generation of like-minded NGOs across the region, pioneering an approach to regional political activism that was also grounded in community-led initiatives in ecological farming.

The depth of the experience, and the power of fusing community practice with policy advocacy, first became evident to me in 1996 on the Deccan Plateau of south-central India.

Crops of truth

The landscape looked bone-dry when I dismounted from a white Premier Padmini, India's classic four-seat sedan, in the village of Pastapur an hour north of Hyderabad. Satheesh was relaxing on a bench built into the side of a mud building, an IBM ThinkPad at his side. He was sporting a goatee, facial hair I later came to favour as well.

The building was the Pastapur office of the Deccan Development Society (DDS) and home to one of the most remarkable grassroots organizations I have ever come across. It recently won two of the world's prestigious environmental awards for its work with Dalit women farmers—the 2020 UNDP Equator Prize and the 2021 Prince Albert II of Monaco Foundation Award. I was there, more than twenty years ago now, to participate in a Biodiversity Festival organized to share the results of one of the first Using Diversity Awards.

Satheesh spoke with the precise diction of his training as a media journalist. "Local people", he said, "call the traditional post-monsoon

Begari Laxmamma, sorghum farmer, Deccan Plateau. Central photo by the Deccan Development Society; background by D. Buckles

crops *Satyam Pantulu,* which means "Crops of Truth." The phrase refers to the hardiness of the crops, even in the driest of conditions and on the poorest of soils common in the Deccan. "The people are hardy too," he continued, "staying here whatever the misery, whatever the wretchedness. Crops that demand nothing, like the farmers, are crops of truth—to be celebrated and cared for."

Research on the seed types and seed sources of dry land agriculture in the Deccan and the mixed cropping practices used to cultivate them had been led by Dalit farming women over the previous years. First, they made maps of their fields, using coloured chalk to represent the different species and varieties combined on their land. A high diversity farm like that of Gangwar Manemma might include four varieties of sorghum, three varieties of pigeon pea, three varieties of cowpea, three varieties of foxtail millet, little millet, finger millet, two varieties of hibiscus, dollochis lablab, yellow cucumber, groundnut, four varieties of redgram, three varieties of field beans, niger and horsegram, all on a plot a little over a hectare in size.

Chandramma, a Dalit woman I met several times over the years, facilitated scoring and analysis of the crop characteristics. She and other women made a huge matrix in chalk on the ground and used stones to rate specific crops against a long list of potential uses. Ground

Jayappa, Chandramma and China Narsamma mapping village soils and crops.

Mural in Pastapur Village, showing the caravan.

democracy, they called it. The results, Chandramma said, show that: "There is no seed on our farms that does not answer the need of medicine or fodder or food or nutrition or ritual. Every crop we use is good for the soil, good for human beings and good for the animals. It is this relationship that sustains agriculture."

Sharing the results of the research funded by the Using Diversity Award was dynamic and meaningful to people imbued in an oral and visual culture. DDS hosted a *jatra* (fair) that brought together over a period of three days some 5,000 women and men farmers from dozens of neighbouring villages. Many arrived in carts drawn by oxen with painted horns and plaited braids as local bands played in accompaniment. The processions converged on the fairgrounds, a large field planted with dozens of crops and surrounded by temporary shelters.

The shelters housed displays and events which people wandered through as though in a village marketplace. One was a livestock pen, with traditional breeds of cattle, goats and chickens, and piles of diverse fodder crops. In other shelters farmers used coloured chalk, seed, leaves and clay figures to recreate miniature versions of their farms as living versions of a PowerPoint presentation. Every crop was matched to a particular soil type. They explained to visiting farmers and other guests what and why they grew what they grew, and the recipes used to turn harvests into food. I saw some visiting women cry when they held in their hands the seed of a crop they no longer grew and realized the seed wealth they had lost.

Toy ox cart, Pastapur, India. Photo by Justin Wonnacott.

I too was overwhelmed. The food venue was spectacular, with huge vats cooking curries and a clay tandoor built for the occasion churning out *roti* flatbread from the flour of millet and sorghum. Colourful mats were laid out in long rows for people to sit. Somehow, every day for three days, the cooks fed hundreds of people, each served with a range of pulses, cooked vegetables and *roti* on a banana leaf plate. Dances, films about local biodiversity and painted motifs on the buildings added even more colour to the experience.

The festival concluded with a pledge, called out by Satheesh and responded to in unison by 2,000 women farmers and several hundred invited guests. We had formed a human chain around the mixed crop field at the centre of the *jatra* and called out in response to Satheesh's lead, "We pledge that we will continue to preserve and promote diversity on our farms. We pledge that we will ban chemicals from our farms."

After the first Biodiversity Festival in 1998, DDS switched from holding the event in a single location to organizing it as a caravan of ox carts filled with colourful displays of local seeds and agricultural implements. Today, each village welcomes the ox carts at the village entrance and takes responsibility for the celebration until the next day. They then hitch up their own bullocks and take the carts to the next village en route to more than a dozen other villages in the region.

People put holy marks on the bullock foreheads and wash the animal's feet in a ritual of gratitude. Singers, dancers and drummers

P.V. Satheesh, during the Mobile Biodiversity Festival, Deccan.

join in, bringing their own stamp of novelty and creativity to the caravan. The songs they compose are sung in front of the temple, the mosque, the church and the Sufi shrine, embracing all faiths in the celebration of crops, seed, livestock and agricultural implements. Substantive discussions on food and farming futures are also organized, particularly when the caravan stops at a *mandal* town (representing a group of villages). This brings farmers together with village, *mandal* and district level officials.

Evenings are marked by screenings of films on local agriculture made by local women farmers, attracting huge crowds. The organization, thanks to Satheesh's media training, has pioneered participatory video production, with Dalit women farmers as both the subject and the directors behind the camera.

The first film I watched is called *The Sangham Shot* and is a masterclass on why people's own analysis and self-expression matters to understanding the true range of human experiences. It examines, in the words and images created by a small group of women farmer-filmmakers, three distinct camera angles. The "slave shot" is taken from the ground looking up, as though at a powerful overseer. The "patel shot" assumes the opposite position, looking down at a subject it examines and commands. By contrast, the "sangham shot" shows the perspective of equals, eye to eye between subject and object, speaker and filmmaker, living being and living being.

Filmmaking by women farmers, spoken of but rarely practiced in international development, has, in my view, achieved its highest expression through decades of production at DDS. It has inspired farmers throughout the region, including those associated with the SANFEC organizations, to make films celebrating the biodiversity of their farming systems. These tap into deep oral traditions while at the same time erasing the barriers of literacy.

China Narsamma, a farmer-filmmaker who visited my home in Ottawa one time, spoke plainly about the power and advantages of film as a means of communication in villages. "Neighbours who receive printed media may think that we are the ones causing the problems. If we film the same story, people will get a clearer idea that a person from this or that village has these definite problems and that she spoke to this particular person. Since we are speaking face-to-face we can clearly understand each other's problems. Pictures and sound can say all this."

China Narsamma, a farmer-filmmaker.

Years after attending my first biodiversity festival I asked Satheesh why DDS had shifted the Biodiversity Festival format from a village fair to a mobile caravan. He replied, "The mobility ensures unprecedented participation." Now in its twenty-second year, the caravan passes through more than sixty villages, touching the minds and hearts of at least 100,000 farmers every year and etching for itself a permanent place in the cultural calendar of the community. It has also elevated farmer concerns to the national stage. "Over time," explained Satheesh, "the farmers have become very clear about what they will accept from governments and what they will reject. Top agricultural scientists, bureaucrats and politicians now come to the festivals to learn new perspectives on agricultural biodiversity and gratefully honour farmers."

From these simple expressions of awareness among officials, small and larger shifts in policy perspective have emerged. One of the more significant was a decision by the state government to allow locally grown millets and sorghum into the Public Distribution System used to distribute subsidized grains among the poorest segments of the population. Previously, only wheat and rice imported from other parts of India had been included, a bias that placed these crops above others and by-passed the contributions of local farmers. "Farmers did not see themselves, and their crops, in this government policy," said Satheesh. "Now they do."

My own understanding of the link between policy change, grassroots mobilization and connection to cultural identity was forged in this creative exploration of the crops of truth. I wanted to bring the truth home to Canada.

The future of agriculture

Salt Spring Island sits off the west coast of British Columbia among a smattering of other small islands between the City of Vancouver and Vancouver Island. Today it is a fabled place of expensive real estate, relatively protected from the open ocean and connected to Vancouver Island by a ferry. When I went there with SANFEC members, Salt Spring Island was still a haven for back-to-the-land advocates, adventuresome retirees, artists and craft makers. It was also a hot spot of organic farmers, seed savers and entrepreneurs connected to the emerging food movement in North America.

We were on Salt Spring Island as a caravan of South Asian and Canadian farmers and political activists to develop common ground on principles and practices of sustainable agriculture. I had convened the group in coordination with SANFEC and InterPares, a Canadian NGO dedicated to solidarity among equals as an approach to international cooperation. Abra Brynne, a long-time British Colombia food activist, provided expert local knowledge of farmsteads and arranged the local logistics for various stops on a tour of southern British Colombia. It culminated in Victoria where we presented a collective vision of the future of agriculture at the 2001 Organic World Congress.

We travelled, ate and learned together over a period of ten days. South Asia was represented by eighteen farmers and allies from India, Bangladesh, Pakistan, Nepal and Sri Lanka, including Satheesh and Farhad. The Canadian farmers came from Quebec, Manitoba and British Columbia, accompanied by Abra and Dominique Caouette, a friend who had worked with me in the Sierra de Santa Marta, Mexico and was now with InterPares. The experience, captured beautifully in a video by Chinna Narsamma and other Dalit farmer-filmmakers, was a remarkable moment for its insight into the biodiversity crisis we live today and the power of food to unite across boundaries.

Begari Laxmamma preparing to interview a Sri Lankan farmer in an orchard on Salt Spring Island, Canada.

Two observations by South Asian and Canadian farmers involved in the "Dialogue on the Future of Agriculture" illustrate the connections and the importance of agricultural biodiversity as a tool for food security, regional reconciliation and global peace building. The first observation started with Cathleen Kneen, who co-hosted the launch of the process in a small hotel conference hall outside of Vancouver. Cathleen was described by Oxfam Canada in a 2016 obituary as "a food hero" and "the grandmother" of grassroots food security organizing in Canada. Not surprisingly, seed saving was top of mind for her and many seated around the circle. Saving money, controlling your own food supply, adapting seed to your soil and climate, preserving genetic diversity and asserting farmer rights to use open pollinated seeds were among the various reasons to save seed that people listed during the session.

Everyone knew of the Percy Schmeiser v. Monsanto law suit in full swing at the time, and the profound implications of the outcome for the rights of all people everywhere to save their own seed. Monsanto started the row by suing Percy for using its patented Canola seed without a licence. Percy claimed the seed had blown into his field from a neighbour and contaminated his own seed with their product. He counter sued.

The first ideas for the declaration *Our Common Ground: South Asia-Canada Dialogue on the Future of Agriculture* presented at the Victoria conference were focused on seed and farmer rights to save their own seed free from harassment by corporations.

A few days later, at the Foxglove Farm on Salt Spring Island, we sat again to discuss the role of seed and biodiversity in farmer livelihoods and food systems. Michael Ableman, who ran the farm with his partner Jeanne-Marie Herman, explained his perspective as we sat on the neatly mowed grass next to his house. Michael had for twenty years managed Fairview Gardens in Santa Barbara County, California, helping to establish urban agriculture as a pillar of the 1990s food movement in North America. His 1998 book *On Good Land: The Autobiography of an Urban Farm* chronicles the life of the one-hundred-year-old farm and the struggles to save it from urban development. Now, he and his partner run a model farm catering to food tourists. Like many of the market garden farms we visited in British Columbia, the grounds were impeccable, with carefully tended garden beds and rows of vibrant and photogenic vegetables.

What surprised the Canadians, as we went around the circle sharing impressions from the caravan, was an observation by Jahanara Begum, a Bangladeshi woman farmer in her sixties. Dressed in a dark Borkha, and speaking through translation, she said simply, "You have lost so much." Far from being impressed with the beautiful Canadian farms she had seen during the caravan her tone and message was one of sympathy.

There were no animals on Michael's farm to provide manure and milk. Among the many vegetables in the gardens there were few grains or pulses critical to food security. Other farms we visited had similarly narrow niches and limited production practices, isolated from each other and from the full range of biodiversity native to traditional agricultural communities. To her, Canadian farming, including organic farming, was sterile and vulnerable compared to the richly integrated practices of her tiny biodiversity-based farm and village life in Bangladesh. It was a shadow of what it could be, dependent on distant markets and with key components of life missing from the ecological and social landscape.

This theme—the poverty of food policy driving the loss of agricultural biodiversity—became a rallying call for the group. John Wilcox of Duck Creek Farms on Salt Spring Island put the solution succinctly on the film record. He said, "We commit to recreate community," referring to the community of plants, animals and humans that make up the agricultural landscape.

His own farm focused not on extracting the maximum amount of product from the field but rather attending to the myriad relationships he understood bound him to the land and people around him. This included the beavers on his land that sometimes damaged his crops but also created a water balance necessary for the long-term health of the land and the crops. It included as well the neighbours he worked with to protect farmer rights to save seed.

Robin, a young woman with a soft voice and strong back who was new to farming at the time, also acknowledged the importance of recreating diverse plant and human communities. Without any land of her own, Robin's market garden depended on her relationships with older generations in her community in suburban Victoria. They provided access to land she did not own in exchange for a share in the harvest.

Cathleen, Michael, John, Robin and other small-scale Canadian organic farmers we met during the caravan also spoke out strongly against the corporate take-over of the achievements of the organic food movement in North America. The risk was evident at the Organic World Congress in Victoria where large corporations occupied prominent positions selling their products under the organic label. Lundberg Family Farms, for example, was there with a large booth. The corporation started as a family farm in 1937, but by 2002 they controlled a large part of the global organic rice market through a vast network of suppliers. Today it manages rice monocultures with organic inputs on a massive scale, bringing hundreds of farms and communities under a single system of technological and corporate control. While easier on the land and water than conventional agriculture, the corporation is inexorably centred on feeding itself rather than feeding the world of food producing communities.

We brought the problems of corporate control over food systems directly to congress organizers and participants through a plenary presentation, where we read our manifesto. Satheesh first pointed out that small scale farmers around the world, not corporations, are feeding the vast majority of the world's population. This is true even today everywhere outside of North America where industrial farms dominate. These same farmers, he noted, including the thousands of small-scale farms in France, Italy, India, Kenya, Mexico and many other places, are also doing the hard work of transforming conventional farming into sustainable farming. They are doing the practical experiments, developing the local understanding and conserving the plant genetic resources necessary to the future of agriculture, guided not by theory but rather by trying to solve real problems, in the concrete. "But the gains," Satheesh said, "are vulnerable to the greed of corporations seeking new profits in organic food production."

The disconnect between the origins and values of organic farming and the financial interests of the global food system is even clearer today, with green investors building brands on a food movement they did not initiate and do not represent in spirit or practice.

Our collective stand against corporate control in the realm of food and farming impressed a farmer from Pakistan travelling with a delegation headed by Shahid Zia, a prominent SANFEC member and founder of the Lok Sanhj Foundation. The farmer, a man in his fifties from the Punjab region of Pakistan, had been sharing accommodations with a Bangladeshi farmer of a similar age. Mixing farmer accommodations across national boundaries was a deliberate strategy of the tour, not without some risk considering that the governments of some countries were in conflict. Memories and misunderstandings regarding the 1971 war that separated Pakistan and Bangladesh were painful for people even thirty years on.

The two roommates struggled at first to understand each other, speaking Urdu on one side and Bangla on the other, with a few English words along the way. They kept knocking at Shahid's door in the next room, even up to midnight, to ask for translation of this term or that idea. They were particularly excited by the caravan discussions about seed and rights to save seed as well as the role of animals in helping to sustain agriculture.

By the end of the tour, the two were fast friends. The Pakistani farmer said to the whole group in a closing meeting, "I no longer see the West as my enemy. I now have friends in the West, in Bangladesh, in India, in Sri Lanka and in Nepal who are also opposed to the violence of transnational corporations." He conveyed for many the excitement generated by the dialogue and its statement of solidarity across political, economic and cultural boundaries.

Common ground on the future of agriculture seemed possible, bridging as well to Indigenous movements against patents on life forms, social movements to rebuild local communities, consumer movements for safe and healthy food, and urban movements for a new form of urbanization based on sustainability and inclusion. On the day we left, the two farmers had tears in their eyes as they hugged each other.

Learning across boundaries

From the late 1990s to 2007, SANFEC organized, with their own resources and with funding from IDRC and InterPares, a dozen cross-border farmer exchanges. Canadian farmers made a reciprocal tour of Indian and Nepali farms, meeting along the way with government officials to share their struggles with biodiversity loss and policies favouring large scale farms. A caravan of farmers from Pakistan picked up farmers in India and Bangladesh, who carried on together to Sri

Sundaram Verma (left) from Rajasthan, India visiting Chaina, Anwara and other farmers in Bangladesh.

Lanka before returning home. Dozens of women farmers from India, Sri Lanka, Nepal and Pakistan converged in Bangladesh for ten days of visits with their sisters in farming communities throughout the country. The caravan concluded, on International Women's Day, with a large rally in Dhaka dedicated to bringing farming women onto the centre stage of the urban women's movement.

The way people survive was a complete surprise to visiting farmers. Bangladeshis were amazed to see the agriculture of farmers in Andhra Pradesh, where there is almost no water. Indian farmers could not believe how Bangladeshis cultivated with so much water around. How Nepalis managed to protect their fields on steep hillsides was astonishing to people from the plains.

National and regional events under the banner of SANFEC included seed festivals and food festivals bringing together women farmers, policy makers and middle-class urban women nostalgic for lost foods and lost food arts. These were celebratory in tone and content, and always included policy dialogue with agricultural scientists and government officials on national and international policies with impacts on agriculture, food and farming women.

Regional representation in SANFEC events made it easier for national hosts to say that they were not alone in raising these concerns.

Podiliname, a Sri Lankan leader of SANFEC.

Podiliname, the SANFEC animator in Sri Lanka said, "Getting heard by the national government on why we should oppose Genetically Modified Organisms (GMO) is something we could not have achieved on our own. Having Indian, Pakistani, Bangladeshi and Nepali NGOs all saying the same thing meant they could not dismiss us so easily."

In the hands of thoughtful organizations, farmer-based research, farmer-to-farmer exchanges and dialogue between farmers and scientists were not simply an extravagant curiosity. They were a conscious attempt to build peace in a fractious region and a catalyst for profound human-to-human learning and practical advocacy. The process disseminated ideas, including the elimination of false ideas about the other. Farhad, reflecting with me on the exchanges, said, "Directly meeting people, and the kind of relationship you develop from meeting people, is always superior to other forms of human interaction. Even fanaticism and other forms of extreme conservatism can be neutralized through people-to-people relationships."

The need was clear. The Pakistan-India relationship has been fraught ever since the partition of British India in 1947, and was very tense in the late 1990s and early 2000s when I travelled in the region for IDRC. Both countries had armies sitting ready on their borders and equal numbers of nuclear warheads. The movement of citizens between the two countries was restricted. Exchanges even among scientists were difficult to arrange. Bangladesh and Pakistan also harboured long-standing hostilities rooted in the 1971 war and subsequent famine in Bangladesh.

Migration from Bangladesh and Nepal into India, and trafficking of women and children from both of these countries, were particularly sensitive issues at the time. They were, and today still are largely hidden forms of modern slavery.

The South Asian Association for Regional Cooperation (SAARC), which also includes Afghanistan, Bhutan and the Maldives, was set up by governments in the late 1980s to help manage some of these tensions. As with many bodies of this nature, however, it lacks real power and suffers from a bureaucratic lack of imagination regarding what, concretely, can be done to address areas of common concern. SANFEC, in parallel to the annual SAARC meetings, did what it could to draw attention to the insights coming from the network's collective experience.

For a decade SANFEC organized the SAARC People's Forum in cooperation with several regional social justice organizations. Street protests outside the venue of the official meetings were a common tactic, along with parallel conferences on the contributions of traditional agriculture to food security and meetings to strategize on ways to influence national governments. SANFEC routinely ensured that women farmers occupied centre stage in numbers sufficient to make their presence not only seen but meaningful. Celebration of food cultures and sharing of food were part and parcel of the practice of personal connections imbued in the activism.

SANFEC responded to the fraught geo-political environment of the SAARC with positive initiatives and novel thinking about even the most difficult issues being addressed at the policy level, such as migration and trafficking in women and children. These, the network members argued, are not primarily political or cultural issues. Rather, they are directly linked to the destruction of local food sources in regions where there are few economic opportunities. Food sovereignty was the central counter-demand.

The poverty of food policies of the WTO and an international scientific bias towards industrial agriculture ignores a cornerstone of peace building and social stability. Efforts to strengthen food producing communities offer an alternative vision, one based on an understanding of the relationship between food, ecology and self-confident communities. In short, safe-guarding the conditions for peaceful co-existence among peoples begins with local control over food, a policy even more relevant today in the context of the global climate emergency, migration and the coming food crisis.

A chance to show quality

The mid- to late 1990s witnessed the emergence of a global movement of protest against the worst effects of globalization and industrial agriculture experienced by rural and urban communities. The hardships experienced by communities united diverse social movements, from the Zapatista Army of National Liberation in Chiapas, Mexico to a series of global, anti-capitalist protests at meetings of the WTO.

Credible researchers in both the Global North and the Global South were riding, and in some cases leading, that wave of protest. This could not be ignored by funding agencies that had their eyes open. During the 1990s and early 2000s, IDRC supported research initiatives with sharply political implications in many regions. Broad funding envelopes approved at the level of the IDRC Board of Governors, and administrative tools for small exploratory grants, provided staff with the flexibility they needed to take intellectual risks and follow their interests and passions.

Senior management went along, so long as the work was grounded in credible southern perspectives and kept IDRC out of the limelight. Reputations for research excellence among staff also created space for research outside of the political mainstream.

By and large I walked the line between policy advocacy and political activism. I knew that Farhad and Satheesh were firebrands, and so did other members of the program initiative. Their sharp views remained largely invisible to senior managers until I crossed the line by signing the *Our Common Ground* manifesto, developed on Salt Spring Island and in Victoria. Two IDRC communications officers that had joined the caravan and signed the statement also had their wrists slapped.

The manifesto was replete with the tactical language of political activism. It was anti-imperialist and anti-capitalist while at the same time clearly articulating an alternative path to a future that includes agrarian societies and lifestyles. These, we argued, feed the world and ensure survival in ways corporations cannot.

What I learned from being disciplined at IDRC, in addition to the limits of independence in a government institution, was that it was not enough to simply articulate new perspectives on development alternatives and inform policy advocacy, as IDRC was mandated to do. Social change also requires of us that we put skin in the game.

Farhad Mazhar, more than anyone else I know, showed me what courage and integrity of thought and deed looks like in the context of political activism. The first sign of this from him came when, some months after I met him in New Delhi, I asked for background on a letter about him I read in the New York Times. It was signed by Jacques Derrida, a major figure in postmodern philosophy, and several others.

In the letter, they demanded Farhad's immediate release from jail. He was being held for criticizing the Bangladesh government's ruthless suppression of a strike over low pay and unfair treatment in the ranks of an auxiliary police force, the Bangladesh Ansar. More than thirty members of the poorly armed rural contingent were killed in their barracks by a much better equipped and better trained paramilitary force, the Bangladesh Rifles, sent by the government to put down the strike.

"We want to insist at once that this rebellion was just," wrote Farhad in the Bengali magazine *Chinta*. His analysis of class struggle and state abuse of power was clear:

> *The state, in its attempts to preserve law and order, gathers manpower from the oppressed subaltern class. The armed forces built with these very people are then used to further the rule of the oppressing and ruling classes over poor farmers, labourers, and the working class. Their revolts are suppressed. Killings are carried out. The BDR soldiers that shot and killed the Ansars are also the same 'farmers in uniforms.' And yet, the BDR soldier did not realize that he had just killed his own brother.*

The cruelty and callousness with which human life was treated by the state, and the muted response by the Bangladeshi intelligentsia, were the centre of his outrage. "Is there no one in this cruel society to listen to the Ansars?" he wrote.

In my conversation with Farhad he told me that when he was put in jail under the Special Powers Act and the offending issue of *Chinta* banned, he feared for his life. A group of prisoners immediately approached him and insisted he be moved to the infirmary where they felt he would be safer from government reprisals against him. After a little more than a month, he was released by the court under the pressure of a deluge of international attention from protectors of press freedoms.

What struck me the most from his story, beyond the perspective on the class dynamics of the rebellion, was the integrity of his action. He knew very well that the Ansars were also brutish and responsible for many abuses in villages during the exercise of their routine policing tactics. They were not a sympathetic group in and of themselves. Yet he spared neither government nor the silent progressives and culture of hypocrisy in his midst. "If a son of the middle or upper classes dies, even if a rich man's terrorist son is killed in a brawl, the entire city is in mourning," he said. "And yet there is no action when Ansars are shot like animals. The same people who love to chant formulas of 'democracy' and 'human rights' did not get busy to condemn their murder."

Connecting principled thoughts with principled action takes courage, but so too does the willingness to show compassion. Both are needed to stand up for one's beliefs.

9

Cultivating Peace

When I joined IDRC, Flora MacDonald, a former Cabinet Minister with two Progressive Conservative governments in Canada, was the Chair of IDRC's Board of Governors. She had been a contender for leadership of the party and Canada's first female foreign minister. She was also a celebrated humanitarian, winning many awards, including the Pearson Medal of Peace shortly after she left IDRC.

Flora was a "Red Tory," with views I could respect even if they differed from my own. Communitarian social perspectives, a degree of fiscal discipline and respect for social and political order—the values of my father—are not so foreign to me.

Crossing a footbridge near Pokhara, Nepal.

A few months before Flora MacDonald's term at IDRC ended she invited me to her office on the top floor of the IDRC Headquarters. She wanted me to describe for her my experiences with a project in Nagaland, a remote and conflict-ridden state in northeastern India. It needed board oversight, in part because a staff member tasked with managing research components had been fired for complaining publicly about the political and military situation in Nagaland. The political views of IDRC staff, expressed in India without due constraint, didn't go down well with Indian government officials or IDRC management, and almost derailed the project.

The Naga, a famously ferocious tribal people, have origins shrouded in mystery. They are comprised sixty-six distinct ethnic groups, each with a traditional dress, dialect and cultural traditions more closely aligned to the mountainous regions of Southeast Asia and the Philippines than India. They came reluctantly under British rule in the nineteenth century and have been fighting an independence struggle with India ever since the British left. In addition to their cultural distinctiveness and claims to national autonomy, most Naga are Baptists, converted in the mid-1800s to Christianity by American missionaries.

I had been assigned to take over support to the research, which at the time focused on generating alternatives to shifting cultivation on the forested hillsides of the state. The Indian government wanted to convert a complex, community-based agroforestry system into a sedentary practice based on the private ownership of land, as in mainstream India. The Naga State Government had a different reason to partner with IDRC—they wanted research on the merits of the current communal system and ways to improve it gently. My experience in Mexico with cover crops, living fences and the use of agricultural biodiversity in hillside agriculture made me a good fit, as did experiences with community engagement and collective land tenure.

I told Flora that on my first trip to Nagaland I spoke with an elder we met along the roadside near Mokokchung. He was holding a *dao*, a traditional Naga sword. It is a practical farming implement much like a machete but also part of a history of men being ready to defend from attack by other tribes as the women worked in the field. Villages are located on hilltops, for a similar defensive reason.

I learned that he was a member of the Aö tribe and part of the all-male village council. The council, made up of male elders, determines where community members will be allowed to clear land for

Naga man near Mokokchung, India.

cultivation. This collective governance ensures that village farming is concentrated in one area at a time. Paths can be cut through the surrounding forest, fires controlled, crops protected and fallow periods respected long enough for the land to fully recover. Defence from raiding villages was no longer necessary but the massive presence of the Indian Army in Nagaland created its own vulnerabilities.

Flora, a socially conservative feminist, remarked on the gender and age dynamics of this practice. She also seemed to acknowledge, through her own reluctance to judge, that respect for other cultures meant bracketing our own cultural definitions of equality: the wisdom of the elders should not be discarded out of hand even if it is tainted with elements of patriarchy and gerontocracy. I brought this anthropological perspective into later work on community-based natural resource management, a framework that is sometimes caught between wanting to treat all social imbalances with suspicion while at the same time holding up the positive role of local authority structures.

I was fascinated by Naga history and society and deeply grateful for the opportunity to travel frequently to the region. It was a unique experience because in the late 1990s Nagaland was off limits to both Indian and foreign nationals. A bitter and violent struggle with the central government had been going on steadily since 1960 when Nagaland became a state within the Union of India. The isolation of the people in remote forest villages was almost complete. One elderly farmer I interviewed told me as we parted, "Since the Japan War, you are the first White man I've seen."

I later visited a war cemetery in Kohima, the state capital. The town had been the site of a bloody battle between the Japanese and their Indian allies invading from Burma. British India soldiers, made up primarily of members of the Naga Angami tribe, suffered terrible losses. British and Canadian soldiers also died in the 1944 conflict, which successfully stopped the Japanese from advancing into India. The sacrifice added to the sense of betrayal during the partition of British India after the war, redirected against the Indian Government when Naga autonomy was denied.

On my last trip to Nagaland I was driving the project Jeep between Tuensang and Phek near the border with Burma. The day before I had

Naga shawl and a *dao*, a traditional Naga sword and farm implement.

attended Baptist church services and been gifted a warrior's blade and numerous Naga shawls, the most prominent of Naga crafts, by village heads along the way. These were packed into my hard sided suitcase on top of the Jeep.

The Naga project lead was taking a rest in the passenger seat. He had a sly sense of humour. Knowing I was a vegetarian, he was fond of reminding me that "Nagas will eat anything that moves." I understood his double entendre, referring to both the Naga's history of head hunting and the large white grubs, frogs, dog meat and monkey meat for sale in the market.

Two IDRC colleagues were in the back seat while I drove. I came bumping around a bend in the narrow, dirt road through the thick forest and suddenly encountered a group of twenty or so men standing facing us with machine guns in their hands. I stopped, disengaged the clutch and put the vehicle in park.

The scene made my heart race. Trees created strong contrasts of light and dark on the figures ready for action. A man approached, dressed in green with a dark blue Che Guevara-style beret on his head. It was adorned with the red star of Mao Zedong's China. The men around him shifted to fill the space from edge to edge.

A conversation among the Naga followed and after fifteen minutes or so we were waved through to continue our journey. What I learned from my colleague was that he had forewarned the rebel leadership of our planned travel route and received approval for safe passage. We were not Indian nationals. The project was a Naga project, rooted in traditional Naga farming practices countering the Indian government's narrative that the Naga are indiscriminately and irresponsibly cutting down the forests. We were allowed to pass unharmed.

The tragedy of the commons

I never met with Flora again, and after a few years no longer had a role in Nagaland. Nevertheless, the experience helped me understand how broader conflicts over political autonomy and national independence are connected to local governance, culture and sustainable livelihoods. Peace is not justice if these connections are not examined and addressed.

In 1998 I had the opportunity to pursue this theme at the World Bank. My former boss at CIMMYT, Derek Byerlee, was working at

"The Bank," an association that led to various introductions and, eventually, to an invitation to co-organize a conference on the role of communities in sustainably managing forests, pastures and fisheries. The relationships offered me an opportunity to reach into big policy institutions with novel ideas from community experiences.

The conference, in Washington, D.C., brought together some two hundred policymakers and researchers from about fifty countries for four days of discussions. As with events I had organized in rural Mexico, Bangladesh and Benin, I encouraged my co-hosts at The Bank to start deliberations with an activity outside of the conference hall. We planned a day visiting Chesapeake Bay. The nearby communities were facing serious environmental problems (pollution and over-exploitation of fisheries) and related social and economic conflicts in one of the largest and most storied estuaries in the United States. I wanted visitors from the Global South to know that the challenges, and opportunities presented by local institutions, were ubiquitous.

The weather didn't cooperate. It was damp and cold and most participants were dressed in suits and fine shoes. Many remained huddled in the buses rather than venturing out to talk and explore with the locals. I was better dressed for the occasion and made the most of it by meeting with the watermen and waterwomen of Chesapeake Bay waiting for us in their oilskins and rubber boots. Their efforts to protect local traditions of resource management and address external sources of pollution affecting the fisheries and their livelihoods were not unlike pressures faced by rural people elsewhere.

The conference turned out to be consequential in other ways. The book I edited from one of the sessions, *Cultivating Peace: Conflict and collaboration in natural resource management,* presented a timely alternative perspective on the so-called "tragedy of the commons," the theory that if many people have unrestricted access to a resource, they will quickly and inevitably exhaust it, making everyone lose. In this view of the rational economic man, where everyone pursues their own individual interests ruthlessly, fishing the open coastal waters of a rich habitat will continue unchecked until the last fish is removed because every fisher naturally feels, tragically, that "If I don't take it, someone else will."

The Bank and most other development agencies at the time had already acknowledged the limitations of direct government

Conference participants, Washington, D.C. 1998. Photo by the World Bank.

management of common-pool resources such as fisheries, pastures and forests, the so-called "command and control" solution. It creates conflict in settings where state authority is contested and fails where government institutions are too weak to be effective enforcers or too costly to be financially sustainable.

Instead, The Bank was investing in a "market-based" solution by championing policies that establish individual, exchangeable property rights in a resource—licensing and quota systems, private sector ownership and distribution of water rights, privatization of forests. Privatization was the cornerstone of much international development policy during this period, before the failings of neo-liberal policies were widely understood. However, markets too depend on state authority and, importantly, create their own set of individual winners and losers by running roughshod over collective and traditional systems of resource management.

Conflict between the state and communities over private control and decision making can undermine sustainable use, displace legitimate resource users and create deep and long-lasting resentment. Violence is a too-common result, illustrated in *Cultivating Peace* with stories from the Nuba Mountains of Sudan, the homeland of the Chortís of Honduras and the Nusa Tenggara uplands of Indonesia.

Overall, the arguments we developed were that collectivities have a history of successful natural resource management. Individual members of these collectivities also have a vested interest in avoiding over-exploitation because they depend upon sustainable use for their livelihoods. This suggested a third solution, neither market driven, nor government controlled, but rather based on community institutions and group-based decision-making.

The book was popular, immediately selling several thousand copies in English, French and Spanish and later being downloaded countless times from the IDRC website. It connected readers around the world to a theme that was bursting onto the international scene at the time and that needed a variety of credible voices.

I did my best to create space for these voices, commissioning case studies from Africa, Asia and Latin America along with concept papers on the implications of community-base management for public policy, peace building, culture and research methodologies. For example, a chapter focused on the direct and often unintended negative impacts of international aid on peace and conflict outcomes.

Creating the book was consequential for me personally in another way. I had invited Jacques to co-author a chapter on the cultural assumptions of community-based management. While it was clear to me that past solutions to the tragedy of the commons were failing, I also realized that there was a certain smugness in the alternative we were thrusting into the limelight at the World Bank and elsewhere. I wanted to be aware of and challenge hubris on our side too.

Jacques' training in anthropology and critical perspective on the discipline made him more than qualified to outline the issues. Also, he was ready for something tangible. He had just completed a series of books in the field of semiotics, the theory and study of signs and

Along the banks of a Bangladeshi fishing community.

symbols as elements of language. He told me that his father, a Quebec judge of considerable renown, joked with him about the books. "You are smarter than Einstein" he would say. "Only three people in the world understood him. Only two in your case."

Our renewed working relationship resulted not only in an original chapter in the book but also a small project on doing stakeholder analysis. The question of stakeholders—who is affected and who has influence over a given situation—was poorly developed in the case studies in *Cultivating Peace*. Researchers focused on environmental issues often didn't know how to situate the problem in the context of local power dynamics and competing economic interests. A chapter I commissioned from Ricardo Ramirez, a Mexican-Canadian social scientist I came to know well in later years, outlined the concept but more was needed to give researchers the tools to actually do the analysis, in collaboration with the stakeholders themselves.

In the months that followed, Jacques created a research tool for doing stakeholder analysis that non-specialists, including the people involved, could use to examine social obstacles to change and develop strategies to overcome them. It married the requirements of critical thinking with those of pragmatism, becoming the model for a wide range of new social research tools.

By then I had been doing participatory and action-oriented research with farmers for nearly a decade, and worked closely with leading practitioners such as Satheesh in India. The experience had driven home the realization that how research is conducted, and who with, matters as much as what it is focused on. However, I still didn't fully appreciate the potential of the approach for research on other social problems or the strategic value of participatory research tools. Thinking about the challenges of conflict and collaboration over land and water provided that wider canvas, and launched a decades long journey into the heart of participatory action research (PAR) and significant turn in professional life for both Jacques and me.

9/11

When planes struck the twin towers in New York, we were in Costa Rica. Many would argue that this moment, September 11, 2001, and the U.S. response over the following years, changed the face of peace and conflict across the globe. It narrowed the possibility of cooperation across boundaries of all kinds, with endless war, closed immigration doors, big surveillance and culture as the enemy. Only today, with Vladimir Putin's war on the Ukraine, have we reached another such turning point.

Jacques and I were co-facilitating a workshop, one of the first of hundreds we led, together and independently. The week-long event with two dozen researchers from across Latin America was organized by the Conflict and Collaboration program of research I had launched with IDRC funding after the Washington conference, a program managed by the University for Peace.

The small university, based in Costa Rica, was established by the General Assembly of the United Nations under the leadership of the President of Costa Rica. It had been training small cohorts of students in Alternative Dispute Resolution, a legal practice first developed in the United States focused on resolving disputes through negotiation, mediation, arbitration or similar means, as opposed to litigation. Adapting these techniques to the Latin American context had proven to be difficult, however, raising the question of whether or not there was a uniquely Latin American approach to managing conflict over natural resources.

The program sought to answer this question by examining the causes of conflicts in dozens of settings and drawing lessons from efforts to manage them. To support research on water wars in Bolivia, industrial over-fishing around the Galápagos Islands of Ecuador and eviction of the urban poor from the outskirts of big cities, the program offered small grants, training and networking similar in style and scope to the South Asia Using Diversity Award. This was typical of IDRC's "funding, plus" approach to grant making and capacity building at the time.

I asked Jacques to offer the PAR training, a task he dove into with characteristic enthusiasm. The result, informed by our complementary knowledge and skills, was a process that blurred the lines between action, research and capacity building. It did all three at the same time: learn new participatory techniques by applying them to real life problems and using the results to imagine and plan potential follow up actions. Later work together in Honduras consolidated the training approach.

Woman with her child on the outskirts of Tegucigalpa, Honduras.

Stakeholder Analysis CLIP (for conflict, legitimacy, interests and positions) was a featured tool in the Costa Rica workshop, combined with a range of other social analysis tools Jacques had drafted. I contributed knowledge of the topics and the researchers involved and my own experiences with participatory methods and facilitation. It was easy to work together, with a level of trust and friendship that guided us past disagreements.

We designed a session in Costa Rica aimed at creating an analysis of the types of conflicts being addressed through the program, starting from a list of words used colloquially in Spanish to refer to conflict. It elicited seventeen terms, each with a slightly different nuance depending on whether the conflict was more or less violent, more or less polarized, short term or long term, more personal or more public in nature. We were all blown away by the ease and speed with which the group co-created a sophisticated picture of a Latin American world view on conflict.

The tool for supporting the discussion, called *Domain Analysis*, became a staple in workshops and an advanced form of analysis useful in studies I did later with the Katkari in India and tobacco farmers in Bangladesh.

The events of 9/11 came near the end of this discussion, a day before participants were scheduled to depart. A few people, frightened by the enormity of what had happened, left the hotel immediately, hoping they could get a flight home. Others stayed on, playing music and talking late into the night. The common question was, "Why?"

Jacques and I met over food and drink, talking about the horror of what we had watched on the hotel lobby television. The full meaning of what had just happened was beyond anyone's understanding. It was not lost on us, however, that dialogue across boundaries, the core of what we were both trying to do with participatory action research, needed to be part of the global response.

We later wrote in the introduction to our first book on the topic: "The global epoch we have now entered will embrace many forms of wisdom and dialogue, or it will not be. To survive and flourish in a world fraught with uncertainty, we must create synergies among the living knowledge of people from all parts of the world. This includes the more than one billion poor or marginalized people wrongly branded as 'have-nots' and 'know-nothings' with little to contribute to human history."

Our current crises show we have still not made that turn towards cultivating respect, justice and peace for all.

Feng shui

My time at IDRC was rewarding, not least because I was able to support worthwhile research and work with remarkable people, both inside and outside of the organization. It was an environment that acknowledged the complexity of international development, forcing staff to go beyond their disciplinary silos and blind spots. *Agenda 21*, an action plan of the United Nations and key product of the 1992 Earth Summit held in Rio de Janeiro, Brazil, had helped to push the organization towards interdisciplinary approaches and ground funding in leadership by credible organizations in the Global South, including non-scientists and organizations outside of universities.

Founded in 1970 by an Act of the Canadian Parliament, it was a unique organization with a reputation for funding high quality and often novel research by and with developing country institutions and researchers. David Hopper, the first President of IDRC said in his first speech as President, "They (institutions and research workers), not we, are the best judges of what is relevant to their circumstances. If this (approach) is successful, we will have pioneered a new style of international cooperation that can remove the stigma of charity and donor control from the support of research in development."

Much like in a university, staff were encouraged to think independently and to pursue projects that not only fit the corporate programs and southern mandates but also their own perspectives. Unlike in a university, we were also encouraged to think and work like teams. This created a powerful chemistry.

I enjoyed the job immensely. At a time when IDRC was developing new fund raising strategies, others and I drew the Canadian International Development Agency (CIDA) into a joint program in Honduras, integrating research by local institutions into conventional anti-poverty projects following the devastating Hurricane Mitch of 1998. This marriage of research and mainstream development programming was novel at the time.

In addition to funding research, we had opportunities to promote diverse strategies for communicating research results—policy briefs, video productions, audio files, group tours and university curriculum. I sponsored a guide to writing for research purposes and writing for policy advocacy. It was a way to support lead authorship by developing country researchers, many of whom had little training of this nature and struggled to write in English, the globally dominant research and policy language.

Over several cycles of organizational planning, I did a lot of writing for the IDRC teams I was involved with. While not expected of IDRC staff, I also managed to write, edit and publish four books with IDRC partners.

The office was not without its internal struggles, however, something to be expected in any organization with a large proportion of staff holding PhDs and the ambition to go with them. Like others, I jostled for position and influence.

Late in my tenure, when the organization had new leadership and significant change was afoot, I was reassigned from the programs of my choice to a program that at the time held little interest to me. Sitting with a senior manager in my office, I respectfully declined the reassignment. I was offered the position again, and respectfully declined. Then I was offered the position a third time, with the caveat that if I didn't accept it I would be fired.

The exercise of authority has always troubled me, making me a poor fit in a hierarchical institution. Being told what I would do with my professional life set my teeth on edge. In all, I held out for precisely three and a half minutes, sitting face to face with the senior manager for what seemed like an hour before accepting the reassignment.

The new home turned out to be in an interesting program with a great title: "Cities Feeding People." The brainchild of Luc Mougeot, a longtime IDRC specialist with a background in urban geography, the initiative brought the same concern I had for small-scale agriculture to the challenges and opportunities of producing food in and on the outskirts of cities.

To ground myself in the new topic, I made one of my only IDRC trips to Africa, visiting an urban agriculture project in Kibera, Africa's largest urban slum on the outskirts of Nairobi. While I thought I knew a thing or two about agriculture, the experience opened my eyes to a new world where food and urban poverty collide.

In this neglected and grim community, people produced food, typically leafy greens and plants such as beans and tomatoes, in tiny garden plots on unused municipal land. It was important to their nutrition and to their livelihoods. I walked along narrow pathways to observe the plots and to see the source of the irrigation water higher up the slope.

The water came from a metre wide cement sewage pipe that had been perforated with a hammer. The sewage seeped out onto the ground and began its journey down the slope through small channels to irrigate the garden plots. While I was familiar with the use of animal manure in agriculture and, as a child, had seen German farmers spread human feces on their fields from "honey pots," the rawness of the Kibera practice took me by surprise. "The plants looked healthy, but are they safe to eat?" I asked myself.

When I returned to Ottawa and reported to Luc on the situation his response surprised me too. "Yes," he said, "you've asked the right question. The best way to find out is to study the sewage. Does it come from residential neighbourhoods or from industrial sources? This makes all the difference to whether or not the food plants are likely to end up with dangerous chemicals in them."

To me, this line of inquiry represented the best of IDRC's way of working. Luc's commitment to intellectual risk-taking recognized that producing food and making use of the available water and nutrients in the sewage water was a matter of survival in Kibera. His perspective was also free from moral judgements regarding the use of human waste and focused only on how to support what people were already doing by making it safer. I decided to stick it out in his team, withdrawing applications for jobs in other parts of the organization.

When Luc moved on and his leadership position came up, I applied but was passed over. Part of the reason was my participatory approach to grant making. New leadership was moving the organization towards fewer and larger grants, and a more directive approach to defining research topics rather than being responsive to ideas coming from researchers in the Global South. Grant competitions with precise expected outcomes, rather than program areas open to unsolicited proposals, was the new *modus operandi.* This reflected in part the high transaction costs of managing many small and novel projects, including the expectation of considerable travel by IDRC staff.

The shift was also due to pressures to bring IDRC programming more firmly under the machinery of Canada's official foreign policy (a trend that intensified once Stephen Harper came to power as Canada's twenty-second prime minister). I thought this was a mistake, and didn't hesitate to say so. Large projects, I argued, would discourage novel but riskier initiatives and shower attention on a small number of well-established research institutions with a capacity to write good proposals. IDRC's bottom-up approach to scouting research talent grounded in pressing local and regional realities, and commitment to gradually building institutional capacity, would be left behind. This could turn researchers of the Global South into consultants for agenda's set in the Global North.

It is for IDRC staff that stayed through the years of Stephen Harper's conservative government and beyond to say whether or not I was right about approaches to grant making. Some, I understand, believe that without bowing to a more assertive federal government the IDRC would have been disbanded and folded into CIDA, the primary aid arm of the Canadian government.

The direction of the culture change towards pre-defined, IDRC-led programming was already clear, however, in 2005. My ambition for a greater leadership role blocked and major institutional change in the air, I began to search in earnest for an exit.

My wife, Debra, found one in Feng Shui, a Chinese system to promote good energy or "chi" in one's environment. "First," she said, "you need to declutter so new things can find a place in your office." Piles of unread and dusty papers sitting for years on shelves and knick-knacks from around the world tucked away in drawers needed to go.

"Second, you need to change the orientation of your desk and chair so that you are facing the door rather than staring out the window." I did a tour of the three main floors of IDRC and found that almost everyone had their backs to me as I walked by their open office door. "I need to concentrate," was the common explanation for the desk orientation. "Bad chi," said Debra, "and a clear message to the world that others are not welcome. It says you are afraid to face whatever might come your way."

A few weeks after decluttering and changing the orientation of my office space, a senior manager came through the door with another offer I couldn't refuse, although this time it took no time at all to accept. The golden handshake was delivered with grace and generosity. "IDRC staff should be encouraged to contribute to university life in Canada," he said. "You have that potential," he went on. "We want you to stay but if you are determined to go we can help you make the transition."

A month later my wife and I were doing Feng Sui adjustments to my office at Carleton University. IDRC had authorized a major supplement to Jacques' grant on social methods for participatory action research. The grant now paid my full-time salary for two years. This was later extended for two more years by Canadian Partnerships at IDRC, and then again, with a part-time salary, for another two years through a project with IDRC's program of Research for International Tobacco Control.

I never made the transition to a tenure-track university position, remaining an Adjunct Research Professor (an unpaid position) to this day. The track I took was better suited to my desire for direct and collaborative work with people on issues important to me. Through the funded research position at the university I had all the freedoms and credibility of an academic life without any of the administrative or teaching requirements.

Unfortunately, I never learned to lecture a class of students with authority and, except for teaching a few courses here and there, I missed out on the joys of guiding university students as I had been guided. Nevertheless, I hit my stride as an anthropologist, combining detailed and rigorous research with a level of activism impossible to achieve at IDRC or in a university.

Art remained a background hobby, sustained only by the ubiquitous camera in my travel pack and occasional paintings at our Temagami cottage. Image-making no longer occupied a prominent place in my day to day experience. After leaving IDRC, reconciling the inner and outer life took a new path, one which had a spiritual turn grounded in South Asia and in my own backyard.

10

Fighting Eviction

My return to anthropology after ten years at the International Development Research Centre (IDRC) began at a difficult moment in Jacques and Michelle's life. Signs of trouble started in Goa, an Indian state on the southwestern coast best known for its beaches, nightlife and world heritage architecture. In mid-April, 2005, only a few weeks after I had joined Carleton University, we were to meet up in Mumbai and then jointly facilitate a training session I had arranged with partners from various parts of India, Bangladesh and Nepal.

Jacques and Michelle were in Goa leading a different training session when Michelle became sick, vomiting whenever she tried to eat. She had a septicaemic infection due to a ruptured appendix. "My IQ dropped to around fifty even as I tried to help with the training for a couple of days," she joked with me recently. On the plane from Goa to Mumbai she developed an embolism that remained undiagnosed until a later return to Canada. I met them at the airport in Mumbai, where she was whipped into life-saving surgery and remained in intensive care for two weeks before she was well enough to fly home. Jacques stayed with her in hospital and asked me to run the workshop. I did, even though at that point I had never been a lead trainer.

It was a baptism by fire. With Michelle's life hanging in the balance and dozens of workshop participants praying for her daily, I felt strangely confident and resolved to do my best. It turned out to

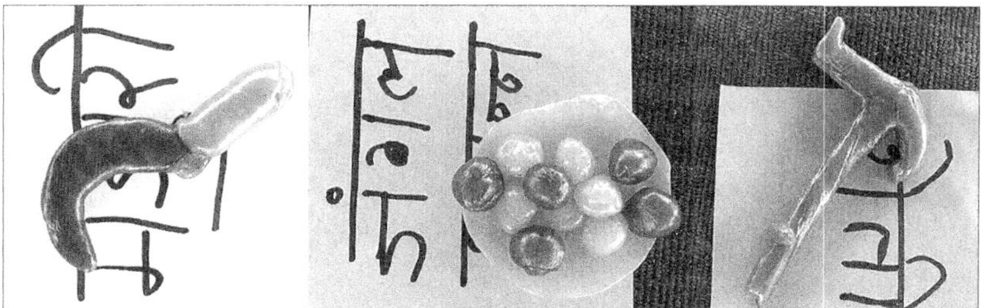

Wax figurines created to discuss livelihood options.

be not only the first but also the most consequential training event I ever facilitated.

The workshop was also my first exposure to the humour and wisdom of Mullah Nasruddin, a philosopher, Sufi and wise man born into the high medieval Turko-Persian Sunni Muslim empire in 1208. He is much loved today by people of all religions in India for his funny stories and anecdotes in which he is variously portrayed as witty, wise and often the butt of his own jokes. Ardhendu, the oldest and wisest of the participants in the workshop, made effective use of Nasruddin stories by leaping to his feet to tell one whenever a break was needed or he could see an opportunity to reinforce the pedagogical lesson I was trying to convey.

After teaching a technique exploring levels of trust among stakeholders—who is trusted by others and who shows trust towards others—Ardhendu asked everyone, "Do you know about Mullah Nasruddin's donkey?" "Yes!" came the reply, as the Mullah famously rode a donkey wherever he went. So he told the story known as *Whom do you believe?*

> *A neighbour came to the gate of Mulla Nasruddin's yard. The Mulla went to meet him outside.*
>
> *"Would you mind, Mulla," the neighbour asked, "can you lend me your donkey today? I have some goods to transport to the next town."*
>
> *The Mulla didn't feel inclined to lend out the animal to that particular man, however. So, not to seem rude, he answered:*
>
> *"I'm sorry, but I've already lent him to somebody else."*
>
> *All of a sudden the donkey could be heard braying loudly behind the wall of the yard.*
>
> *"But Mulla," the neighbour exclaimed. "I can hear it behind that wall!"*
>
> *"Whom do you believe," the Mulla replied indignantly, "the donkey or your Mulla?"*

Ardhendu had been invited to the workshop by Rajeev, a man I had come to trust completely and respect deeply. We had worked together on the Using Diversity program initially funded by IDRC. He picked up coordination of the program and kept it going when

Carrying bricks to the brick kiln, Maharashtra, India.

IDRC funding ended, drawing on his contacts with European donors. Over the years, he gave of his time and caring attention to some eighty grassroots organizations documenting unique traditional farming practices and local uses of biodiversity. More than anyone I have ever met, Rajeev embodies the quiet and loving resolve needed to bring about social change in the most difficult of situations.

During breaks in the workshop, we challenged each other at ping pong. Thin and wiry, Rajeev was a bicyclist as a youth before the highways outside of Mumbai became too dangerous to cycle. He still carries himself with the grace of a long distance athlete. As the ball bounced back and forth between us, he told me the story of how the Katkari were the brick makers of Maharashtra.

Katkari men and women carry loads of up to fifty kilos on their heads, stacking bricks to be fired or loading them onto trucks for transport. They have literally formed with their own hands the majority of the bricks making up Mumbai's towering structures, modest middle-class homes, and vast slum communities. Later, I witnessed the brick-making effort directly, along with other miraculous acts of strength by this remarkable people living on the edge of survival.

"How is this possible?" I thought as I watched women carry heavy loads of bricks on their heads all day long and men threshing the harvest of others.

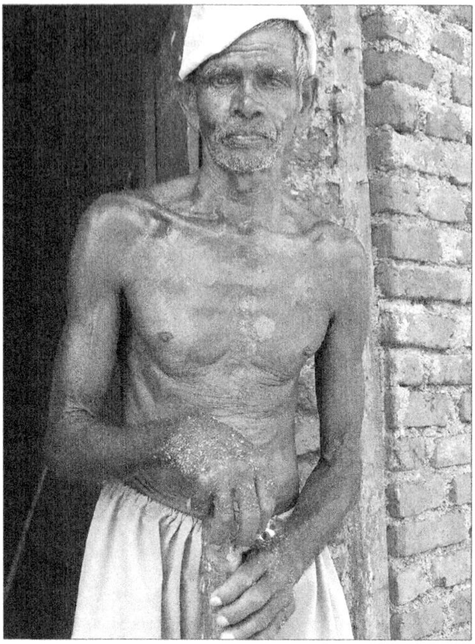

Shripat Waghmare, a Katkari man, resting after threshing rice for a landowner.

"What joy in bodily struggle!" I thought as I watched a Katkari youth on home-made stilts walk up and down a rough and inclined track in the village, barefooted, sweating and laughing. Other youth, unemployed and landless, urged him on as he performed the difficult feat as aptly as any star with the Cirque du Soleil.

The Katkari attribute their strength and long life, qualities well-known among the farming castes of Maharashtra that hire them, to the consumption of rodents. They are the only tribal group in India that eats the Little Indian Field Mouse (*Mus booduga*), the Servant Mouse (*Mus famulus*), the Black Rat (*Rattus rattus*), the Brown Rat (*Rattus norvegicus*) and the Greater or Indian Bandicoot (*Bandictoa indica*). Farmers contract them to clear rodent infestations in their fields and fill the burrows with mud to close channels that syphon water from the rice paddy fields.

The collective hunt starts by burning dried cow dung and hay inside one of the burrow openings, and clubbing the rodents as they rush out of other burrows. As some animals die of smoke inhalation, the Katkari dig to collect the dead rodents along with loose branching clusters of rice that have been stored inside their burrows. The Katkari can collected as much as twelve kilos of rice from a single hunt, collecting food planted by farmers, harvested by rats and repurposed by the Katkari.

Smaller rodents are roasted immediately and eaten in the field while the larger adults are taken home, roasted, cooked in the form of curry and eaten with rice or bread. The rodent's intestines and liver are cooked separately with salt and turmeric and consumed as a tonic for stomach ache.

In October or November, after crops are harvested, the Katkari celebrate the *Undir Navmi*, a Hindu festival dedicated to the rodent. It is not a popular festival in the cornucopia of Hindu deities that include Ganesh, the elephant man, Shiva, Brahma, Vishnu and many others. The food habits and related cultural practices of the Katkari set them apart from all other caste communities in rural Maharashtra to such an extent they have no standing in any village hierarchy. In direct and subtle ways, the distinctiveness of the Katkari collectivity is used by others to exclude the community utterly, leaving them in a lower position than the lowest castes and other tribal groups who have some form of membership in the village system.

When I told an Indian colleague in the New Delhi office of IDRC about the Katkari penchant for rodents she couldn't believe me and even seemed to recoil from me physically as I outlined the details. A feminist herself and committed to justice for India's many exploited Indigenous and low caste populations, eating rodents was beyond the pale and could only be reconciled in her mind by the thought that they had no choice. "No," I said, "they are not starving when they do this. The practice, which is a service to the agricultural community, is a statement of fearlessness." A Katkari saying is,

> *We put our hands in the mouth of the tiger, open the jaws, and count the teeth of the tiger. We are the Katkari.*

The origin of the problem

The Katkari are a former "Criminal Tribe," labelled as such by nineteenth century British lawmakers and sociologists who believed that the offspring of nomadic groups were born to criminality. If your father or mother was a criminal then you were likely to be one as well. The Katkari carry this stigma even today, enduring exploitation and exclusion from many aspects of village life, including basic rights of residence.

Evictions of the Katkari from their own homes and hamlets, and Katkari resistance to the injustice, became the subject of a five year study by Rajeev, his colleague Bansi Ghevde, a legal expert and land rights activist, and myself, published by Cambridge University Press.

In the months and years following these various introductions—to Mulla Nasruddin, to leading training in participatory action research methods and to the Katkari of Maharashtra—I immersed myself in the details of a people that are at once raw, ingenious and strong beyond belief. Writing a book about their situation, with Rajeev and Bansi, became an obsession. Rajeev's remarkable sensitivity to the voices of the marginalized and Bansi's powerful resolve to achieve justice, combined magically with my knowledge of action-oriented research tools to foster a rich dialogue between ourselves and the Katkari and among the Katkari themselves.

We began our work with a visit to the hamlet where Bansi had first been confronted with the problem. It was a cluster of twelve or so mud houses along the side of a country road in Karjat some thirty kilometres from Mumbai, parched by the hot sun but close to a source of surface water. Barbed wire had been strung on cement posts around the hamlet, hemming in every house with an irregular perimeter fence and leaving only a single small gate for people to enter and leave. A group of five women had approached Bansi when he stopped in the hamlet to drop off a caste certificate he had processed on behalf of a family, a service he had been providing in the region for some time.

A religious trust from Mumbai, dedicated to one of India's many yogis, had recently purchased several properties, including the land of the hamlet. They planned to establish an ashram where the yogi could teach middle- and upper-class Hindus on retreat from Mumbai. The area was in the lightly forested foothills of the Western Ghats, and consequently cooler than the coastal city.

We sat with the administrators of the trust and asked them why they had erected the barbed wire fence and what their plans were for the Katkari hamlet. "They have to go," they said, "because the hamlet is too close to where the ashram dormitories will be built."

Rising before dawn to meditate within close proximity of a hamlet of rat eaters, it seemed, was not conducive to elevating the mind.

We were granted an audience with the yogi, who acknowledged that it was unfortunate the Katkari would have to leave. He assured us that a new site would be gifted to them some seven kilometres away. The women who had first approached Bansi about the situation had told us that the new site was on a hill, with no access to water nearby. They also said that they could not bear leaving the place where their parents had been buried, literally under the mud waddled floor of each of their tiny houses, as was their practice. We knew the land swap would not be suitable or acceptable to the women and their families.

The administrators became angry with us when we persisted in our questions, and particularly with me, asking aggressively for proof that I had permission from the Government of India to be doing what I was doing. We left with the situation unresolved but clearer about the need to strategize with the Katkari on ways and means for them to find powerful allies of their own.

What had started as an isolated case of eviction by the ashram became a flood less than a year after this first encounter. Land prices on the outskirts of Mumbai and along highways towards the mountains

Bansi discusses land rights with Katkari youth. Photo by Rajeev Khedkar.

Land for sale near Pali, India.

of the Western Ghats began to rise sharply in response to a spike in demand for "country estates" and industrial lots. Katkari hamlets on high rocky outcrops with cooler air temperature and views of the land below became prime targets for weekend retreat homes. Roadside hamlets were displaced and the land consolidated into blocks for new industries.

A wave of panic went through connected Katkari communities, giving us a sense of urgency as we came to understand the scope of the problem and stakes for all parties concerned. Bansi criss-crossed the territory by motor bike, satchels filled with paperwork documenting the land tenure of 212 Katkari hamlets, two thirds of which had no title of their own. We mapped their locations using a GPS and calculated that approximately 25,000 people were vulnerable to eviction.

On the road to Pali, a small city known for its shrine to Khandoba, a reincarnation of Shiva, I stopped for tea at an intersection. Before me was a huge billboard advertising land for sale and a man and his bicycle laden with possessions. I took a photograph (above), one which more than any image from my life as an artist, shows the cross currents of art and politics. It became the featured image on the cover of our book, and one which I treasure for the outrage it still produces in me.

Indian law on land rights, which Bansi knew in detail, was clearly on the side of the Katkari. For several generations they had continuously occupied hamlets on the outskirts of agricultural villages, serving the community as labourers. In the eyes of government officials and many villagers, however, they were not legitimate claimants to land. They were considered vagabonds moving about in search of employment and without a history of participation in the formal institutions of village life and governance.

I could understand how that perspective might seem true. When I visited Katkari hamlets in the hot winter season they were virtually empty of all but the elderly and infirm. Able-bodied men and women, and their children, typically spent six months of the year working at brick kilns, sand-dredging and stone breaking operations associated with the construction industry. Many of these were dozens of kilometres away, so they lived at the work site.

Contractors visited their hamlets prior to festivals offering cash advances, putting in place a cycle of debt bondage. Small weekly payments would be added to the advance to cover subsistence needs during the time they worked for the contractor, deducted at the end of the season from the total wages earned. Remaining debt was carried forward to subsequent years, creating obligations borne by the entire family and from one generation to the next. This was the face of modern slavery in rural India.

We stopped one day in a small Katkari hamlet in Sudhaghad *Taluka* (county) near the highway to Pune. Just how vulnerable the Katkari were became evident to me when we talked with an older man I saw sitting in front of a very small, dilapidated mud house in the hamlet. The walls were made from woven sticks of karvi (*Strobilanthes callosa*), a shrub that comes alive only during the monsoon and produces a rare flower that blooms only once every eight years. He stood as we approached him, hanging on to the beam of the thatch room. That is when I realized one of his legs was badly out of alignment and that a set of crutches leaned against the wall.

He told us that he had been hit by a motorcycle while working at a brick kiln and then left at a hospital with no money and no identity papers. The brick kiln operator, who at the beginning of the season routinely collected from his workers caste certificates or other proofs of identity they might have, refused to return these to him. The contractor probably feared charges against the motorcycle driver, or a claim of workers compensation.

Without papers, the injured man had no means to access the medical treatment he had a right to receive. He also had no scope to press charges. Instead, he returned to his village with a leg that never set properly, leaving him crippled and destitute.

I was outraged and heart broken by the story. So were Rajeev and Bansi, although we could not imagine what to do about it other than offer him some money to buy food. Bansi later helped him acquire identify papers showing he existed but later lost track of him.

Stories of equal or even greater tragedy came to Bansi's attention on a regular basis as we documented the Katkari situation. Incidents at brick kilns of beatings, rape, sexual abuse and non-payment of wages were common. When they protested, Bansi told me, kiln masters filed charges of theft against them at the police station, knowing that the reputation of this "criminal caste" would make it difficult or impossible for them to gain police support. Bansi recorded and reported to the police twelve deaths due to beatings at brick kilns over a period of five years. A colleague of Bansi's, a human rights activist, documented several cases where Katkari labourers had been burned alive in a brick kiln furnace after refusing to comply with the master's expectations.

The suffering of the Katkari was visible at every brick kiln and in every hamlet I visited. Children as young as five made bricks while their younger siblings played at doing so with tiny cups of water and mud. The wattle-and-daub walls of the *kuchha* (temporary) houses in the hamlets were rarely in good condition and offered little protection from rain or cold. Dampness and moisture in the home would last for two or three months during the monsoon, making the living space miserable and inhospitable. Barely ten percent of the Katkari hamlets we surveyed had access to electricity, even when neighbouring villages did.

We also found that the majority did not have caste certificates, tribal identity certificates or even ration cards that would give them access to government supports such as fair price shops and basic medical services. Houses were in such poor repair that even those with papers often lost them to weather and neglect. Indian authorities, other villagers and owners of the land the hamlets had occupied for decades felt vindicated in their conclusion that the Katkari were not legitimate members of the community and therefore deserved no protection from eviction.

Organizing and empowering practices

The threat of eviction from house and home was visceral for the Katkari we met, as it would be for any household or community. To start a conversation about housing rights, we drew on a genuine respect for the knowledge and ingenuity of the community, and the work of Rajeev and Bansi on a range of Katkari livelihood and land rights challenges. The relationship created conditions of trust, prompting community members to ask Bansi what they could do in response to eviction.

Bansi responded by pulling together copies of utility bills, caste certificates, village maps and other documents attesting to Katkari presence on the land over time. We knew that some paper trail would be needed to appeal to authorities for assistance. Deeper conversations with groups of men and women followed, using a simple but powerful research tool: *Problem tree.*

It employs a tree metaphor to reconstruct the causes and effects of a core problem. The trunk stands for a problem statement, with roots and branches. Direct causes of the core problem are identified, followed by discussion of the causes of causes, going down deeper to finer and finer roots. A similar mode of questioning maps out the effects, first noting the direct effects connected to the trunk and proceeding to finer and finer branches.

Exploration of the core problem began with a plain statement of the facts: The hamlet did not have legal title to the land. This became the trunk. In meetings with small groups of men and women, I would offer a few pieces of coloured beeswax and invite people to sculpt something to represent what they wanted to talk about. They did this easily and creatively, making beautiful objects that enriched the conversation and ensured that everyone, literate or not, could see and understand the whole picture of the problem we were discussing: a wax hut surrounded by wax barbed wire; team flags pointing

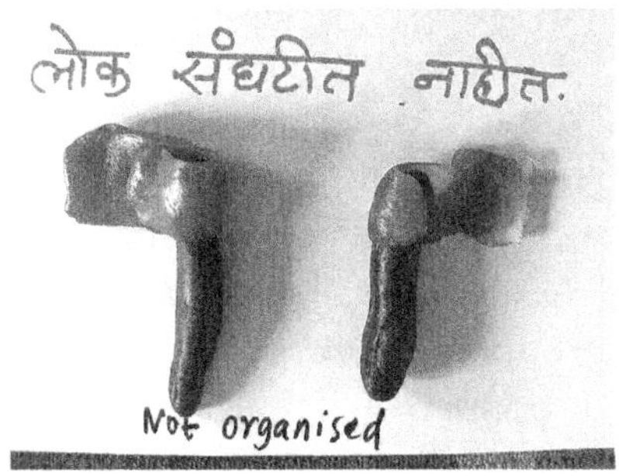

Wax figures created to discuss root causes and effects of the land tenure problem.

in opposite directions signalling a lack of organization in Katkari communities; a kerosene lamp instead of electricity.

On one occasion, the participants explained to us that they depended utterly on local landholders for their livelihood, whether it be access to fragments of farmland or employment as day workers. Debts or anticipated favours obliged them to plant their patron's field when the first rains came rather than planting their own fields. Late planting in turn undermined their own crops and deepened their own poverty, creating a vicious circle.

I had no wax with me that day so I asked them to collect materials from outside to create a picture of the problem. Within a few minutes they built a tableau on the ground from sticks, leaves and small stones showing a large field planted with many green plants and a number of small fields empty and bare. This was their situation, visualized simply and elegantly.

The integration of visual cues into formal discussions with people is a central feature of participatory methods. As an artist, I took to this approach easily and experimented frequently with different materials and different moments in the research process. The practice became important in the ongoing development of our tools and facilitation style, integrated into our teaching and writing.

With the Katkari, we moved from discussions of direct causes of the core problem to an exploration of the chains of causes and then the upward branching effects of not having title to the hamlet. A picture emerged of isolation from local access to health and other services, utter lack of privacy, restrictions on home gardens, dependency and other concrete consequences important to the people involved in the discussions.

In another community, a rising branch of effects, or "children" of the core problem, started with a recent decision by a landholder to block construction of a government sponsored school in the hamlet. His decision led to identification by the local government of a different location for a school a number of kilometres away, where it would also serve children of the agricultural households the Katkari sometimes worked for.

At school, we learned, Katkari children, were ridiculed as sons and daughters of criminals and rodent eaters. As a result, the children did not attend regularly and soon dropped out. The man telling this story went on to say that children not in school are usually taken to work on the brick kilns, where at least they can be cared for on a daily basis. People lamented this situation, which they felt inevitably brought their children into bonded labour at an early age.

The Katkari's own analysis brought them to the conclusion that not having legal title to the hamlet site created multiple chain effects. The picture of the whole, an elder said to us, combined the various situations they face into a single, clear story.

Rajeev and Bansi undertook dozens of problem tree assessments with people in hamlets throughout the region, building consensus on the relevance of legal title even in hamlets that were not yet feeling the bite of eviction. In many sessions, the various causes and effects they identified were later converted into statements of means they could use to secure title and ends that could be achieved if they owned the land. This bridge from problem analysis to planning solutions is part of the methodology, intended to chart a pathway to a better future.

On one occasion, a participant inspired by the positive image of the village that was emerging from discussion shouted, "We could build a stage!" The Katkari have a unique style of music and are very fond of celebrations of all kinds. I was familiar with the music, a storytelling

Dwarkanath Lakhma Ghogharkar (left) and another Katkari musician playing the pitali.

art form not unlike a rap song. The musicians use a wide brass plate and a waxed *karvi* stick to create a wobbling, high pitched droning sound as accompaniment.

The idea of a village stage galvanized others into discussing the means to overcome indifference in their community and achieve the dream, a dream that included artistic expression and an expression of social cohesion.

As a symbol of their resolve, community elders later raised and ceremoniously anointed a *ves* (stone pillar) marking the entrance to their hamlet. They hoped that the gesture would show their resolve to stay while at the same time assuring landholders that their demands would not go beyond that point. "We are here, but no further. So don't fear us," was the message. I photographed the gathering, the anointed stone and some of the wax objects created along the way. Witnessing the excitement of the Katkari and the shift in their thinking from problems to artistic dreams deepened my own resolve to do all I could to make a difference in their struggle.

Katkari men erecting a *ves* (stone pillar) to mark the entrance to their village, Maharashtra, India.

Research-in-action

Responses to the threat of eviction involved demanding and sometimes tedious work by Rajeev and Bansi. Simple things like collecting proofs of residence took hundreds of hours but also turned a cadre of young Katkari into paralegals. They are now able to offer services in their own communities for things such as birth certificates, death certificates and ration cards needed to access even the most basic of government services. I visited regularly, to discuss new siutations and train the team in use of research tools they could use with the Katkari to both understand and transform constraints.

Work on fighting eviction soon broadened to consider how the Katkari could break the bonds of migratory labour and play a more active role in village life. This went far beyond quick-and-easy consultation focused on a single issue to consider complex interactions between economic, social and psychological factors affecting their lives.

We adapted advanced analytical tools to work with non-literate people by drawing on language, concepts and ways of doing things that are part and parcel of Katkari culture. The insights, and action plans, were expertly facilitated by Rajeev and Bansi, with patience, humour and a stunning warmth of character. The details of what we did, how, and why, are published in a scholarly book and journal article we wrote together, along with an outline of the many practical outcomes of the research.

Rajeev facilitating a meeting with Katkari to discuss their views on livelihood constraints.

Bansi provided the key ingredient that helped us turn the corner on what at times seemed like an intractable problem with no end in sight. Evictions touched him close to home when a business owner in Mumbai purchased land from an agent to build a country house retreat, not knowing that part of the plot belonged to Bansi's father-in-law. A member of the Thakur tribal community, Bansi's father had been allocated the land years before under a government program, a process that had not produced a surveyed title document. This made it vulnerable to competing claims and sale.

Bansi's father-in-law was beaten when he demanded a fence be removed from his land, prompting Bansi to file with the police a charge of physical assault. He referenced in the paper work a powerful but little used piece of federal legislation called the Prevention of Atrocities Act, enacted by the Parliament of India in 1989. The Act reinforced articles of the Constitution of India protecting members of listed tribes such as the Katkari and the Thakur from extreme forms of humiliation, exploitation and dispossession rooted in the historical practice of untouchability and caste hierarchy.

The Act characterizes the use of force, intimidation, public humiliation and other acts aimed at asserting caste-based dominance as "hate crimes or bias crimes." While few cases prosecuted under the act over the years included crimes related to land, Bansi convinced the deputy superintendent of police to acknowledge these roots of the case—his father-in-law had been beaten in an attempt to dispossess him of his land. The police accepted the reference to the Prevention of Atrocities Act and passed it up the line for case review.

In time, the charge was seen by a judge and the dispute settled without a ruling. The land had been returned, said the judge. Still, the case validated a powerful legal pathway to fight eviction. By referencing the Prevention of Atrocities Act in filings with the police, Bansi had established a connection between eviction and a specific human rights crime with very severe criminal penalties.

This court case outcome received considerable attention from the regional press, and sent a chill through the regional real-estate industry. Routine encroachment on hamlets and intimidation of Katkari and other vulnerable Indigenous groups by realtors stopped. Just the threat of conviction under the Act became enough to give the Katkari time to take other actions to secure formal titles.

Over time, Katkari hamlets in the areas we worked became moderately more secure than when enclosures and evictions went unnoticed and unchallenged. This was relief and respite to hundreds of hamlets and thousands of very vulnerable and highly marginalized families who had been facing a tidal wave of misery unleashed by a relentless and well-resourced real-estate industry. Katkari in dozens of hamlets, at least forty-five at the time our book was published in 2013, had successfully registered petitions for inclusion into the land base of rural villages. Many individual house plots had also been registered, giving families an inalienable base, a home from which to pursue a livelihood and to hope for a better future.

Rajeev also noted a tangible shift in the level of confidence, self-esteem and initiative of Katkari communities where he has now worked for over thirty years. Katkari resolve to stay in their hamlets is much stronger than it was at the outset. Many, including several women's groups, are making demands for rights to other lands and services that are due to them, a courageous step for a people isolated in silence and hopelessness only a few years earlier.

Katkari women rest on their way to sell firewood in Pali, Maharashtra, India.

I was deeply grateful to Rajeev, Bansi and others in the small team that brought me into their work with the Katkari and who so diligently applied the research tools I adapted and honed to the questions at hand. Being able to travel frequently to India and immediately delve into intimate meetings and planning activities with various Katkari groups was a privilege few anthropologists anywhere enjoy.

It also produced meaningful changes in the material circumstances of the Katkari, an outcome that still amazes and uplifts me. In the years that followed, whenever I doubted the value of what Jacques and I were trying to do by dedicating our time to the development of participatory approaches to action research, I would think of the Katkari, and find courage.

A rightful place to stay

Other signs of a path beyond the constraints of bondage and landlessness appeared on what turned out to be my last trip to India to work with Rajeev, Bansi and the Katkari. I went from Mumbai to Pali for a meeting of the Katkari Forum for Justice, a regional association of eighty-two hamlets formed in 1982. The organization had waxed and waned over the years, doing its best to address matters such as abandonment of young brides by their husbands, feuds between families and harassment by police.

I arrived at a critical juncture in the organization. A year earlier, members of the forum had proposed to build a permanent meeting place for Katkari in Pali, a commercial as well as a religious centre in the region. Other Indigenous groups had similar arrangements, typically a small building where people could temporarily store goods they brought to sell or bought for themselves, spend a night to rest before walking home or wait while family members were receiving medical treatment.

A place to stay in Pali also meant they could pursue important paperwork such as an old-age pension or birth certificate through the byzantine workings of the Indian bureaucracy. The town hosted the main police station, the bus stand, schools and colleges, various doctor's offices and clinics and the courthouse, all of which might be relevant to individuals and their families at some time in their lives.

Having a rightful place to stay, rest, eat food and regroup would solve a lot of problems: a missed bus home, a rescheduled medical appointment or a meeting of local leaders from several towns. Katkari, with no relatives or friends with property in town, would mill about the town, waiting for this or that and sleeping along the side of the road. Sometimes this prompted aggression by townsfolk: throwing water on a Katkari near a market stall; pushing others out of a shaded resting place.

Some Katkari leaders had been lobbying political candidates and government officers for such a facility, known as a *samaj mandir*, for more than fifteen years, without success. A breakthrough came through the efforts of a member of our team. They did a *Timeline* history of the lobby effort and *Problem tree* assessment showing the ramifications of the problem of no place to stay. This inspired the Forum leadership to think about new ways they could address the problem themselves, without using the promise of their vote to solicit political party support.

Within two months of that assessment, the forum had raised 50,000 Rupees from families in forty hamlets, asking first for tiny contributions from the poorest of the poor so that they too would have rights to use the *samaj mandir*. They made a downpayment on a small parcel of land and took out a loan against the title, allowing them to also begin construction of a modest structure. It was made from bricks, of course, that Katkari had made themselves.

When I arrived in Pali the building had a solid foundation, walls and a tin roof but no windows, doors, gate or other amenities. Still, a first gathering in this shell of a *samaj mandir* was inaugurated with flowers, incense and the ritual breaking of a coconut. The head of the forum, Dwarkanath Lakhma Ghogharkar, an elderly man and Katkari singer who had presided over the long years of the forum's existence, announced his decision to step down. He said, "We have made progress by helping people break from bad customs. We have also built a Katkari *samaj mandir*. It is important that we continue to look outward, beyond what we have accomplished so far. Now is time for the younger generation to lead."

Building on his speech, we facilitated a strategic planning exercise using another simple yet powerful tool called *The Socratic Wheel*. Twenty men sat in a circle, each representing a collection of hamlets from across the *Taluka* (county). I guided the process, with Rajeev translating and improving on my questions. "What things are going well in your communities? Where have you seen improvements over the last few years?

As clear responses emerged, we invited people to think of and provide an object to represent the topic. One offered his white Neru hat to represent the cleanliness in their hamlets they aspired to and had seen improve in recent years. The flowers brought for inaugurating the building became the symbol for the practice of customs related to marriage and other religious ceremonies. Norms for expenditures outlined by the Forum a decade earlier had helped to control elaborate and costly marriages and dowries, practices borrowed from the caste community and different from the bride price system native to Katkari's tribal culture.

Another pushed into the circle the cane he use to support a damaged hip. "Whenever there was a crime in a village," he said, "the police came immediately to our hamlet and rounded up a few young men. It didn't matter if the men had not been anywhere near the crime. They could be easily intimidated into confessing. Now, the police don't beat us with sticks as often as they used to," he concluded. "This is an improvement."

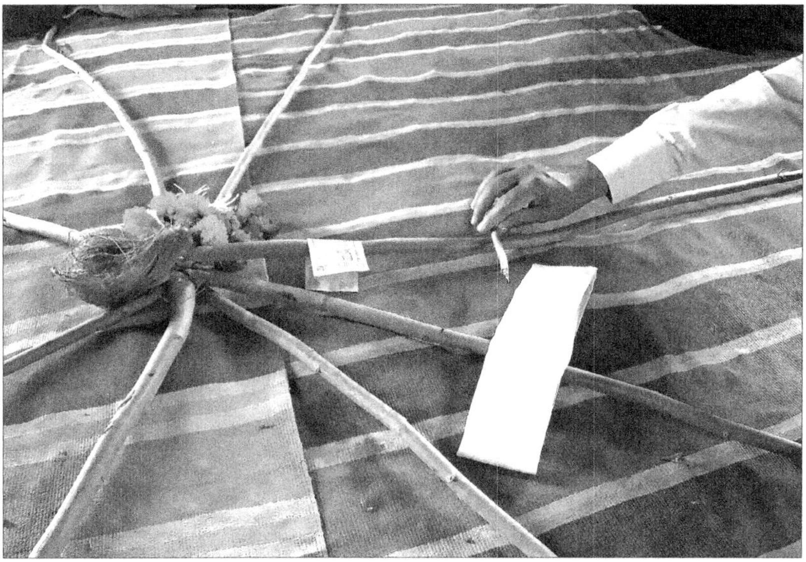

Wheel showing organizational accomplishments and priorities for future action, Pali, Maharashtra, India.

Bricks, a pen, a rupee note and an empty bottle were placed before the group to stand for self-employment, education, small business development and levels of alcohol consumption, respectively, all topics of importance to the Katkari in which various degrees of improvement could be seen.

As each topic emerged and was validated by the group, I placed a long bamboo stick on the rug like a spoke in a wheel, gradually constructing an array of topics up for evaluation. To conclude the strategic planning exercise, the group assessed their progress on each spoke, placing markers to show the current level of progress and a target level for the next year of the Forum's work. This became their strategic plan.

The ease with which a meaningful discussion and plan unfolded gave me hope that Katkari organization was on the rise. Looking back, at the end of my professional life and with few prospects to travel again to the hillsides of the Western Ghats, I can rest a little easier knowing that, like the youth walking on stilts in their hamlet, the Katkari will find a way, barefooted, sweating and laughing.

11

Breaking Dependency on Tobacco Farming

When I was eighteen, I picked tobacco in Tillsonburg, southern Ontario, setting aside money for university in Montreal that fall. I later took a creative writing course at the university with Clarke Blaise, a well-known Canadian-American writer of short fiction. He encouraged me to write from my experience, which I did for my first assignment. This is how it started.

> *The sun slowly evaporated the dew off the tobacco leaves. The feeler of the picking machine bounced and groped its way between the rows. The four seats and the four pickers remained just the right distance from the plants. I leaned back against the steel seat as we skimmed along the ground. My arms became shiny wet with plant juices, and flecked with sticky sand.*
>
> — *"Export A," by Danny Buckles (1974)*

Farmers rating alternatives to tobacco, Bangladesh.

The story was published in the student magazine, the only fiction I ever wrote that made it into print. It was prescient, however, in a personal way. While a coming-of-age tale featuring a girl and an awkward attempt to seduce, it included an account of a mysterious illness I experienced in real life on the tobacco farm: nausea, vomiting and dizziness. Without realizing it at the time, the symptoms match what is known as "green tobacco sickness," a widespread occupational health problem among tobacco workers caused by exposure to nicotine through the skin. The plant juices on warm wet skin bring the water-soluble chemical directly into the blood stream.

Many years later, I learned the details of the illness through work with Farida Akhter and a team of remarkable people in several regions of Bangladesh where tobacco farming is common. I came to understand that tobacco farmers are as dependent on tobacco as tobacco smokers. Debt to the tobacco companies, and the seductive appeal of the incentives they offer, bind tobacco farmers to an industrial monocrop that depletes soils, denudes forested hillsides and compromises the health of field workers and the women and children curing the tobacco leaves. Many tobacco farmers, especially older ones who have seen the impacts on their families and on their land, are desperate to shift into other livelihoods, but don't know how.

Breaking the dependency is not easy. The British American Tobacco Company (BATC), the largest buyer in Bangladesh, is particularly effective at drawing farmers into tobacco farming and keeping them bound. For decades they have been setting up operations in prime food-producing areas such as river valleys and flood plains close to abundant sources of firewood for curing kilns. As they deplete the forest and soils, the company shifts to new areas, leaving damaged landscapes, neglected agricultural markets and indebted people in their wake. From both a farmer and national food security and health perspective, tobacco farming in Bangladesh and many other developing countries around the world is a disaster.

Our tobacco research, funded by IDRC, showed what is fundamentally wrong with global, capitalist, industrial agriculture, but also the challenges of making a transition to viable alternative livelihoods. While the case against tobacco has been strongly articulated and formalized in the Framework Convention on Tobacco Control (FCTC), one of the most widely embraced treaties in the United Nation's history, Big Tobacco has kept the industry alive and thriving.

British America Tobacco Company sign promoting a green image, standing against a deforested hillside, degraded field and tobacco monoculture.

The corporate financial interests at stake are huge, and in the years leading up to the 2003 approval of the tobacco control convention the industry pivoted from denial of the harmful effects of tobacco use to espousing the contribution of tobacco farming to government revenue and local livelihoods. They warned of critical losses for developing country governments collecting taxes from tobacco companies and from the sale of tobacco products. They also predicted unemployment and lower incomes for workers and tobacco farmers, framing both groups as innocent victims of tobacco control policies.

IDRC pioneered research on an alternative narrative through its Tobacco Control Secretariat. Wardie Leppan, the lead on tobacco farming issues until 2014, had been my immediate boss during my final years at IDRC, and an ally. His easy going manner hid a radical political perspective well suited to taking on Big Tobacco.

He and others at the secretariat developed a funding program to challenge the corporate argument about tobacco farming while at the same time going beyond the World Health Organization (WHO) assumption that tobacco control was strictly a health issue. The health focus of the WHO, to the exclusion of other considerations, effectively reduced the problem of tobacco to the ignorance of governments and farmers about the evils of smoking. Education and moral sanction were the policy solutions. By contrast, Wardie and the IDRC advocated for research into the pros and cons of tobacco cultivation and the barriers farmers face when they try to shift out of tobacco.

In many respects, the politics of Big Tobacco are similar to those of Big Oil. So too is the challenge of transition. Both industrial mono crops and fossil based energy demand of us a fundamental break with what is and a leap into an unclear future.

There are lessons here I think for understanding the role of participatory and action-oriented research and activism in creating conditions for this kind of change. The methods, some of which involved advanced analytical techniques, stimulated breakthrough thinking among farmers with little or no formal education. Their ideas, combined with culturally grounded activism by Farida and her team, produced national policies that got the attention of Big Tobacco and changed the course of tobacco farming in Bangladesh. The outcomes illustrate the power of the grassroots to drive change at multiple levels, from the village to the banking institutions that regulate loans to farmers and to the tobacco industry.

The journey began with a song.

A science of the concrete

Farida invited me to join the research on tobacco farming almost a decade after my first visit to Bangladesh and introduction to UBINIG, the organization she ran with Farhad Mahzar. It was a new topic for her too, brought to her attention by Gain Bhai, a farmer from a region of Bangladesh where tobacco farming was common. He had decided to stop growing tobacco because he could see the impact it was having on the soils of his fields and the health of his family and people that helped him harvest and process the crop. To share his concerns, he composed a song, performed with the one-stringed *ektara* in the tradition of Shah Lalon, the late nineteenth century Bangladeshi political and spiritual philosopher.

I first heard the song during the fateful workshop on participatory action research I conducted near Mumbai while Michelle was in hospital with severe appendicitis and Jacques sat at her side. Farida had invited Gain Bhai and several people from her organization to

Gain Bhai singing about the trouble with tobacco and the feeling of being free from dependency, Tangail, Bangladesh.

learn new research tools and plan how they might go about organizing research and advocacy in support of farmers seeking to break their dependency on tobacco. They planned a cultural strategy as well, building on Gain Bhai's song. Tall, with short cropped greying hair and a *longi* wrapped around his waist, Gain Bhai gave a graceful and compelling performance at the workshop and in many other venues I witnessed over the following years.

I became an integral part of the team, visiting farming communities in Bandarban and Cox's Bazaar in the south, Kushtia near the Indian border, Tangail near Dhaka and Ishwardi in the northwest. The experience helped me hit my stride as an anthropologist interested both in global issues and the methods that carry us to research conclusions. Farida and other UBINIG staff organized encounters with farmers, translated my questions and instructions and quickly picked up the participatory approach and detailed methods on their own. Women played a leadership role throughout, sometimes meeting privately as small groups to develop their ideas before engaging with men or other stakeholders.

We started with a simple question: Why do farmers continue to grow tobacco, despite the many concerns they have about its impact on their health, environment and land? The research tool I selected to structure and support the conversation was one of the most advanced in the toolbox Jacques and I had been developing, adapted for group discussion from the work of the Russian-American economist Wassily Leontief. Leontief won the 1973 Nobel Prize in economics for his work on the underlying model, known in economics as input output analysis.

In keeping with the logic of the model, I asked farmers for their reasons for growing tobacco, which we compiled, compared and refined together until we had a list of clearly expressed and distinct reasons. We then used a tree metaphor and diagram with roots (causes) and branches (effects) to ask to what extent one reason caused another reason.

This required more complex reasoning than a classic *Problem Tree* method because it focused attention on the interdependencies between things, not simply their linear relationship. A numerical rating of the interaction of reasons like "tobacco growing makes good use of family labor" and "the tobacco company pays us with a lump sum for our entire crop" produced a matrix of scores and then a diagram showing the overall system of reasons for growing tobacco.

Some reasons were powerful causes while others were mainly effects, or both causes and effects of the system of reasons binding farmers to the crop. Farmers explored the picture and decided which reasons to focus on changing, in light of their causal weight and whether or not they or UBINIG could do something about them.

This was pretty amazing stuff, with non-literate farmers making practical use of an advanced economic model that had earned Leontief a Nobel Price.

While the details of the factors, ratings and discussion are best left to readers of other publications, farmer-based analysis converged around the conclusion that decades of tobacco company dominance had undermined farmer capacity to innovate their way out of the conundrum. There seemed to be no alternative to tobacco, in part because farmers were not trying new things and the national agricultural research system was not providing new options.

This conclusion led the group to decide to collectively design and implement experiments with potential cash crops and to evaluate outcomes together. If the universities, research centres and tobacco companies would not help them come up with options, then they would do the technical research themselves. This is what small-scale farmers the world over have been forced by circumstances to do: find their own way.

As I had learned in Mexico, conducting field experiments is no small matter for farmers, even on a small scale. Land and other resources dedicated to an experiment expose farmers to risk from the loss of income if the experiments fail. For small scale farmers already living on the edge, even small losses could be devastating.

To help minimize the risk we needed to plan experiments that might work economically and technically while at the same time offering farmers something new. Radical innovation was needed to break through the inertia and dependence on the tobacco companies.

The challenge led me to a different method in the methodological tool box, this time adapted by Jacques and his wife Michelle from the field of Personal Construct psychology. It is based on a theory of personality and cognition developed in the 1950s by the American psychologist George Kelly.

What appealed to me for the question at hand was its potential to tap into traditions of local knowledge and ways of learning—what farmers actually know about crops and their capacity to "think outside the box." My contribution to the method was to find a way to do the detailed and complex reasoning with non-literate people steeped in an oral tradition and knowledge system most researchers knew very little about. What emerged was a variation on the game Twister and X's and O's.

The core idea is simple and fun. Three different crops are chosen at random, represented by small pots of seed or a cutting from the plant. People are then invited to indicate which two have something in common, different from the third. This generates a contrasting characteristic or descriptor. Of three friends, for example, two may be great sports buddies while the other is someone to sit down with when facing a hard choice. From this point of view, the world of friends is made up of people to play with and people to plan with, a contrast that can help create a map of friendship.

The discussion of contrasts produced a matrix of crops and crop characteristics, sometimes as many as ten columns wide and six deep. We organized these on the ground for farmers to then rate each crop on each contrasting characteristic.

While the tool typically relies on numbers for the ratings, I developed a three or five-point grey scale to show a range of ratings without

Male farmer comparing crops using the triad method, Chakaria, Bangladesh.

Wax figures of alternatives to tobacco, Bandarban, Bangladesh.

relying on numeracy. Cards from an art store made the pattern of black, white and shades of grey visual in a way that helped people participate directly in the analysis. For example, farmers could see for themselves from the pattern that crops "requiring added fertilizer" tend to be "monocrops" and also "need extra water." Crops that "help fertilize the soil" clustered around other contrast such as "grow well mixed in with other crops".

Domain matrix on crop comparisons, Bandarban, Bangladesh.

Domain matrix on crop comparisons, Chakaria, Bangladesh.

Farida and the team watched as farmers debated the ratings. They then recorded the final score for each crop on each contrast until we had enough scores to fill the matrix on the floor. I sat nearby, entering the data into a computer program used in social psychology to do cluster analysis with this kind of data, validating the patterns farmers observed directly and drawing attention to other patterns less obvious but potentially interesting for discussion. It took us most of the day, broken up with tea breaks, walks on the grounds of the UBINIG centre, and a meal.

The practical implications of the research were subtle but significant, producing an unexpected and pivotal insight when we realized that some crops combined characteristics in unusual ways. We found that jute and peanuts, for example, are similar in many ways to other "food and fodder crops for local markets" but also, like tobacco, have "well-established external markets." Also, they do not "compete for space with tobacco during the same season" but rather "straddle the tobacco season," either before or after. This put them outside of the general category of "alternative" cash crops that farmers could simply substitute for tobacco and insert during the same season.

One of the women farmers in the group, Sheuli Begum, gave shape to this shift in thinking with an example. She explained that recently she had seen a spice in the market that she and other rural women regularly buy. It contained seeds of three different plants not currently grown in her region. She decided to germinate and grow all three, and then chose one (*methi*) that she believed could be easily grown in a mixed cropping system. She noted that it needed to be planted before the tobacco season and would help create some cash

Sheuli Begum (sitting) and friends, Chakaria, Bangladesh.

income at a time when she would be tending to crops that would be harvested later on.

Inspired by this insight, farmers and the project decided to also search local markets for crops that combine with each other in novel and fruitful ways over the long growing season available to Bangladeshi farmers. It prompted us to include in our study cropping patterns and crop rotations over the entire calendar year, rather than limiting the research to a single substitute crop that would magically change everything for tobacco farmers.

We realized that change could come from creating the conditions for a broad *transition* from one state to another over a defined period of time. Developing a transition strategy with diverse crop combinations, rather than finding a single substitute crop, became the new guiding narrative. The discovery paralleled the psychological process of "breakthrough thinking" central to George Kelly's Personal Construct Psychology.

The exercises, repeated in different tobacco growing regions, launched several years of practical experiments by and with farmers. It created a novel and effective approach to transitioning out of tobacco production. The experiments were rooted in a science of the concrete, producing nuanced, systemic and locally adapted solutions to the problem of farm transition.

The research approach was different from what scientists normally do to identify solutions to technical problems: draw on theory to find solutions. It also differed from conventional anthropological studies of local knowledge systems based on naming and classifying discrete components of a system, as ethno-botanists might do for native plants. The approach was participatory. The method reflected what is known in systems theory as a "soft system" perspective: the system described emerged dynamically and evolved in unanticipated ways. The spirit of the exercise was also in keeping with the therapeutic purpose of the underlying theory—how do we understand the world around us and how well does that understanding help us predict and adjust our personal and collective actions?

I'm not sure why farmers in Bangladesh tolerated this and other detailed research activities I introduced over the years, although I do think they appreciated the focus on a common purpose. Furthermore,

Farmers rating different cropping options, Chakaria, Bangladesh.

the results were shared immediately and transparently. The discussions, animated expertly by Farida and other team members, were also lively and respectful. Laughter came easily. Also, everyone's intelligence was respected, regardless of their literacy or education.

These features reflect a key principle of our approach to participatory action research. Too much structure and not enough conversation undermines participation. The opposite is also true. Not having a structure runs the risk of losing sight of what people are going for, and why Jacques coined the term "structured conversations" to capture this balance.

From field to policy

Researchers often think that their job ends when new knowledge is created. It is up to policy makers to do the right thing with the knowledge, in the context of the political process defining the general directions of society. Typically, that direction is rooted in the values and the owners of capital, making systemic change extremely difficult.

The Bangladesh tobacco study bridged the gap between research, policy and political change through a positive and culturally specific alternative vision: Food for people, not a harmful drug for companies. It articulated that vision forcefully and relentlessly, once the basic outline of the technical research was clear.

Women were the driving forces behind the activism, on the streets and in the machinery of government. World No Tobacco Day, celebrated by the WHO on May thirty-first every year since 1988, became an early focus for use of the tobacco farming research. It was a rallying cry for policy advocacy, uniting middle-class proponents of anti-smoking laws and former tobacco farmers in marches on the streets of Dhaka. Most of the marchers were women with first-hand experience of the human suffering from both ends of the product cycle, growing the product and dying from using it. They lifted the concerns and options emerging from the research out of relative obscurity, mobilized thousands and provided a powerful critique of the industry's sales pitch.

Journalists covered the unusual and photogenic alliance of urban and rural women and integrated into their news stories a broad range of related issues. The food security and environmental impacts of tobacco farming, and in particular the company practice of targeting prime agricultural land near forested hillsides, made for compelling media.

These negative impacts were also tangible and measurable. Traditional food-basket regions of Bangladesh such as Kushtia were experiencing exponential growth in tobacco farming, as were politically and culturally sensitive forested regions such as the Chittagong Hill Tracts. Suddenly, the true scope of tobacco's harm to the security of the nation was apparent in a single image of women of different classes and occupations walking together to protect the land.

Farida told me of a health worker, married to a tobacco farmer, who spoke out against tobacco farming in a television interview. She was later confronted in the local health centre by an angry British American Tobacco Company representative who demanded she explain why she was supporting the anti-tobacco campaign when her family benefited from the industry. She responded, "I am a health worker so I can see all the health effects of tobacco farming. I have to see that."

Some policy changes came quickly. In 2011, the Bangladesh Bank ordered all commercial banks to suspend new loans to individuals and companies for the purpose of tobacco farming. It cited the threats to public health from the use of tobacco products but also noted the negative impact of tobacco farming on the food crisis in Bangladesh. That same year, and in subsequent years, the Ministry of Agriculture suspended individual subsidies on fertilizer for tobacco production and the Ministry of Industries reduced its fertilizer subsidies for tobacco companies. These are actions no national government has yet taken with the fossil fuel industry but that must and will come.

Officials in tobacco growing areas such as Bandarban made use of local administrative procedures to ban tobacco cultivation on government-owned lands. Several municipal-level governments announced bans on cutting trees to cure tobacco. The effects were visible enough to prompt representatives of the British American Tobacco Company to visit Gain Bai, the singer and former tobacco farmer, at his home in Kushtia. Much as they did with the woman health worker, the representatives complained about the anti-tobacco campaign. He replied, "Tobacco is not a food crop. That is why I'm opposed."

Deeper policy change was longer coming. In 2016, ten years after the research was launched, Farida was invited to sit on a newly formed committee charged with drafting the National Tobacco Cultivation Control Policy. Coordinated by the Ministry of Health and Family Welfare, the committee has the complicated task of negotiating agreement among multiple arms of government, from the National Board of Revenues to the Ministry of Labour. It needs to work as well with the Ministry of Agriculture, a partner of tobacco companies for decades. The long and torturous process, typical of controversial legislation in any government, also points to the ongoing influence of the tobacco industry lobby.

Thanks to women's leadership from within the Ministry of Health, and Farida's ability to engage with political leaders from all major parties, the policy initiative survived and is now in its final stages. More and more members of parliament and government officials are routinely speaking out against tobacco cultivation. Only a few government officials, swayed by the BATC, continue to stand in the way. "They will not succeed," Farida says.

Cape jasmine (*Gardenia jasminoides*), an edible flower of South-East Asia.

Once enacted into law, the Bangladesh policy will be the first in the world to take a firm stand against the cultivation of tobacco, in concert with policy supports to address structural constraints and kick start a transition to sustainable agricultural systems. A nation of the Global South, wracked by enormous other problems, is getting the practice of transition right.

The experience continues to inform my politics and my advocacy, and remind me that multilayered and multifaceted research, advocacy and activism are central to policy change in a complex world.

12

Skillful Means

When I was still with IDRC, living in Ottawa with my wife and raising a son, I began to exercise a new skill: standing in front of a crowd to listen and guide a conversation. Sam Kaner, a California-based facilitator, had opened my eyes to the art of facilitation during a two day workshop at IDRC. "Support people to do their best thinking," he told us, and "Hold the space but don't think you have to do everything for others."

Daniel Bowling, a mediator for the Alternative Dispute Resolution Program of the US District Court for Northern California, was another early source of inspiration and training. A book he authored, called *Bringing Peace into the Room: How the personal qualities of the mediator impact the process of conflict resolution,* raised a powerful question and reminded me to be aware of my own feelings and body posture when facilitating. I learned to focus on the feeling in the room, and to smile more easily.

Educators weighing in on proposals, Montreal, Canada.
Photo by Justin Wonnacott.

Daniel, who gave a workshop at Carleton University, also shared with me an icebreaker I have used a thousand times since: "Tell us something you like about your name," he said. This invitation to share a simple yet intimate detail always brings a smile to people's faces and is a powerful reminder that we all have a story to tell, if we wish and are given a chance.

One of the first opportunities I had to apply training in facilitation was not in a professional setting but rather at my son's school, where I was a member of the Board of Governors. My wife and I had pulled our son out of the public school system when he was ten, bored, he said, in a classroom of thirty-two where the teacher had no choice but to manage the class around the most troublesome students.

Our son was virtually invisible to the teacher in the public school system, so we moved him to a private Rudolf Steiner School where small classes and teaching to the individual were core values. It was a great experience, turning him into a positive learner. It also introduced me to pedagogical uses of drawing, sculpting and physical movement I later adapted to my professional practice as a facilitator.

The core Steiner approach to experiential learning—using all of our faculties to learn, with head, hands, and heart—also moved me in a way I could not have learned from facilitation books and training alone. It was my son's experience. It was personal.

The teachings of Rudolf Steiner, Sam Kaner and Daniel Bowling came in handy when I volunteered to facilitate what proved to be the final meeting of our son's school before it went bankrupt and closed down. Thirty or so parents, and the full contingent of eight teachers, had gathered to discuss the financial situation and tensions between parents and teachers over discipline. The teacher council had decided to expel several students for persistent rude and disrespectful behaviour, even though their parents had a long association with the school and the loss of revenue would be critical.

People initially talked past and over each other, escalating the conflict to a point where no resolution seemed possible. I was in the middle, listening and turning to one then the other as they expressed their distress. I remained calm, hands at my side or held lightly together in front as Sam had modelled. I acknowledged what was said, paraphrasing if need be or simply repeating the words I heard until everything that needed to be said had been said.

The circumstances called on me, as the facilitator, to suspend judgement and my own pragmatic orientation in the face of principled disagreements and attempts to negotiate compromises.

No magical solution arrived. Collectively, parents and teachers arrived at an intractable "No." The teachers would not relinquish their stand on Steiner philosophy and pedagogy and the children that had been booted out for persistent misbehaviour would not be reinstated. The remaining parents would not accept higher fees to compensate for the loss in revenue. Closure at the end of the school term was the only option, and that was what happened a few months later.

Facilitating dialogue when the stakes are high, and the stakes should always be meaningful, does not mean arriving at a happy resolution at any cost. Getting to no can be just as right as getting to yes. The consensual focus of group processes, I came to understand, can miss or obscure diverging interests and the actual exercise of power. The loudest voice, or normative pressure, may hold sway over marginalized voices and displace legitimate local and traditional ways of thinking, learning and deciding.

A common problem I witnessed as a consultant to international development projects is that participatory elements are used to legitimize agency-driven agendas, making too much of participation and too little of who decides and what actions are ultimately taken.

This does not mean that our own beliefs and commitments as facilitators be dropped into a cloud of cultural relativism. This is another anthropological trope that justifies total inaction and tolerance of all forms of social behaviours and organization, from machismo to extreme imbalances in wealth. For an anthropologist, or facilitator, genuine curiosity and a degree of equanimity is a better place to start if dialogue is to happen. Taking a stand may also be necessary.

It is a demanding and exhausting task. Over the years I facilitated hundreds of group events, learning to patiently hold a space for difficult group conversations. Usually I did my job successfully. Occasionally it ended with poor results.

I also learned not to panic in the middle of conversations filled with uncertainty about what comes next. The "groan zone" Sam Kaner called it; those moments in a problem-solving process when the way forward is unclear, calling on people to work harder and do their best thinking.

Structured conversation among stakeholders, Canada.
Photos by Justin Wonnacott.

A few personal tricks were helpful. To start a meeting, I would organize chairs in a perfect circle. This allows everyone to see each other easily and is a reminder that the group can work together as a single body if it chooses to do so. I often placed an object of focus and beauty in the middle: flowers, a colourful silk scarf, a bowl of apples.

I made flip charts of event objectives and agendas, with colours and lettering easy to read from a distance, and enclosed the words in an attractive border. I invited people to use art-quality paper and art-quality colours to visualize core challenges or resources, or to sculpt these with beeswax or modelling clay. Instead of relying on the spoken word only, I invited people to vote with their feet to show support for priorities or options.

The research tools helped enormously. Visualizing the questions and responses of a group using physical objects and by moving their bodies combined beautifully and effectively with ranking and rating, Cartesian graphs and concentric circles with tools for ranking the visual character provided a way to draw people's attention to the topic at hand and discuss data and understandings emerging from the process, rather than the personalities in the room. While not a panacea for the facilitator's nightmare—a loud and domineering participant—an external point of reference such as a number in a graph or object representing the title of the gathering offers a bridge back to the matter at hand.

I learned the spirit of serious games for facilitation from sources more closely aligned with the New Age fringe than the latest *Facilitators Handbook*. Debra and I did periodic retreats with yoga teachers and practitioners of "energy work" such as *The Dances of Universal Peace, Tara Dances,* and *The Wave Work*. We used *The Circle Process* and went regularly to see a neighbourhood troupe doing a form of improvisational theatre known as *Playback Theatre*. These unorthodox and creative forms of expression gave me a direct and personal understanding of experiential learning and how it can enhance teamwork, leadership and innovation.

Rather than reproduce these practices, however, I learned to select and adapt elements to support discussions, celebrate others in the room or illustrate core ideas such as systems thinking, brainstorming, empathy and positive psychology. Facilitation took on the character of a Steiner education: engage hands, heads and hearts.

I also learned from facilitators and professional coaches with The Ginger Group, a Canadian cluster of friends involved in organizational change inspired by the ideas of David Bohm. Bohm helped to establish the science of quantum physics and flesh out the challenge it presents to Cartesian thinking—the view that the mind is wholly separate from the corporal body and that the senses are simply illusions of the mind. Bohm also collaborated for more than a decade with Jiddu Krishnamurti, an Indian philosopher I read closely as a young man. While I did not integrate poetry and creative writing, one of the tools of the Ginger Group, into events I organized, the experience showed me the relevance of intimate sharing to the change process.

Jacques and I realized together that these tricks of the trade, common among some facilitators, could easily fall flat if they were used simply as energizers with no link to the task at hand. Inviting people to pantomime, tell a story in sequence or create a drawing of a vision statement can be fun but will only fly if they also contribute something useful to the immediate goals of the group. *Declare yourself! But versus And. I failed! Safety zone. True or False. Status Cards.* These are fun and energizing tools of improvisational theatre but a distraction if they are not also appropriate to the moment. For facilitators, the choice means exercising judgment in context.

Sometimes an energizer needs to remain invisible or turned towards the facilitator. To lift my own energy, I might wow the crowd by drawing a perfect circle freehand on a flip chart, and then add two more to make a Venn diagram. Before leading a final plenary session towards the end of a demanding day, I might imagine a cone of light entering through the top of my head, a source of energy from outside to carry me through feelings of anxiety and exhaustion.

Watching a pantomime exercise that feeds into a quantitative assessment, Montreal, Canada. Photo by Justin Wonnacott.

On more than a few occasions, I revealed my own facilitation mistakes by proclaiming them with relish, inviting applause and taking a deep bow. Making friends with failure, I learned, is part of risking enough to succeed.

Learning to facilitate events, large and small, from that first experience of intractable difference at my son's school to meetings of scientists concerned about invasive species and aquatic diseases, prompted a shift in approach to my task as a researcher. Instead of trying to convince others to join me in my projects, I took to joining theirs. I became less concerned about getting things done and more concerned about responding with what is appropriate in the moment.

Over the course of a decade, I went from being a generalist at IDRC to being an anthropologist among farmers in India and Bangladesh and then on to being a specialist in the design and facilitation of participatory action research (PAR) and processes for public engagement. I claimed no technical expertise in fields other than agriculture and the art of collaborative inquiry. This became my consultation practice, which today I'm happy to teach but reluctant to practice. It is just too exhausting.

SAS^2 dialogue

In 2005, I created a company with Jacques and Michelle to provide the legal and accounting framework needed to support a consulting business. The separate legal identity was a vehicle for us to "scale up" our experience with participatory action research beyond what was possible for university-based researchers with time-bound project funding.

Marketing and promotion included branding the name of our approach. We called it SAS^2 (Social Analysis Systems squared) to signal both the tools for social research and the means to apply them socially, that is, in a participatory manner. This double entendre distinguished our collaborative approach to research from conventional social science methods such as surveys and questionnaires. Surveys fragment the analysis of problems and isolate responses, and people, from each other. The name also emphasizes a systems perspective on social change, necessary in a complex world. The term "dialogue" was added later by Michelle, to create a more inviting statement of what we had to offer that also worked in English and French.

Branding is a curious fashion in the international development industry, as are hybrid business models involving universities and private organizations. While the hubris and irrelevance of sustaining the branding effort eventually became apparent to us, we were

Conversation among teachers at a small agricultural university in Honduras. Photo by Laura Suazo.

genuinely excited by the reception SAS^2 Dialogue was receiving. For a time, the name created a buzz in some research and development circles, including among Canadian and European organizations and in Latin America and South Asia where we both had long and credible track records. We saw no harm in the marketing approach to our work so long as the products of the publicly funded research remained free to the public, which they always have been.

Beyond the formal branding exercise, the company charter lay largely unused while I worked with the Katkari of India and tobacco farmers of Bangladesh, activities funded by the IDRC grant to Carleton University facilitating my transition to university life and position there as an Adjunct Research Professor.

Jacques and I collaborated on common publications, including several books consolidating and presenting the theory and methods of participatory action research and our particular contributions to the field. By publishing with leading academic presses, we hoped to showcase the overall integrity of our approach to research and create permanent resources for university teaching and training. One book, published by Routledge in the United Kingdom, is now moving towards a third edition, earning me a royalty of about 800 dollars a year. Such are the riches of academic publishing.

Thanks to funding early on from IDRC, we had the rare privilege of working with outstanding partners in ten countries, receiving support from them for the continuous development and improvement of our approach to PAR and PAR training. The exposure we had to a wide

Partners in Pokhara, Nepal, planning ways to use a new PAR tool in their work.

range of topics and diverse practical needs and capabilities among partners also stimulated production of an ever-expanding handbook of tools we thought were useful to community based researchers and facilitators of group-based problem solving.

The handbook, a free PDF on our website (www.SAS^2.net), has been downloaded more than 8,000 times, making it a best seller not only in our publishing experience but also for many specialized publications in the field.

Jacques drafted many of the tools in our toolbox and formulated most of the theoretical foundations on which they are based. My contribution lay mainly in a deep practice in a wide range of international development settings, an aesthetic of simple and direct language and a visual and kinaesthetic orientation to facilitation. Both of us maintained throughout a sharp focus on making a difference to the situations and people involved.

We complemented each other perfectly, fleshing out together what neither of us would have done alone. The partnership meant we could not only try to change the world, as activists intend, but also try to make a difference to prevailing ideas and mindsets in the social sciences and international development.

One theoretical contribution I made to our collective body of work proved to be consequential. It is derived from the Sanskrit expression *upaya-kaushalya*, meaning "skill or cleverness in means" used in Buddhist traditions to refer to the careful and caring use of questions or actions to help people on their road to greater wisdom.

A Zen koan (riddle) inviting meditation on the sound of one hand clapping, or an offer to help a thief who has broken into your home find the money hidden in your dresser can, through paradox, shake people out of their habitual frame of reference. The questions or actions produce "ah ha" moments and the possibility of a shift in thinking, or, in the spiritual context, sudden intuitive insight. These means become skillful, however, if and only if they are both expedient and fit the situation and the potentialities of the people involved. A thief who cannot reform himself even when presented with an opportunity will inevitably get arrested.[1]

1 Chapter 76 of the Lankavatara Sutra illustrates the Buddhist meaning of skillful means in a conversation between the Buddha and Mahamati Bodhisatva. The key phrase, at least for me, is, "Therefore, Mahamati, fearless bodhisatvas are not attached to language but teach accordingly to what is appropriate." The thief metaphor comes from Akira Kurosawa's film *Dodes'ka-den*.

Comparing perspectives on criteria and indicators for a watershed program, Renfrew, Canada. Photo by Justin Wannacott.

We used this concept and its variations—careful and caring, rigorous and flexible, structured and conversational, fit to purpose and fit to people—to organize and reflect on the competencies needed to create and mobilize knowledge for the common good. Our books on the topic of PAR, training activities and personal practice with partners revolve around these skills in means.

The role of the company changed in 2010 when IDRC project funding ran out, forcing me to flex entrepreneurial muscles I hadn't used since my time as a self-employed artist operating craft stores in Dawson City, Yukon. I sought out international and Canadian consulting assignments while Jacques, who retired early from teaching at the university, focused on Canadian partners in the private and public sector, and new partners in France and Belgium. He worked frequently with his wife Michelle, who added a deep sensitivity to the dynamics of group processes and knowledge of psychology, her field of expertise and teaching at the University of Ottawa. Together, they have engaged with a new generation of researchers in the French tradition of psycho-sociological interventions, especially in education.

None of us had an interest in developing a permanent institutional home for SAS² Dialogue at a university. It seemed like too much administrative work when what mattered to all of us was doing meaningful work on the ground and the human relationships this afforded.

Together, and separately, we developed and facilitated hundreds of group problem-solving and research-training projects and events

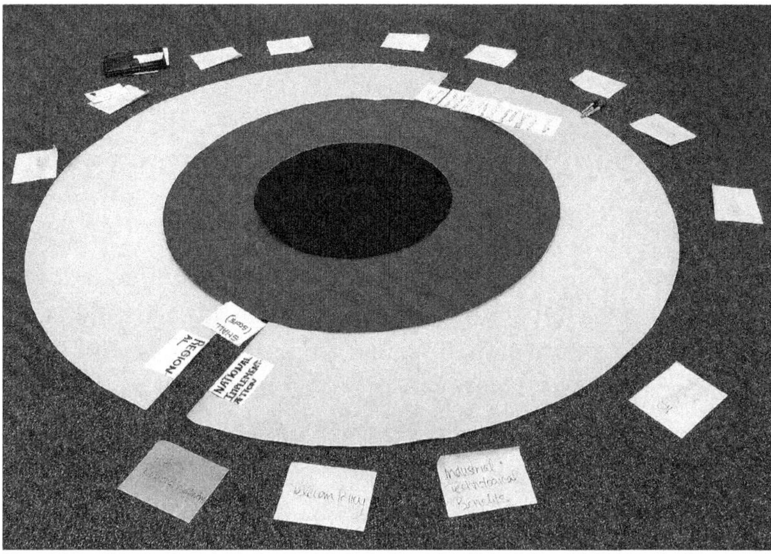

Visual support for a rating exercise among government workers.

for a wide range of clients in Canada, Europe, Africa, Asia and Latin America. Many were one-off relationships, ending when the job was done, while others unfolded over months and even years. Both scenarios were satisfying in their own way, because grounded in the felt needs of others.

Fortunately, I did not need to sell my soul to feed my family. The modest consulting business generated a steady stream of income similar to what I had earned as a senior scientist at IDRC and as a funded Adjunct Research Professor at Carleton University. It was enough, allowing me to work with people whose values were consistent with my own. Along the way, I got to share with the world the excitement I felt for what we were learning about participatory action research and what it has to offer in efforts to solve human problems.

It starts with the simple act of bringing peace and skillful means into the room.

13

Ring of Fire, and Other Stories

The Philippines lies on the Pacific Ring of Fire, a confluence of tectonic plates giving birth to volcanic eruptions and earthquakes. The country is also on the path of regular tropical cyclones with powerful winds, torrential rain, high waves and damaging storm surges. Sam, a native of the Philippines and a Catholic priest-in-training, had witnessed the impact of these natural disasters and been drawn into responding.

The Camillian Ministers of the Sick, a religious order founded in Rome in 1582, offered Sam a vehicle for his work. Saint Camillus de Lellis was an Italian soldier who had turned from fighting to healing the injured on the battle field. He is the Catholic patron saint of hospitals, the sick, nurses and nursing associations. The red cross worn on the black cassocks of members of the Camillian Order is similar to the international symbol of medical care. The Order runs dozens of hospitals and clinics around the world. One is in Manila.

Circle of Camillian priests, nuns and laity, Peru.

Sam had came across our published work on participatory action research in the course of his PhD studies with the Cody Institute in Nova Scotia. He contacted me and extended an invitation to visit the Philippines as a guest of the Order. When a consulting contract for my services arrived at our home from the Rome headquarters, my wife, in her words "a recovering Catholic," joked "Now you are working for the Vatican! What next?"

The Order wanted me to develop a community-based approach to planning for and responding to disasters. Efforts to reduce the loss of life, property and livelihoods depend on a high degree of cooperation and coordination among stakeholders. Emergency plans also rely on people's capacities to independently manage the tasks that must be carried out urgently when disaster strikes. Planning for these is best done in a multi-stakeholder mode, something I could offer despite my limited knowledge of the specific field.

Once I started to plan for the trip I realized that there is a deeper layer to emergency planning as well: What happens before and after the storm? Answers to the question involve paying attention to what makes people vulnerable in the first place and what barriers they face when trying to recover from loss.

People faced with an emergency do not sit on their hands waiting for agencies and authorities to save them. They do what they can, often creatively, to save themselves and collectively care for their own traumas. As remarked by Casey Barrs in his 2010 book *Preparedness Support*, "There is a whole understory of local preparations against harm that we tend not to even recognize." Sam wanted to be sure the Order engaged vulnerable populations in organizing themselves and fighting for deeper changes to situations that make them vulnerable. He wanted them to become the subjects of their own security.

Over a period of several years, I trained members of the Order in facilitation of participatory planning events in the Philippines, Peru, Burkina Faso and Italy. As was often the case with new topics, Jacques and I invented a tool to address the core question: risk management. *Hazards* asks groups to assess the severity of the potential hazard, the probability that the hazard will occur and the current capacity of people and organizations to avoid or respond to the hazard. It uses a Cartesian graph to organize the responses into quadrants.

Through story-telling, map making and hazard assessments, the community planning process tapped into experiences of individual and community trauma and capacities for self-preservation and self-care. For example, a participant in the Philippines workshop highlighted self-organization by the very poor in his account of past storm surges along the waterfront of Manila, the capital. More than 1,300 people live illegally in ramshackle and vulnerable houses at the urban shoreline. They are regularly mobilized and guided to safety during storms through the independent action of a handful of women and elders respected in the community. Connecting with these natural leaders, and bringing them into the formal emergency planning process, became part of the Order's disaster relief and preparedness plan.

The approach to group assessment and planning we developed for this topic, and for problem-solving research in other settings, is very different from university-base research concerned with "interesting" questions. It focuses instead on "useful" questions, where answers can immediately guide action. The methodological assumption is that nothing is solved by simply thinking about it. Learning by solving, or trying to solve, is a more skillful practice than trying to come to an understanding by abstract means alone, even if the solution fails in some respects. All learning is problem-solving, involving a transition from what is to what it can be.

What moved me the most about working with members of the Camillian Order was the opportunity to understand the human experience of disaster—feelings of fear, helplessness and loss in the face of an uncontrollable force. Intense trauma, and post traumatic stress disorder, are, thankfully, not experiences in my own long life or the lives of people close to me.

The nuns, priests and laity I met had all given helping hands directly in the service of people in severe physical and emotional pain. They were intimately familiar with suffering and ways to accompany people experiencing trauma.

The West Africa Ebola epidemic had just come under control when I facilitated a workshop in Burkina Faso and learned to do "the Ebola shake" (elbow bump) instead of holding hands gently as is the normal greeting in West African culture. The epidemic had killed more than 11,000 people across the region, devastating individual families and entire communities.

A Spanish psychologist and former priest who attended the workshop in Rome helped me to understand the skills needed to respond appropriately to trauma. Instead of speaking of empathy as an attitude people should adopt, he turned empathy into a verb for a skill that could be learned progressively. "Empathy is something all people have," he said, "an innate quality of a human being." Providing an empathetic response skillfully, by contrast, is something people can learn.

Empathetic response as a skill starts with reflecting the words and emotions you receive. No editing, no elaboration. A deeper level is to link and order the words and emotions received. Patterns are created. Deeper still is to identify a metaphor rooted in the words and emotions received from the person in trauma. A shape emerges.

His insight prompted me to invite the group to co-construct an original tool for self-assessment and peer-to-peer learning based on our *Socratic Wheel* framework. Other active listening skills were added to the spokes of the wheel: unconditional welcome; being present; being authentic to honour the dignity and sacredness of the person and; silent self-reflection. Through these words, the group gently offered a spiritual perspective on attentive listening.

Camillian insight into caring for the sick through attentive listening and helping hands is summed up in *Ten Commandments of St. Camillus*, a list I read from an old mural on a wall at their monastery in the Philippines. The third commandment reads, "Remember to forget yourself," an idea that resonated with me and helped me form a deeply personal practice from all of the elements I'd learned about the qualities of a facilitator.

My work with the Camillian Order on disaster relief planning provided me with an experience I treasure for reasons other than my work. I was invited to Rome to give training to a small group of Camillians doing disaster preparedness work in Italy, France and Spain. My son Ryan, twenty-three at the time, came with me.

It was the second father-and-son trip to faraway places, carrying on a tradition my father had started with his three sons. When I lived in Germany between the ages of twelve and fourteen, my father took me in the Dakota transport aircraft he flew to Sardinia and Pisa in Italy and, on another occasion, to Stavenhagen on the coast of Norway. It was a bonding experience with many fond memories, including sitting in the cockpit while flying low up a Norwegian fiord, dropping a coin off the edge of the Tower of Pisa (no longer safe or allowed) and eating pizza together during a windy night in Cagliari, Sardina.

I did something similar with my two sons. On our first outing, Ryan and I went to Valparaiso in Chile where I facilitated a workshop on

Ryan at Machu Picchu, 2007.

Daniel at the Taj Mahal, India, 2022.

the country's coastal fisheries. Afterwards, we hiked to Machu Picchu in Peru with a friend from Lima. He was nineteen, a gregarious young man but self-conscious of his lack of worldly experience. He was keen to distinguish himself from friends leading normal teenage lives in Ottawa. The trek, and requisite photo with the ancient city's iconic buildings in the background, gave him the confidence he needed at the time, adorning his Facebook page for a year or so. For me it was a skillful means to being a father.

My son Daniel and I had fewer opportunities to bond on long distance trips when he was a boy and youth living with his mother in Mexico. We did, however, go to his grandmother's farm, and years later to Merida on the Yucatan peninsula. By then he was already a mature man. We spoke often of hiking together in the Himalayas, but by the time it was feasible for him I had already stopped travelling to the region. Still, we planned his itinerary together when his work took him to India.

A second opportunity to model my father's teachings with Ryan came when he was also more independent, travelling on his own to Switzerland to meet some university friends and then joining me in Rome where I was giving a workshop. We stayed in the Rome monastery of the Camillians, attached to the Church of St. Mary Magdalene less than one hundred metres from the Pantheon in the historic centre of the city. I'd arranged to help pay for the trip by offering a second workshop open to the general public, using a basement meeting room in the church. A small number attended, including a woman from Action Aid in the U.K. I later worked with and a scientist at Bioversity International, one of CIMMYT's sister organizations focused on biodiversity conservation.

The scientist and I met with her daughter and Ryan for dinner. When I returned to the austere monastery room for the night, Ryan went off with the daughter for a drink. By two in the morning he had still not arrived at the room. Worried and frustrated that he was breaking all the rules of the monastery, I texted him without any of the carefulness I had been teaching all day. By 2:30 a.m. he was back, excited by the music and conversations that had just wrapped up, and puzzled by my worry. With no harm done, I decided to suspend judgement and forget myself, knowing that he was safe. I also decided

Fountains in Geneva. Photo by Ryan Huron.

to recognize, as a parent, that he had the capacity for self-preservation and self-care needed to keep himself out of harm's way.

Gross national happiness

Bhutan's 1971 announcement that "Gross National Happiness is more important than Gross National Product" set out a vision for building an economy and society based on deeply felt Buddhist values. The position came at some cost to the country's standing in international financial institutions such as the International Monetary Fund and The World Bank. How could the country's economic plans be taken seriously?

When I travelled there in 2010, the King of Bhutan and the constitutional government had made Gross National Happiness an official goal. It was continuing the hard work of embedding the concept into the country's institutions, including primary and secondary schools. The previous year, several international conferences and planning meetings among educators from around the world had reviewed the core values of gross national happiness and defined compatible educational practices: holistic student assessment, daily meditation, critical thinking skills and green school infrastructure.

The ideas resembled in many ways the core components of the Rudolf Steiner educational program, including the importance of the student-teacher relationship, working from experience to concept, working from whole to parts and observation of the student (not the test) as the foundation for assessment.

I was invited to Bhutan by a Canadian Buddhist deeply involved in implementing the broader policy. He knew of my work from people at IDRC, and, through the Ministry of Education, asked me to facilitate a meeting of school administrators, teachers and the ministry evaluation team responsible for assessing progress. While I was not an education specialist, I could offer an approach to evaluation consistent with the values they sought to embed in the education system.

By then Jacques and I had begun to develop our own participatory approach to monitoring and evaluation, a technically complex branch of international development and project management backed by an entire consulting industry. Our critique of the field was built around the same questions we brought to the research challenges and public engagement events we facilitated: What is the evaluation for, who is it for and how will it be organized?

We questioned the need for standardized evaluation methodologies, the bread and butter of many consultants. We also felt skeptical about the utility of very broad conceptual guidelines often promoted by academically oriented evaluators. Instead, we charted a middle road, one based on generating context specific methodologies using and creating tools suited to the defined task. Evaluation built to purpose was our mantra.

Bhutan's national game, archery, provided the perfect starting point for design of a methodology fit to the goals of the ministry and the school context. Archery is widely played in villages and town settings, by young and old, and proved to be an effective metaphor for setting goals and assessing progress using indicators, the two key steps in any evaluation.

During the workshop, some thirty teachers, principals and students identified the conditions needed for a happy and harmonious learning environment, represented as arrows pointing to happiness at the centre of a round target. They then discussed indicators of progress for each, which we organized on a continuum along each arrow.

Observations indicating continuous and holistic student assessments or a joyful psychosocial ambience, for example, were placed closer to the centre than student assessments based on a single exam or a school day with no group play or quiet reflection.

The evaluation tool that emerged from the exercise, a variation on the *Socratic Wheel*, was to be used by the entire school body—teachers, students and parents—to assess a baseline, set targets for the school year and plan actions to achieve the targets. Much to my chagrin, however, the design, which I considered useful, simple and elegant, was virtually ignored by the professional evaluators in the Ministry of Education who gathered with me after the workshop to plan next steps. They thanked me for the inputs, and then began selecting elements they could convert into a survey questionnaire to be filled out by school principals.

I was rattled by the disconnect between what was to be evaluated (steps taken to create a happy and harmonious learning environment) and how progress was to be evaluated (a survey, with respondents isolated from each other and cut off from the possibility of dialogue). I raised the question but bit my tongue until they paused for the weekend and agreed to reconvene a few days later.

Tiger's Nest Monastery, Bhutan, 2010.

The break gave me an opportunity to do something I rarely had time to do when travelling as a consultant: I went to see the sites. In Thimphu, the capital, I walked into neighbourhoods on the edge of town, stopping to talk with youth gathered to play outdoor darts, a simpler variation of the archery game ubiquitous in the country. I climbed up to the famous Tiger's Nest Monastery in western Bhutan, passing the young King and his fiancé on my way down as they were making their way up. Another day I took a taxi to the foot of the hour-long trail to Cheri Monastery, built in 1620. The young driver offered to hike up with me as he had never been there himself.

I also visited with the uncle of a Bhutanese friend I had made some years earlier and sat down with the Canadian Buddhist that had invited me to Bhutan in the first place. We talked, amongst other things, about his understanding of *upaya-kaushalya*, the Sanskrit term for skillful means, and what might be appropriate for me to say to the evaluation team.

The experiences helped me settle my anxiety over the turn of events and what was looking like a complete waste of my time in Bhutan. Clearly, it was not my place to insist. I wouldn't be there to implement the evaluation process anyway. This tension is an inevitable feature of one-off and short-term consultancies.

I decided, however, to be fearless, as a bodhisattva is meant to be, and give my design one more pitch. I invited the group to simulate use of the tool for a school they knew well and to explore the implications by comparing one school assessment to another. This was an application of the *Socratic Wheel* I turned to often, supporting an evaluative approach focused on finding common strengths (what particular schools are already good at, for example) and complementary strengths (what some schools can do well and offer to other schools weak in that area).

The exercise worked. When the final plan was brought forward to the ministry for approval some months later it included, as part of an annual survey of schools, a group assessment led by a member of the evaluation team. The *Socratic Wheel* and indicators formed the basis for the group discussion, introducing and legitimizing a new culture of evaluation that includes self-directed, critical reflection and group-based planning. While not as ambitious as I had hoped, the compromise methodology struck a balance, reconciling what was too much and too little for the situation at hand. It settled in the middle of learning journeys that never end.

Beings with souls

Most development projects are limited by narrow mandates, short contracts and extremely precise deliverables. Unlike work with Rajeev in India and Farida in Bangladesh, as a consultant I had no steady partner doing the long term and truly difficult work of deeper system change. Core problems, and things discovered along the way, had to take a back seat to predefined project goals and stakeholders, and specific technical offerings.

My encounters with development projects often had these limitations, although I rarely got trapped into situations I could not live with. When CUSO, Canada's first volunteer sending organization, asked me if I would design and oversee the evaluation system for a climate change project in Cameroon, I was happy to join the team, which included the International Model Forest Secretariat, based in Yaoundé, the capital.

The project focused on diversifying agricultural production in the face of climate impacts by diversifying production and introducing ecological farming practices such as bio fertilizers and cover crops. Unlike consulting on disaster relief, education and other topics unfamiliar to me, with this project I had something substantive to offer as well as knowledge of the evaluation process.

The first meeting in communities was in a Bantu village near Kribi along the coast of Cameroon. Bantu are the dominant farming culture of central and southern Africa, although also a diverse set of sub-cultures and dialects. I knew almost nothing about the country or African cultures generally, having only spent weeks in Benin and Ghana with CIMMYT, and even less time in Kenya with IDRC.

A friend reminded me before I went to Cameroon that many who visit Africa and spend time with the people and cultures believe, after a short while, that they know and understand much of what is going on. The longer they stay, the more they realize that they know less than they thought, perhaps not understanding anything at all.

Shortly after arriving at the village meeting place, members of a different tribal community, a forest tribe called the Bagyeli (formerly

Bagyeli singers, Cameroon.

called Pygmy), took centre stage. Four Bagyeli women began to drum with short, stout sticks against a bamboo log and sing at the top of their lungs. The sound was loud, and the rhythms frantic, supporting a dance by a man dressed in a wild, hairy covering. I was confused by the intensity of the scene, uncertain whether it was a sacred ritual or light entertainment for the visiting westerners.

It was, of course, both and neither. I learned afterwards that the Bagyeli live in a slave-like relationship to the Bantu farming community that owns the land and controls local politics. The Bagyeli and other forest tribes in Cameroon such as the Baka, by all accounts the original inhabitants of the coastal and interior forests of central Africa, provide the Bantu communities they live in with access to bush meat and services such as clearing land and cleaning houses. Their own land rights are not recognized, locally or by the national government.

This situation reminded me of the Katkari in India and their vulnerability to eviction. It also explained why the Bagyeli singers did not participate in the assessments following the opening formalities. "They are not farmers," I was told, "so not really a community we can work with under this project."

I went on to organize a number of community meetings in the Kribi area and then at the more remote town of Lomie, close to the Cameroon border with the Republic of the Congo, the Central African

Republic and Gabon. We used the tool *Problem Tree* in a storytelling mode to explore the central theme of the project: food is becoming increasingly scarce.

A Bantu woman spoke about the challenge of feeding her extended family. While pounded cassava was always available, many other important food items were too expensive or in short supply. To represent the dilemma, she brought a large cooking pot from her kitchen nearby and placed it upside-down on the tree trunk image the team had traced on the hard-packed ground. She then carefully tilted the lid against the overturned pot. "People can no longer easily feed neighbours and family when they come to visit," she said, referring to wedding feasts and family gatherings.

The image of the overturned pot and lid inspired others to delve into discussion of the roots of the problem and the many effects. Factors such as proximity to a French-owned palm plantation and a new industrial port under development, both with large numbers of workers that needed to be fed, and the declining fertility of the land, provided a solid basis for food and market related interventions possible through the CUSO project. I repeated the exercise several times in other villages, gradually turning facilitation over to project team members.

One day I decided to organize a *Problem Tree* assessment in a Bagyeli village on the coast near Equatorial Guinea. Rachel Thibeault, a University of Ottawa researcher I had invited to help with the project,

Bagyeli exploring land rights challenges.

facilitated the meeting, bringing an empathetic and warm spirit to the discussion while I listened and took notes. She is an Occupational Therapist and recipient of the Order of Canada for her work with landmine survivors, war-affected children and people living with HIV/AIDS and leprosy. I was thrilled she found time to travel with me to Cameroon, and in awe of her extraordinary sensitivity to and understanding of people living with trauma. She was also a specialist in the gender dimensions of development, knowledge that helped to fill gaps in my own background.

When the discussion with the Bagyeli village community began, it immediately became evident that the participants were uninterested in the problem of food scarcity, the project core mandate. One young woman reacted angrily, saying that Bantu claims to all of the land around their villages, including the more remote forests, made it impossible for her people to follow their own burial customs. Unlike the Katkari, who bury their dead under their houses, the Bagyeli prefer to leave their loved ones buried where they die, and to then move their temporary villages to another location. Where once they moved through the forest uninhibited, now they had fewer places to go.

Rachel and I were unprepared for the challenges raised by the discussion, different from the food scarcity mandate of the CUSO project and grounded in an historical conflict between the two cultural communities. The Bagyeli were treated as an outcast community in their own territory and had become entirely dependent on the

Bantu for employment and income. They did not want to talk about current pressures on the regional food system. Instead, they wanted to talk about a possible world that did not yet exist—a place where their land rights were recognized.

All Rachel and I could do was follow the discussion with empathy, feeding back to participants the words and emotions we heard and felt. We did not try to imagine links to the project we represented or make promises other than to draw attention to the land problem with the project managers. I later tried to launch a pilot project on land rights with the Bagyeli but without a constant presence in the country or strong mandate from CUSO it quickly fell away.

The impossibility of the CUSO project to connect the dots from climate change to land rights and historical patterns of exclusion was disappointing but not surprising. Even well intentioned and well facilitated participatory development rarely adapts to fundamental challenges to pre-defined project assumptions and funded activities.

Cultural Survival, in a brilliant little illustrated booklet called *Here We Go Again*, notes that the underlying logic of development interventions is "rooted in nineteenth century colonialism (notions that 'we know best') dressed up in twentieth century 'politically correct' euphemisms." Development is often conquest by another name, tinged with deeply held attitudes of racism and the unilateral exercise of power. Changing these forces of disempowerment and disconnection is a skill the development industry has yet to acquire.

Timbuktu

The international development consulting years of my professional life were humbling but also rewarding personally. Work in Cameroon buffed my limited French enough to be able to facilitate conversations among groups of stakeholders. I couldn't carry on an extended personal conversation in French particularly well, my grammar was too faulty and my vocabulary too limited, but with help from others I could stand in front of a large group and outline the tasks at hand.

A good friend in Ottawa, Gisele, helped me prepare by teaching me key phrases and translating the bones of the instructions I planned to give. Sometimes I could deliver my lines with humour and fill in gaps with words adapted to French from Spanish.

West Africans, who have their own style of French informed by the African languages they also speak, were incredibly gracious and forgiving. It helped that the participatory processes were new to them and were focused on topics they felt strongly about. I didn't really have to perform as an orator so much as create a welcoming space they could step into for their own discussions.

In 2014, Cornell University hired me to partner with Sanou Día, a Burkinabé researcher with a PhD in nutrition and a position at the University of Ottawa. He coordinated the West Africa component of a pan-African research project focused on addressing barriers to collaboration between different sectors and government departments with policies and programs to combat malnutrition.

The stakes could not have been higher. In many parts of West Africa acute malnutrition rates exceed the World Health Organization's crisis threshold. In Mali, nutrition factors were the underlying cause of up to forty-five percent of childhood deaths, a situation that has not changed in subsequent years. I travelled twice to Mali and to Burkina Faso between 2014 and 2015 to design and facilitate inter-sector dialogue among national stakeholders.

The topic and approach reflected the growing realization in policy and development circles that chronic malnutrition, including child stunting, is a multi-faceted problem that cannot be addressed through interventions by one or two sectors or departments. Government agencies and NGOs working in silos have little impact on child stunting even if other project outcomes are achieved. More food from agriculture, even when combined with nutrition education, cannot address the interrelated causes of malnutrition when clean water, sanitation and hygiene practices are missing.

The problem of malnutrition is complex, and demands crosscutting and coordinated interventions among all relevant sectors. The same is true of the climate emergency and many other problems of the modern age. What is required of us is a deeper appreciation for the interaction of sectors and policies needed to create synergies and produce desired outcomes.

Our first workshop was in Ségou, Mali, half way between Bamako, the capital, and Timbuktou. The location was intended to come as close as possible to government regional offices in the north where malnutrition is acute, without putting participants at risk.

At the time, there was optimism among the Malians I met. The armed conflict between the central government and Tuareg factions seeking independence for the vast northern Sahel Desert region seemed to be winding down, with a cease-fire signed in 2013 and shortly afterwards a peace agreement initialled by the government and the main Tuareg rebel groups. This promised to put an end to the latest of a half dozen Tuareg rebellions dating back to the early twentieth century.

We travelled in a small caravan of cars filled with other workshop participants, arriving in Ségou before dark. French soldiers passed us heading north towards Timbuktu.

The ancient city had occupied my imagination since I was a boy. My father had drawn it to my attention when he gave me an assignment on the eve of a long trip to circumnavigate the world. He was piloting a Canadian Air Force Cosmopolitan aircraft with dignitaries on board, and told me to follow his flight path on a map. I was to create a journal with the longitude and latitude, time zone, flag and an historical site from each place on route. It was skillful parenting of a boy worried about his father's long-distance travel.

Timbuktu was one of the cities on his journey. I dearly wanted to go there after the workshop, but could not due to safety concerns.

The Tuareg, a Berber ethnic group of pastoralists, were not the problem. The United States was the problem. In 2011 Hillary Clinton, during Barack Obama's presidency, resolved to change the Libyan regime of Muammar Gaddafi and in so doing destabilized the entire Saharan region from southwestern Libya to southern Algeria, Niger, Mali and Burkina Faso. The civil war in Libya that followed the American intervention, and the collapse of the supports to regional governments Gaddafi's oil-rich regime had provided, allowed Islamic extremists linked to Al Qaeda to gain control of vast tracts of the Malian Sahara, and strike deep into neighbouring countries. Architectural artifacts of Mali's pre-colonial history—buildings and statues that had stood against the winds of the Sahara for centuries—were destroyed by extremists.

The night before the workshop a conversation with one of the participants inspired a metaphor we used to ground the event. In Mali, a *ferekene* or "public market" is where diverse goods and services are exchanged. Our goal was to facilitate exchanges and cooperation

Workshop participants, Ségou, Mali, 2014.

between different sectors and government departments—agriculture, water and sanitation, education, health, social protection and university-based research.

The centrepiece of the workshop was the SAS^2 Dialogue tool *Negotiation Fair*. It uses the mechanics of a postcard sent to each party to consider and act on offers and requests. We used the postcards to explore and coordinate work by different agencies. Dozens were sent to and from different departments and organizations, followed immediately by negotiation and agreements on specific offers and requests. The reciprocity built into the tool—the invitation to join the project of others through an offer and to receive support for your own project through a request—helped to break through the silo mentality and show the possibility of connection and cooperation.

Near the end of the event we had an unexpected visitor. The Secretary General for the Ministry of Health, and one of the highest political figures in the country, arrived unannounced during a break in the proceedings. The Malian convenor summarized the progress so far. The novelty of the methods and depth of the analysis seemed to surprise the visitor, prompting him to open himself up to frank discussions about his perspective on the barriers to implementation of a national action plan on malnutrition. The few hours he spent

Me and Anabdide Ag Tabalboulele, outside Ouagadougou, Burkina Faso.

with the group energized the discussion and linked the technical considerations we were exploring with the broader political process. Change seemed possible.

While I was unable to realize the dream of being in Timbuktu, I appreciated the colours of the desert landscape and opportunity to come to know the Malian workshop participants. I wanted to photograph them, and wondered what time of day and setting might be best. I'd read about how the history of colour science and the evolution of early photography at Kodak had worked against making portraits of Black people. The photographic chemistry and white-skinned references for colour balance failed to register details in dark skin compared to lighter skin. Cameras also interpreted black skin tones within a dark orange range, a technology imposing its own racial bias. New research shows that A.I. is repeating the same kinds of racist and technology-biased patterns.

Before we left Ségou, I invited each participant to pose against backgrounds that emphasized the range of colours characteristic of Malian desert art. Soon after, Día and I met over a late breakfast. He had been talking on the phone with his father, a medical doctor, and mentioned that I did not own a cell phone. His father was incredulous, and insisted he buy me one. It was a flip phone with no smart capabilities but perfect for checking in with local contacts and in case of an emergency.

The friendship with Día faded outside of our working relationship but I maintain links to a Malian Tuareg, Anabdide Ag Tabalboulele, who I met in a United Nations refugee camp outside of Ouagadougou in Burkina Faso. I was in the camp with the Camillian Order because they wanted to develop a stronger relationship with the Malian refugees near their community centre. They used my training in community-based emergency planning to explore how they might do that.

Anabdide had lost his leg in the Malian conflict, but brimmed with positivity and intelligence. We spent the day in the camp exploring how people living with disabilities could better prepare for new emergencies in their lives.

Later, I raised funds for him to purchase a welding machine, small anvils, hammers and snips he needed set up a welding business. He makes chairs and tables for a local market, an effort I continue to support. The money is not an expression of charity. We text occasionally—I now have a smart phone. What I get from this is the joy of being in relationship, sharing what I can and discovering how to communicate, carefully and with care.

PART THREE

BELONGING

< A Champlain Oak, Ottawa.

14

The Wealth of the Social Landscape

From the moment of my first visit to Bangladesh in the mid-1990s I was uplifted and strengthened by people involved in the *Nayakrishi Andolon* (New Agriculture Movement) and UBINIG, the organization that supports it. The movement revolves around some 300,000 farmers in different parts of Bangladesh engaged in ecological farming. Their farming practices, and the political and spiritual ideas of the region, opened my mind to a hidden and hopeful world.

Travel to Bangladesh initially focused on cultivated agricultural biodiversity—the thousands of locally adapted varieties of crops that still make up the vast majority of the seeds used in world agriculture. The topic was central to my work at IDRC on the stability and productivity of food systems. Along the way, I became fascinated with the culture, landscape and people of this improbable country.

Farmer's market near Bandarban, Bangladesh.

My passport accumulated three and sometimes four Bangladesh visas a year for several years. I learned key phrases in Bangla for introductions, food items and basic agricultural operations, creating the unwarranted impression among Bengalis that I spoke the language. There was even a room in one of the agricultural centres I stayed at known as "Daniel's room." Farhad fondly chided me recently for not visiting in some time, saying that when he sleeps in the room people ask him, "Why are you using Daniel's room?"

Every morning I would rise just before dawn and enter the common room to sing the poems of Lalon Shah, a nineteenth century philosopher who shared his insight through song in the tradition of the *Fakir* Saints of Bengal. These popular cultural and oral discourses, recognized by UNESCO as "a masterpiece of the oral and intangible heritage of humanity," challenge various forms of hierarchical oppression. Lalon criticized ideologies and perspectives on caste, class, race, patriarchy and religion that separate individuals on a material and spiritual level. Even during the height of the nationalist, anti-colonial movements in the Indian subcontinent, he continued to reject nationalism. His music mocks identity politics, which can polarize society and encourage violence.

By contrast, Lalon's words call on people to be mindful of our fundamental unity with nature and responsibilities as human beings. The songs bridge divides and connect people to the emotional and intellectual states that reflect life itself, something true of all great music.

Farhad, and his partner Farida, have carefully and lovingly reclaimed the teachings of Lalon for modern times. The daily singing ritual at the UBINIG centres acknowledges the Muslim practice of morning prayers, and provides a culturally appropriate way to start the work day for UBINIG staff living in village settings. The practice, I learned, had been established early on in UBINIG's organizational life to create safety and cultural connections for the young, unmarried men and women who work for UBINIG in villages and live at the centres.

Morning sessions draw on quiet and reflective songs, launching the day with peaceful intent. A small harmonium (reed organ) is a constant in every centre, along with the *ektara*, the single stringed musical instrument Lalon himself used to accompany his songs. In the Kushtia centre in western Bangladesh, located near Lalon's grave,

Belu (left), daughter and Roshan (centre), with other Lalon disciples sharing Lalon's teachings in song.

many more instruments enrich the musical and spiritual experience: the *tabla* drum, the two stringed *dotara*, tiny cymbals, a reed flute.

The Kushtia centre also runs a school of music for peasant children and hosts an annual gathering of thousands of Lalon disciples from all over Bangladesh. While attending one of these, I met Farhad's spiritual teacher and many other disciples. Most, as is common in the tradition, lived and travelled as male and female couples, equals in a life devoted to each other. Farhad and Farida integrated Lalon's teaching of respect for the feminine root of life into UBINIG's operations by making women's leadership central to its organizational practice.

Evening sessions in the centres accommodate a wider range of expression, including humour and storytelling. During one of the first I attended in Tangail, a region with a long tradition of weaving textiles, a tall, thin villager did a pantomime based on a trip to Paris, France. A weaver, he went there with UBINIG staff to promote traditional hand-loom products and traditional textile designs. Tailored to the needs of the fashion industry, the hand-loom textiles garner higher prices than those from mechanical looms, helping to revive a hand-craft that had been in decline.

The weaver's evening performance reproduced the movements and gestures of female models walking down a catwalk as they showed off the clothes of Parisian fashion designers. It was hilarious, conveying the outlandish qualities of the industry but also the pride of Bangladeshi weavers in having their fabrics shown with such pizazz.

Guests at the evening sessions, such as myself, were encouraged to share songs or stories from their own traditions. I brought lyrics and music from the Unitarian hymn book where Debra and I taught Sunday school for almost a decade. It too is an inclusive religious practice, with songs from many world religions.

One song in particular proved to be immensely popular among UBINIG staff and was translated and added to the flipchart of lyrics for songs at the Tangail centre. It was written by Natalie Sleeth, a composer of hymns and choral music used in a number of Methodist, United and Unitarian churches. It is normally sung as a round:

Go now in Peace, go now in Peace
May our love and care surround you
Everywhere, everywhere
You may go.

During the evening sessions I also performed magic and told children's jokes I'd learned from my brother Steve. I had experience. At about age seven I had become obsessed with magic, charging a nickel to attend a magic show in our basement in Ottawa. My most dramatic childhood trick, performed for a grade eight class, was from my father's days as a science teacher, before he had rejoined the Air Force. It required a one gallon can with a screw top, commonly used to hold cooking oil. Boiling off a small amount of water in the bottom of the can, and quickly sealing the screw top, created a vacuum inside the can. I would announce to the audience that I could crush the can from a distance, using only my mind. Properly timed, the vacuum in the can would comply.

While I never performed the trick in Bangladesh—the right can was not generally available for destruction—my tricks grew increasingly sophisticated every time I travelled to Bangladesh. I learned new ones and practised them in our front yard in Ottawa for my son Ryan and his neighborhood friends. Eventually I had a fifteen-minute repertoire of cut-and-restore rope tricks and an effective disappearing coin trick I learned from Jacques. These always ended with laughter as the secrets behind my tricks were unveiled by prying eyes or my

Me, near Kushtia, Bangladesh.

gags touched the funny bone. I felt embraced by the warm response, even loved by people I could barely communicate with in their own language. If music is a universal language, so too is laughter.

I felt not only welcome in the UBINIG centres but also at home in the rural landscape. For the most part, Bangladesh is a lush and green country, more water than land at some times of the year. The fields around Tangail in central Bangladesh, the centre I visited most often, are bound by narrow bunds and simple dirt tracks connecting people and villages. Human figures dot the landscape in all directions, collecting grass, shepherding a few goats, carrying a head-load of jute stalks or simply walking to and from their homes. These byways are literally roads to nature, so different from the roads to the cities congested with machines and toxic fumes. Everything in the rural landscape seems linked in a slow dance, bathed in the sun and embraced by humidity.

My response to the heat of rural Bangladesh was to relax and let the sweat absorb into the long cotton shirt or *kurta* Farhad had

Children of Tangail, Bangladesh.

ordered for me. In the privacy of the walled centre, I wore a *lungi*, a bolt of cotton cloth wrapped around the waist like a skirt. I loved the feeling of air moving on my legs, though I had to constantly adjust the knot to keep it from slipping off to the ground. Pants were safer when visiting and facilitating work in villages, which at first focused on the study of traditional seeds.

Seed wealth

The *Nayakrishi Andolon* is guided by ten rules. These are the foundation for what the farmers and the movement describe as the path to a joyful life, *shohoj ananda* in Bangla.

The first rule is "Keep seeds in your hands, Sisters." By keeping their own seed, farmers remain self-reliant and ensure access to a wide range of food items good to eat at different times of the year. This kind of farming is a ready-made supermarket: nutritious eating, tasty eating, varied eating, culturally satisfying eating.

In the early morning I would visit the "community seed wealth centres" established in every UBINIG centre. A sturdy bamboo and palm structure, the centres are stocked with samples of hundreds of plants adapted to local conditions. Vegetable seeds are stored in small glass bottles suspended in colourful macramé holders to maximize the storage space. Gourds are their own protective shells. Sitting on lattice shelves that allow air to circulate, each one stores a unique variety of pumpkin or squash seed.

Rice varieties are stored in clay pots made by local potters, thereby reinforcing economic ties between neighbours and different livelihoods. For longer term storage, the pots are sealed with a mixture of mud and neem leaves to control insects.

The depth of women's knowledge embodied in seed keeping is breathtaking. A knowledgeable seed caretaker can easily distinguish between dozens of different rice varieties, most of which look the same to my untrained eye. In addition to size, shape and colour, the taste of the seed and how it breaks between the teeth can be tell-tale signs of varieties distinguishing between deep water types and upland types adapted to the seasons of Bangladesh.

Seed caretakers at the centres periodically empty the pots and spread the stored seed out on woven palm mats to dry, choosing sunlight for some species, shade for others and moonlight for more delicate seed types.

The term "community seed wealth centre" is a political manifesto in and of itself. It acknowledges and communicates the collective

UBINIG poster on seed saving, Bangladesh.

origins of all agricultural seed, developed over centuries by farming communities. It also celebrates the idea of abundance or wealth for all.

By contrast, the term "seed bank" associated with the Green Revolution centres where I worked in the early 1990s, is a commercial metaphor. Seeds in these banks, including a "Doomsday Vault" inside a mountain in Norway, hold examples of most of the world's agricultural diversity "in trust for the world." While a good idea, much of what actually happens with the collective intellectual property bound up in these seeds benefits commercial seed companies with private, and sometimes nefarious, agendas.

The most common of the changes to plant traits offered by global seed companies is resistance to herbicides sold by these same companies. This binds farmers not only to purchased seed but also to the chemical products the companies make most of their profits from. It is a vertical integration of farming technologies dangerous to global food security by virtue of the control it hands over to private corporate interests and unsustainable farming technologies.

Keeping seeds in farmers' hands creates autonomy for farmers and keeps the seeds alive in other ways as well. In farmer's fields, crop genetic resources are actively managed by farmers as opposed to being frozen in time in "ex-situ" seed banks. While both are important to conservation in case of major disruptions to the global food system, seeds planted every year stay relevant to living farming systems, co-evolving in a specific environment. This is known as "in-situ" conservation of agricultural biodiversity.

The steady stream of farmers I saw at the Bangladesh seed wealth centres exchanging seed for a different variety they wanted to try, gave a human face to the technical concept. So too did the reasons they gave for their visit: to replace a seed type lost after a recent flood or untimely rains, a memory of a variety with a special taste, a search for a variety resistant to a pest. As Farida explained, "the seed types conserved by farming women in the centres and in their homes are there to support others. This is why we must keep seeds in our hands."

This rule extends as well to animal breeds. I learned that certain breeds of chickens do better at fending for themselves than others, making access to the diversity key to success. I poured over a collection of photographs of chicken breeds created by UBINIG and tried to match them to individuals I saw at homesteads by their colour, shape and distinctive feather arrangements. Try as I might, the differences were too subtle for me to do anything but guess. Still, it was fun and drove home an appreciation for animal breeds I could not have acquired from books alone.

For the poorest of farmers, chickens offer a good source of income when integrated with small fish ponds and ecological farming practices. Free range rearing of chicks reduces the use of purchased or cultivated grains: some seventy percent of their food comes from grass, cow dung and insects on the land. Open spaces also eliminate the use of antibiotics and helps manage the excreta, deposited on the land in the day and into the water of fish ponds when the chickens are roosting overhead at night. Fish eat the algae blooming from the waste, completing the cycle of nutrient outputs and inputs. "There is only one problem with our approach," Farida told me with a smile, "there are many more cocks in the flocks. They shout all day."

There is no weed on our land

When I was a young child my mother would occasionally serve me green peas from a can. When she was not looking, I would take a few in my fingers and crush them into an edge under the table, out of sight and out of my mouth. Only later, in the 1970s, when frozen peas became readily available, did I learn to tolerate green peas. While I have fond memories of other food my mother made for me, peas and green vegetables are not among them.

My experience of industrial food, common fare for North Americans, is very different from the experience of most South Asians, regardless of age and socio-economic class. Nostalgia for mother's food includes a wide range of dishes made with leafy greens, small tubers and roots, leaves of trees and hearts of stalks and grasses collected from the land or purchased in the market place. They are called *shak*, an inclusive term for delicious green curries.

The range of foods from these sources is striking. *Bhaji* is a curry made without the ubiquitous preservative turmeric and is to be eaten immediately after cooking. A *bhorta* is a preparation of tender leafy greens mixed with onion, garlic and green chilies, mashed and only

Shak, tea, *chili*, onions and salt, Kushtia, Bangladesh.

partially cooked. *Ghonto* is a dish that involves mixing cultivated and uncultivated plants in boiling water to extract the nutritional and medicinal properties of very bitter or tasteless parts of plants. The tastier plants render the others more appealing. *Charchari* is a dish of greens cooked over a very hot fire with mustard oil, small uncultivated fish and spices such as coriander or chili paste. It is ready when the combination makes a distinctive "char char" sound indicating that the water has dried up and the greens, fish and oil are properly mixed. The small fish used in the preparation are susceptible to rapid decomposition, a kind of fermentation that, when carefully monitored, enhances their nutritional qualities. I came to enjoy all of these, and to suck the juices from fish heads.

The availability and safety of *shak* is driven in large part by another rule of the *Nayakrishi Andolon*: no chemical pesticides or herbicides. "Pesticides are poison to health," proclaims one of the many t-shirts from UBINIG I collected and continue to wear at my home in Ottawa.

Hand weeding instead of spraying, while costly in time, is a viable option on the hundreds of thousands of small-scale farms spread across the Bangladesh landscape. The benefits are multi-faceted. Occupational health risks from the use of herbicides and pesticides can be severe among farm workers and their families, particularly where poor knowledge or financial circumstances limit the use of protective equipment. I had learned this first hand when Alvaro, a farmer I worked with in Mexico, died from herbicide exposure.

The risk, and the associated health costs, are avoided by firmly rejecting pesticide use. Spending scarce money on chemical inputs is also avoided. Damage to crops from pests, which can be devastating in a mono-crop, is limited by using crop diversity and mixed cropping as the first line of defence. The physical distance between infected plants of the same species created by high diversity reduces the spread of pests and diseases. If one plant is damaged, other species nearby can take their resources (water, sunlight, soil nutrients) and grow more vigorously, a response that partly compensates for losses.

Frequent crop rotation, feeding the soil to produce healthy plants, insect traps and the use of insect predators, among other techniques now common in organic and regenerative agriculture, also manage pests. They have their roots in traditional farming practices, continuously updated and improved by *Nayakrishi* farmers.

The rule against chemical pesticides, while initially focused on the harms to people's health and the health of the environment, took on an entirely new dimension when we worked with the poorest women in rural communities. Landless and with few resources other than their knowledge and labour, this segment of the rural population is routinely by-passed by development agencies. Farida told me that even finding them to interview was difficult at first. "When we asked, where are the poorest of the poor, the answer came back, '*Chak*' meaning 'out there.'"

The women were collecting their family's daily nourishment from the borders between fields, along roadsides, in small patches of forest or fallow land, in ponds and other water bodies as well as in the cultivated fields and homesteads. As they moved through a cultivated field doing weeding for the landowners, they made two piles of weeds: plants for humans and plants for animals. Both came home as part of their wages from nature.

Even the secondary parts of cultivated crops such as jute leaf, pumpkin leaf, amaranth leaves and the tender leaves of potato are collected without damaging the main crop. Animal feed and fuel are also drawn in large part from uncultivated sources. There is a steady demand for all these items in local markets during the monsoon when cultivated vegetables and protein sources are scarce and expensive.

Cleaning collected greens; young woman farmer, Bangladesh.

The research we eventually published with IDRC and Academic Foundation—*Food Sovereignty and Uncultivated Biodiversity in South Asia*—found that uncultivated food sources, including plants from the land and small fish from open water bodies, make up, on average, sixty-five percent of the food by weight consumed by the poorest twenty percent of the rural population. This is an astonishing contribution to food security in an agricultural system.

"You do not need to spend money for the uncultivated food. It is available," reported Saleha Begum, a young Bangladeshi mother responsible for feeding herself and two children while her husband was away for long periods working as a labourer.

Satheesh led similar research on the use of uncultivated plants on the dry Deccan Plateau in India, initially sponsored by IDRC and the South Asia Network on Food, Ecology and Culture (SANFEC). "What do you mean by weeds?" asked Eeramma, an older woman farmer he spoke with in the village of Shekhapur, Medak. "There is nothing like a weed in our agriculture. We eat whatever grows on our land. If we can't, our cattle eat them. There is no weed on our land."

Farming women of the Deccan use some eighty different species of uncultivated leafy greens as food. These are outstanding sources of vitamin A, calcium, zinc, magnesium, manganese, copper and phosphorous important to human health. Many of the plants collected are also rich in iron and therefore helpful in the prevention of iron deficiency anaemia, a condition especially harmful for pregnant and menstruating women and their babies.

Taslima collecting greens (*Dhabi shak*) to supplement a morning meal. Photo by Abdul Jabbar.

"This relationship with cultivated and uncultivated spaces and the gifts of nature," Farhad told me, "was initially hidden by our own biases and a narrow focus on the cultivated components of agriculture."

The relationship also places women's knowledge at the centre of agriculture. Collection and harvest merges seamlessly with the science and technology of cooking, linking plant genetic resources directly with the local cuisine system. Mothers and grandmothers are the main repositories of the knowledge of transforming plants into food, the inedible into the edible. As they light the *chula*, a conical clay stand used to concentrate fire on the cooking pot, they send the girls and boys in the household to collect the plants they want for the meal. Within fifteen to twenty minutes the items are sorted, checked for spider eggs and other insects and washed until the water is clean of dirt. The plants are cooked as soon as they are collected.

The poorest of the poor not only consume what they collect, they also exchange plants for other things they need. For reasons of class and caste, better-off women do not go out themselves to collect uncultivated items they want to add to foods prepared for their families. Instead, they exchange small amounts of rice, chili and pulses for leafy greens and small fish needed for daily meals. The uncultivated food sources are also exchanged for rice husks and rice straw, making it possible for the poor to keep hens, ducks and goats without having

Woman preparing a meal with uncultivated leafy greens, fish and rice, Bangladesh.

to purchase feed and fodder. Livestock then become a source of cash income to purchase soap, oil, salt, spices and clothes.

I was amazed to see ducks gobble down snails, shell and all, gathered from fields and border lands. The margin between the cultivated and the uncultivated, domesticated and wild, edible and inedible, had lost its sharp edge. All were gifts of nature. For this group of people, unreachable in government schemes for alleviating the deepest poverty, uncultivated plants and animals provided virtually one hundred percent of their livelihood.

Invisible expressions of social reciprocity also became apparent to me in conversation with Farhad, Satheesh and Farida. Stopped along the road overlooking flooded fields in Bangladesh, Farhad asked me, "Who do you think owns the water?" The question had never occurred to me and my response turned first to the owners of the flooded land. Then I noticed boys fishing in a culvert below the bridge and dozens of lift nets scattered across the landscape as far as I could see.

A "beel" (large depression) where uncultivated fish and edible water plants are available.

"Bangladesh is a land of water," said Farhad. "When the land floods during the monsoon, water flows in and out of the fields. This converts the private land into common property available for fishing to any member of the community."

Satheesh offered other examples of social solidarity. "It is a common sight in the Deccan to see women go with one or two goats when they leave home for weeding in someone else's field and graze them in a limited area while they are working. The farmer is happy with this arrangement because the animals deposit urine and dung on her farm, increasing the fertility of the soil." The worker need not spend any money on feed for their animals.

The castes on the margins are also a part of the system of reciprocity. "The Begaris," Satheesh wrote in our book on the topic, "are the grave diggers for the community and the Madigas do the 'undoable' jobs like disposing of cattle carcasses. They come to the field the day after the harvest and go straight to the threshing floor where any grain leftover is theirs, no questions asked. They are also entitled to go around the harvested fields collecting fallen grains, an activity that can easily result in thirty to forty kilograms of grain over a few days."

The story made me think of the 1857 painting "The Gleaners" by the French artist Jean-François Millet. It depicts class strife on a large-scale farm, a critical political message that in French culture gradually became veiled in nostalgia tinged with guilt. By the turn of the nineteenth century, the work had become part of the cultural legacy of *la France profonde*, a patriotic and touristic embrace of what France had been and what they dreamed it could become again.

Satheesh offered a very different interpretation of the nature of the relationships he experienced on the Deccan, one which was sympathetic but not blind to suffering and class or caste conflict. The ecological and social relationships built up by rural communities over the course of human history, he suggested, while imperfect, fashion a "social landscape," a kind of safety net and community builder, that ensures survival for all, no matter how difficult that may be.

This perspective, and documentation of the huge portion of food coming from uncultivated sources, had a profound impact on my understanding of agriculture and food systems. Living in the Yukon and hunting for caribou had shown me the value of "wild foods" and their role in the contemporary culture and diet of Indigenous peoples and some rural Canadians. I also knew about "famine foods" referenced by humanitarian agencies as making the difference between those who live and those who die during times of extreme hardship.

What rocked my understanding, however, was the realization that attention to uncultivated foods was not simply a preoccupation with

Small species of fish collected from common water bodies, Bangladesh.

the agriculture of the disadvantaged. Food security, the elusive goal of international development organizations across the world, was being ensured for the entire community, poor and better-off, simply by practising biodiversity-based, mixed farming in an environment free of pesticides.

The real-life outcome suggests that the totality of both cultivated and uncultivated biodiversity, and its availability, matters, not just the performance of a particular component. This conclusion is compatible with a whole range of traditional, regenerative and biodiversity-based agricultural and agroforestry systems I was familiar with in other parts of the world. These pay attention to the productivity of the whole food system and address questions of food access. Far from being an exercise in romanticism and nostalgia, it is a lens through which to examine agricultural policies and programs and question the core premise of industrial agriculture.

A food system perspective on agriculture raises a fundamental question regarding how to feed people everywhere, especially in a era when food insecurity may require us to forego eating certain global foods and better share what is already available locally. Is industrial agriculture, which destroys all life except a few privileged food sources, the best way to feed the world? Or can we begin to see nature and agriculture not as a specific set of resources, like a bushel of potatoes in a sack, but rather as a landscape that nurtures us in myriad ways.

Being ecological beings

Research on uncultivated foods, launched by Farhad and Farida in Bangladesh and deepened by Satheesh on the Deccan and by other members of SANFEC in Nepal, Pakistan and Sri Lanka, is the most original I have had the privilege to be part of. My skills in participatory action research were not really called upon as most of the field work was undertaken by others, using conventional methods and their own ways of engaging with local people. My contributions were limited mainly to writing up and sharing the findings, including placing the work in the context of the literature on food security.

The impact on me, however, took on a whole new dimension when I began to engage with Farhad in discussions on how the practices of *Nayakrishi* farmers relate to the spiritual teachings of Lalon, the nineteenth century Bengali philosopher. Farhad's interpretation of the bridge between agriculture, modernity and the human experience, shared with me in conversations over the course of two decades, clicked into place with my own world view.

What we could see from the real-life experiments of *Nayakrishi* farmers was that waste has no existence in nature. Living things mobilize the available sunlight and soil fertility and balance the interplay of all organisms, like the relationship between the snake and the mongoose, the rabbit and the fox. Surface water, flowing in and out again, creates a new social landscape for fish, fishers and fertilized soil. Uncultivated plants become food or fodder and unused parts become compost or fuel.

Farhad put the broader statement of facts this way:

> *Nothing separates the material world from itself. This includes the human body we inhabit in nature, and are therefore part of. Nayakrishi farming is a powerful metaphor for this way of being and belonging in the world, erasing the separation of nature and mind, self and the world about us.*
>
> *The practical dimensions of non-separation and the intimate relationship of all things are profound, elevating to another level everything we do as individuals and as a society to create a sustainable and just world. When you are taking your food, consider how it is related to nature and to others, what you are taking, from whom you are taking and how it was produced. When you are in a dwelling, your house, know how your house was built and what this has destroyed. When developing and using a smart phone, consider how this is related to nature and others. Is it harming or not harming?*
>
> *The realization that we are part of nature and that nature is part of us is a practice through which we evoke the kind of subjectivity we want to cultivate within ourselves and within our society. That is what we need to bring forward, what has been lost, a kind of ecological ethics, in contrast to the modern industrial path.*

Relating to nature simply as a resource to be extracted and consumed has never been an organizing principle in my life. A commitment to

Farhad resting during a boat trip to Kushtia, Bangladesh.

voluntary simplicity, self-provisioning and careful food choices, first considered when I lived in the Yukon, has been central to my adult experience.

Treating nature as something sacred but external to me, a common perspective of Western science, religion and romantic traditions in art, is also a misunderstanding of the relationship. I moved beyond this when cancer threatened to take my life. Meditation and the visualization of the healing process drew me directly to the unity of my life with nature. These experiences helped me eliminate vestiges of both dualistic and romantic understandings of my belonging in the world.

What I have gained from a relationship with the *Nayakrishi* and with Farhad is a sharper question: What are my responsibilities, both for living my life but also creating my community and how I belong in the world? What do I *do* when I realize I *am* nature? What change in myself and my engagement with the world emerges when I see that the boundary between the self, the other and nature is erased, when I realize that there is no weed on the land separating me from myself?

15

Polar Bear Country

The experience of belonging to Canada, my place of birth and heritage, has rarely been difficult for me. As a white man from a middle-class family and with an advanced university degree, I face none of the barriers of racialized or under-resourced communities. I enjoy all of the benefits the state affords to citizens.

My family roots in Canada are deep. My great, great, great Grandmother Honora O'Grady came to the Ottawa area from Tipperary in central Ireland in 1820 with eight sons but no husband and no daughters. I can't imagine what this was like for her, to leave her home and broader family ties, but the act of courage gave rise to the Canadian lineage of my mother. It remained a family of Irish Catholics until she married my father, a Scottish Presbyterian with the ancestral name MacRae blended into the Buckles monicker after arriving in Canada in the 1830s. My DNA, mapped by a popular ancestry service, is 99.4 percent Irish and British Isles. The rest is Western European.

Child's toy on the ice.

There is no doubt about my settler status in Canada. While based on a longer residency than most Canadian anglophones, my ancestors are not from the lands where I make my home. These were stolen from the original peoples of North America, under European laws and in the name of European monarchs. In Canada, armies and settlers gave their bodies to enforce the thievery through conquest and possession. Only after the Royal Proclamation of 1763, issued by King George III following the surrender of North American territories by France to Britain, did thievery give way to negotiated agreements, all of which were subsequently broken in one way or another.

The personal implication of this history was not something I had any inkling of growing up in various communities in Canada. Indigenous people and communities were absent from my childhood experience of the world, even though embedded in the landscape. Now I can acknowledge my debt to the original peoples of this land.

I was born in Tkaronto (Toronto) on the lands of the Mississaugas of the Credit, first signed over to the Crown in 1787 but not finalized until 2010.

I then spent two years as a toddler on Cree and Saulteaux (Plains Ojibwe) lands, claimed by English royal charter in 1670 by King Charles II of England and handed over to his cousin, Prince Rupert of the Rhine and first governor of the Hudson's Bay Company. The transaction happened without any consideration of rightful users of the land.

When "Rupert's Land" was transferred, for a large fee, to the newly formed Government of Canada in 1869, the Métis people of Red River, whose territory included Moose Jaw, Saskatchewan where my father was assigned to an Air Force base, resisted. The Red River Rebellion ended when the Assiniboia provisional government led by Louis Riel negotiated an agreement with Canada and entered Confederation as the province of Manitoba. Riel's death by hanging came a few years later.

Other Indigenous territories where I lived as a settler Canadian include the Tyendinaga Mohawk Territory on the Bay of Quinte where I went to grade school, the Haudenosaunee (People of the Longhouse) in present day Montreal where I first studied Fine Arts, the Tr'ondëk Hwëch'in of the central Yukon, and the Anishinaabe, an

Algonquin speaking people living up and down the Ottawa River in eastern Ontario and western Quebec. My few years as a teenager in southern Germany, and a decade in Mexico, were the only periods of my life when I did not benefit from colonialism through settler citizenship.

As an anthropologist, trained in the 1980s, the need to decolonize research practice had not really penetrated the discipline. I could see for myself what displacement from the land had done to the Tr'ondëk Hwëch'in of Dawson City, but I had a much deeper knowledge of Indigenous colonial experiences in Mexico and India than I did for the places I grew up in and lived in for most of my life.

This shifted for me partly in response to the Truth and Reconciliation Commission led by Murray Sinclair, which brought the abuses of the residential school system into sharp focus for all Canadians through tens of thousands of hours of testimony by residential school survivors, their families and their communities. The ninety-four Calls to Action issued by the commission also provided a roadmap for ways to redress the legacy of residential schools and foster the process of Canadian reconciliation with Indigenous peoples. Understanding and acknowledging the traditional territories of Canada's First Nations, and respecting treaty rights, are key steps on that path.

A new awareness of Indigenous political sovereignty and Indigenous identity was brought to life for me by my wife's experience. As a young woman and a feminist, she changed her French-Canadian name Pilon to Huron, after the Great Lake, as a way to honour her great grandmother, an Anishinaabe of the Manitoulin Island region of Ontario. This ancestor, Marianne Bemanakinang, had lost her Indigenous rights when in 1875 she married a non-Indigenous man, Debra's great grandfather, Francois Xavier Pilon.

A series of court rulings and legislative amendments ultimately eliminated sex discrimination under the Indian Act—the same rule did not apply to Indigenous men that married non-Indigenous women—making it possible for Debra to register for Indian status, which she did in 2022.

In the late 2010s, Debra spent several years as an ally to Algonquin leadership opposing the commercial development of islands in the Ottawa River a few hundred metres above Parliament Hill. The islands surround *Akikpuatik* Falls (Pipe Bowl Falls), a natural feature of the Ottawa River that rivalled Niagara Falls in grandeur until it was dammed in the early twentieth century to power industrial plants built there. In the 1990s, the islands were slated to be turned over to the Algonquins, who considered the site sacred and in need of decontamination from its industrial uses. William Commanda, an Algonquin elder, spiritual leader, environmental advocate, and recipient of the Order of Canada, had championed the vision for decades.

The struggle was picked up after Commanda died by Douglas Cardinal, the Blackfoot architect of the Canadian Museum of History (Gatineau) and the National Museum of the American Indian (Washington, D.C.). Then, in 2012, a Conservative Federal Government rejected those plans, allowing the sale of the land to a private company for condominium development. Debra helped with communications and mobilization of opposition among settler allies.

The challenges posed by the political and personal projects of Indigenous peoples brought into focus my own experience and responsibilities as a settler. Decolonization, I realized, means not only demanding that the Canadian government honour the treaties but also changing my own understanding and way of being in relation to Indigenous peoples.

Up until that time, I had largely avoided working with Indigenous communities closer to home, partly because my networks were international and partly because I was fearful. Funding for consultants is often motivated by priorities of the Canadian government, not the Band Council. I had been warned by other consultants that Indian Band leadership could be uncommitted to the task and capricious with the hired help. I did not want to run the risk of having my work sit on a shelf. While this can happen with any consultant-client relationship, I did not go looking for consulting work with Canadian Indigenous organizations. Eventually, though, I realized that without risking a deeper relationship I could not go very far on the path of reconciliation and belonging.

A good way to organize research

In late October 2016, I was presented with an opportunity to face my fears. I got a call from George, a consultant with Indigenous ancestry. He was the main advisor and fund raiser for the Chief of Eagle

Sound, a northerly First Nation.[1] He invited me to work with him on a housing policy for the community. The experience that unfolded over a period of two years drew me into a relationship with individuals and community life that was both sweet and bitter, deepening my understanding of dynamics endemic to Indigenous history in Canada and my responsibilities as a settler ally.

The journey started with a Bearskin Airlines flight from Thunder Bay to Eagle Sound, with stops in Sioux Lookout and Pickle Lake. Winter already held the landscape in its grip, giving the frozen ponds and stands of Black spruce a uniformity belying the richness of the flora and fauna on the Hudson Bay floodplain below. It is the world's largest continuous wetland, from Manitoba to Quebec, and habitat for millions of migratory birds. I love swamps and was excited by the prospect of getting to know this one.

No one met us at the airport, breaking with my experience in the Global South where partners made sure I arrived safely from the airport to a hotel. George arranged a ride to town, depositing us at the band-run hotel in time to make a quick dash to the Northern Store to buy food for the next few days. There were no restaurants in town. The collective kitchen in the hotel, equipped with a few battered pots and pans and a fridge half-filled with spoiled food left behind by previous guests, was warm. I had eye covers to keep out light from the porch at night and ear plugs to muffle the nighttime barking of dogs. The view from the hotel second floor was filled with the rusted hulks of front-end loaders and broken-down dump trucks next to the community machine shop. A brand new school, the heart of the community, could be seen down the road, bordered to the far side by a community ice rink.

The Cree community of Eagle Sound was established as a result of Treaty 9, a post-Confederation arrangement to make way for white settlement and resource development in Northern Ontario. It consolidated Swampy Cree populations dispersed on the Hudson Bay plain and eventually deposited them in a place where shipping access was possible. Beluga whales and ring seals from Hudson Bay gather nearby in late summer while polar bears move north along the open shoreline waiting for the salt water bay to freeze.

---

1 The names of individuals and places have been changed to make them less easily identified.

Swampy Cree were the first to settle in the community, but three other Cree and Ojibwe linguistic and cultural communities, from other places in Manitoba and Northwestern Ontario, had also become part of the Indian Band. These linguistic and kinship differences accentuated tensions in a community connected to the wider world only by air and a seasonal winter road.

Before I accepted the job, I asked George what the chief expected out of me. I wanted to be sure that the invitation was genuine, and potentially useful. When we met the next day, Chief Matthew introduced me to members of the Band Council in the office and gave me a stack of letters. Some dated to the previous council, but most were from the six months he had been in office. They asked him for access to new housing, and explained why. "My sons can't be sleeping in our closet forever as they are growing up each day," wrote one mother. Another young couple with a baby wrote, "My mom is trying to kick us out constantly." And a young man noted "I sleep in the living room where there is no privacy or rest."

He then gave me a tour of the construction site in town where new houses were going up. Progress had been slow, but several were nearing completion. Two pre-fabricated houses delivered over the winter road were sitting on foundations but not yet hooked up to sewer and water, or electricity. The promise of spring construction of four more houses had created excitement in the community. The housing supply was growing, financed by a Canadian government shamed into acting on this perennial problem.

The challenge now, he said, was finding a way to assign houses without creating conflict within the community. People were constantly asking him and other council members who was going to get what house, making it difficult for him to focus on other things he wanted to get done. Every Band Council election cycle, he said, was rife with demands for housing and offers of votes in exchange. What he needed from me was a housing policy and governance structure that was fair and could withstand community scrutiny.

I was thrilled with the mandate. I also felt up to the task. Three decades of experience developing and delivering participatory and action-oriented research gave me confidence that I could design a methodology fit to purpose and appropriate to the cultural context. The tools of my trade and general approach to consulting seemed

A community hall prepared for a meeting to discuss housing challenges and opportunities.

made to order, with many of the features recommended by Indigenous scholars: do useful research organized in a culturally appropriate way.

To start, I met with dozens of members of the community, including Band Council, staff in the office, construction workers on the housing site, health workers and school teachers (both Indigenous and visiting non-Indigenous). It was easy to talk with them about housing. Housing was in a crisis, as it is in many First Nations in the Canadian north, and affected everyone and everything, to some degree.

Along the way, I met Bertha, a woman in the Band Office responsible for maps and other things. She was also the senior Canadian Ranger in the community, a cadre of volunteer reservists with the Canadian Armed Forces that act as a local counterpart for the Coast Guard and Canadian military throughout Canada's North. The Canadian Rangers assist in search and rescue efforts, respond to forest fires and floods, and conduct other activities in Canada's sparsely settled regions.

When I told her I wanted to know how many houses there were in the community and how many people lived in each house, she opened an Excel file on her desktop. It contained a partial list of households and houses in the community. "I want to be sure no one is left behind if we have to evacuate the whole town," she said. A call for evacuation could be triggered by flooding, a forest fire or contamination of the town's water supply, incidents that are endemic in Indigenous communities across Northern Ontario.

We struck a deal to help each other, sharing my basic knowledge of how to do a community census and manage a spreadsheet with her knowledge of the households and her head start on a database. We began to construct a list of houses and occupants, including gender, age and the number of rooms in each house. Facebook Messenger was her go-to tool for getting details, drawing on her network of families in the community. Such an exercise had never been done in the community before.

My interest in a housing census, while not normally a priority in work I had been doing internationally, was prompted by my reading of the literature on housing in Canada and discovery of the National Housing Standard. It defines a standard of occupancy based on common sense notions that, above a certain age, girls shouldn't sleep in the same bedroom as boys, and teens and couples should sleep in rooms separate from their parents and grandparents. Measures of the degree of overcrowding, as defined by the standard of occupancy, could provide an independent basis for ranking housing needs.

Overcrowding was not the only complaint about housing I heard from people. Early in the process I sat down with a group of eight or so young people signed up for a course on basic carpentry, and invited them to draw a floor plan of their house. They took their time, drawing images on quality paper and with quality art pencils that showed who slept where and noting structural problems with their house: the presence of mold, dishevelled foundations, water failures, sewage failures and electrical failures.

Chief Matthew had no time to be directly involved in the project process, but he had set up the meeting with the youth and supported Bertha's contribution. He also agreed to convene a committee of five women to work with me, including a hunter, a health worker, a Band Office administrator, a young single mother and an elder. We reviewed the database together and corrected errors. We also discussed the National Housing Standard using a set of house floor plans I made from art boards and toy wooden figurines from my son's time at the Rudolf Steiner school. The set, which I gave to the committee, made it easy to map out and visualize different housing arrangements and compare one household to another and to the national standard.

Gradually, between the database and discussions with households, we built up a picture of the housing situation in the community, determining that 248 people, more than half of the population, lived in housing that did not meet national housing standards for occupancy. Along the way, many people commented on how over-crowding and dilapidated houses created conflict between generations, spread respiratory illnesses and added to the stress and depression of isolation and unemployment.

Some health workers from the community quietly raised concerns that living arrangements including unrelated men posed risks to children and elders, especially when the household was rocked by substance abuse. There was a duty of care, they said, that should be considered when allocating new housing.

Walking in the community, from the hotel to the Band Office, the Northern Store and the various new housing projects in town, occasionally resulted in an unplanned conversation. Some people asked what role I might be playing in the allocation of houses. I assured them that my task was to develop a policy, selection criteria and a process for making decisions on the allocation of houses, and that the Chief and Council were in charge. Still, the question made it clear to me that I was exercising power in the context of an issue of vital importance to many.

To avoid misunderstandings, I prepared a short report on the project goals and what I had heard to date. My wife, a specialist in the principles of plain language communication, edited and formatted the report to make it very easy to read. I then hired and trained several youth and unemployed people I had met to distribute the report to every house and conduct a short survey on key housing problems and views on the draft criteria and governance options. Again, this was something that had never been done in the community.

A community meeting, convened on the heels of the report and survey, invited people to discuss what the Band Council should do to make sure the selection process operated "in a good way." The phrase and full question, written in English and in Cree syllabics, reflected a key concept in Cree and Ojibwa culture known as *mino bimaaduziiwin*, the good life or good way to be. Many people came to the meeting to review maps and floor plans and eat pizza George brought in by air for the occasion. Using a version of the tool *The Socratic Wheel*, I facilitated a group discussion of the proposed criteria for scoring household housing needs and a separate exercise focused on two governance options.

As a final step, I hired my son Ryan to develop a formula for the spreadsheet that could rank households from the most crowded to the least crowded. The ranking was based on the data showing the number of bedrooms in each house in the community and the number of house occupants by gender, age and relationship. His work created a list of households ordered by the degree of overcrowding, presented to the Chief and Council. This was a starting point from which they could make a final determination.

The project design and implementation felt to me like a skillful performance, making the most of my expertise and facilitation skills. The problem had been defined by Indigenous leadership and the research had been organized in a good way: attention to voices from different sections of the community with particular expertise, group-based analysis distributed across various divides and procedures that report back to the community respectfully. There was even a capacity building effect as Bertha developed her skills with database management and others involved came to understand the mechanics of the National Housing Standard and learned how to explain it to others.

The presentation also landed nicely with Chief Matthew, confirming his own thinking about where the need was greatest. He hesitated, however, to draw conclusions which did not consider house condition and other factors such as the vulnerability of household members, factors we had noted but not addressed through the ranking exercise. The database couldn't capture sudden changes in household arrangements either, as families reconfigured on their own and some left for points south. These adjustments, I assured him, was where a housing committee, such as the group of women I had been working with, would come in handy. Let's wait and see, he replied.

Before leaving town at the end of my third trip to Eagle Sound, I saw a flyer at the Northern Store inviting people to a reception in honour of a middle-aged man who had died alone on the streets of Thunder Bay a year earlier. All are welcome, it said. When I arrived at the community hall, forty or more people were already gathered. Children ran in and out of the building, elders sat at tables arranged in rows and other adults stood in small groups near the kitchen. A map of the village I had created a few days earlier still hung on one of the walls. It showed the streets of the community, major landmarks and new houses planned by the Band. A woman at the door, the elder sister of the deceased, welcomed me in with a broad smile and offer of food. Pots of moose stew, caribou and goose were on the table, along with bannock. I stepped in thinking, "I like this place. I want to come back."

Standing with people

Photography was a challenge in Eagle Sound. The landscape, especially in the fall and winter when I was there most often, is expansive, with a limitless horizon on land. I had trouble finding features to create contrast with the horizontal lines.

Picture making in town presented a different problem. While rusted out relics of trucks, tilted houses and yards filled with random objects provided visual interest, I did not want to perpetuate in images the stereotype of a disordered Indigenous community. I simply didn't understand the order within.

People pictures became my main outlet, although these too were constrained by the formality of group shots in the Band Office. The intimacy needed for true portraits evaded me.

A few months after handing in my final report on the housing policy, George called me with news that the Band had secured a grant from a foundation to help young mothers complete high school. A pregnancy would typically end schooling for teenage women in the community, making them ineligible for most employment opportunities. Many turned to their families and government supports for survival. Their children, the project proposal suggested, were also at risk of not doing well in school, perpetuating "a cycle of poverty" for the Cree community.

I read the proposal with interest, intrigued by plans to use a prize-winning method for student-centred learning developed in India and to create and deliver Indigenous curriculum for self-paced learning on-line. A novel approach to evaluation, based in part on SAS^2 tools, was also planned, combining the Cree concept of *bimaaduziiwin*, working in a good way, with Western and developing world tools to "break the cycle." The proposal, written by George, used strong language asserting Cree perspectives and Cree leadership.

At George's invitation, I travelled to Toronto to meet Chief Matthew and the new project team during a workshop organized by the foundation for all projects funded that year. "If you join us as the evaluator," George said, "we'll be a dream team," a prospect I began to doubt soon after I met the others.

One consultant in the team, a specialist in on-line learning, was a bright and positive new Canadian living in Toronto. Over lunch, she made it clear that she did not intend to travel to the community because of the cold and her vegetarian food requirements. Her contributions, she said, would be made remotely by putting content together for delivery through a customized Internet program. Her husband, a retired accountant, would coordinate while George looked for a full-time local coordinator. The final member of the team, and the only one living in Eagle Sound, was a young woman who was herself struggling to complete high school.

None of the team members had direct experience with the Ontario high school curriculum or detailed knowledge of the requisites and procedures leading to graduation in the province. Still, I decided to proceed, hoping that an additional local hire, and Chief Matthew's enthusiasm for the project, would carry the day.

I worked cordially with the implementation team over the first nine months of the project, engaging with the young mothers involved and providing the project with quick feedback on initial responses and possible project adjustments, as called for by the evaluation terms of reference. Given the limited presence of the Toronto team in Eagle Sound, I tried to compensate by organizing local meetings with stakeholders, doing local research and reporting back my findings.

It became immediately evident that the project plans to provide support, resources and mentoring were almost completely disconnected from the needs of young mothers in the community and the sets of resources already available to them. The most obvious personal barrier to graduation—access to child care so students could spend time studying—had not been addressed at all. Family networks might have sufficed for some single mothers, but many families were already strained by multiple demands and responsibilities. These constraints had driven the young women out of school in the first place.

Access to appropriate educational resources, the main project offering, was not needed at all. The community was equipped with a well-stocked and well-run Internet high school and a highly competent Indigenous teacher and teacher's assistant. Young adults beyond a certain age could not register there as regular students, but the teacher offered to open the facility after normal hours and mentor a limited number of students for a modest fee. This local resource lay untapped.

There was also an adult high school program and building in the community run by the regional First Nation government, free to use and with ample computers and hours available for adult students to do self-paced study. Both schools, after years of effort by educators and negotiations with the Ontario Ministry of Education, had adapted the official curriculum to the context of life in Indigenous communities in northwestern Ontario, and produced plain language workbooks for all subjects needed. Online and paper-based resources were available, and culturally sensitive, but ignored by the project.

Jordan's Principle, a federal program set up to respond to urgent needs of Indigenous children, including access to educational supports, was also present in the community. The local coordinator was looking for ways to contribute but even after months had not been approached by the project team.

From these explorations, and interviews with the people involved, I came to realize that the project had been developed and funded in a vacuum. Many, including the elementary school principal and head of the adult education program, had not met any of the project leads and knew nothing about what the project had to offer.

I said to George that the community suffered from an abundance of projects and a poverty of coordination. As the key adviser to Chief Matthew and writer of many project proposals, he was partly responsible for this situation.

I also realized from meetings with the young mothers that the project had failed to do any direct assessment of their educational history or their personal strengths and weaknesses as students. Again, I tried to compensate for the poor background research, facilitating an individualized timeline of the path to graduation for each of the registered students and using the *Socratic Wheel* tool to set individual learning goals and form peer-to-peer learning teams. It was a lot of fun to do this work, bringing me into the lives of eight young mothers in the community and learning about the situations of others.

Discussions with the women reinforced my initial intuition about the strategic value of child care, and generated ideas for solutions.

Young mothers assessing their study skills and looking for peer support.

If the Band could not offer day care, then at least the project could redirect some of its resources to pay family members a minimum wage to care for children while the mother was at one of the high schools studying. The women suggested a simple way to avoid abuses: a sign-in and sign-out sheet at the school, validated by the teacher. It could track hours against which payments for child care could be made.

The proposals and early reports on findings were rejected by the consulting leads in Toronto who continued to coordinate the project. George was rarely in the community, and when he was, he was focused on other projects he was developing for the chief. He drew a part-time salary for coordination, but deferred to the Toronto consultants and left much of the day to day operation of the project to the young assistant coordinator.

For her part, the assistant coordinator struggled to connect to the other women in the program, many of whom were older than her and more experienced.

What I initially thought was resistance to project change from the Toronto consultants turned to hostility when I asked them to give me direct access to the online learning tools they were developing for the students. A significant part of the project budget was dedicated to this activity, sub-contracted, I came to learn, to a consulting firm also owned by the couple. I wanted to see, precisely, what content had been generated and how compatible it was with the requirements of the Ontario high school curriculum. Again, my request was denied and my need to know these details challenged.

The situation prompted me to begin to act more as an auditor than a gentle evaluator charged with organizing local meetings and quantifying participation in the project, the role the consultants expected of me. I began to dig into the detailed project plans and spending of the budget, realizing that $200,000, more than fifty percent of the grant, was directed to outside parties, including my own evaluation fees. I couldn't decide if the consultants were scammers or arrogant do-gooders with an unshakable belief in the rightness of their experience, far from First Nations' realities and the Canadian educational system.

After about eight months, I organized an evaluation session with the project participants to take stock of progress to date. A local coordinator had still not been hired, leaving the task of convening the meeting and co-facilitating the evaluation to the assistant coordinator. No other team members came.

What had started for me as frustration over huge errors in the project design grew on that visit into heart break and anger. I had set up a Facebook account when I first started working in Eagle Sound because it was the most reliable and most common means of communication

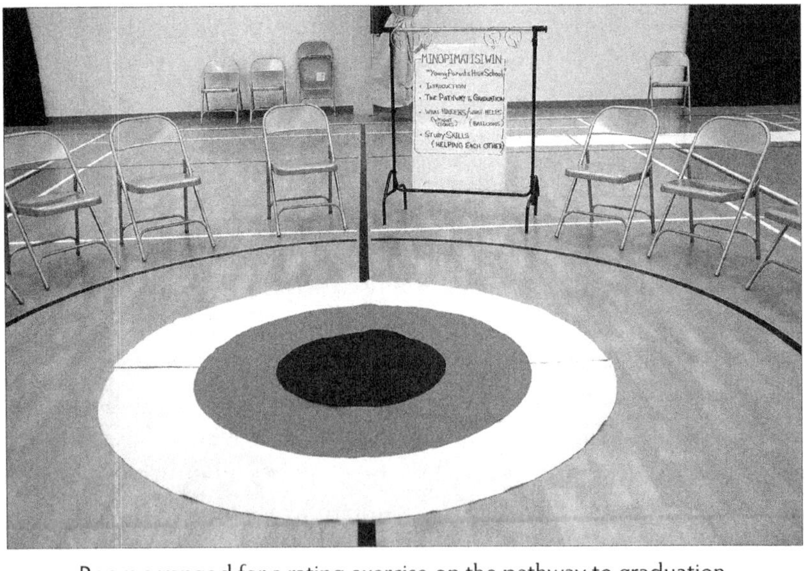

Room arranged for a rating exercise on the pathway to graduation.

in town. My cell phone didn't work because my provider had no coverage in the community, so I relied on Wi-Fi and Facebook Messenger to check in with people when I was in town and at home in Ottawa. One friend on the account, a young woman working on her high school diploma, posted to her own page that she was struggling and wondered what was wrong with her. Two other participants made similar comments to me during the evaluation meetings. "A special project has been set up for me, but I can't seem to make any progress at all. I feel like a failure," one said.

The sentiment, conveyed with tears on another occasion by a woman struggling with addictions, touched my heart and boiled my blood. While my relationship with these young women was limited by time and social distance, I had come to appreciate how difficult life was for many in the community. I'd been in their homes, been offered tea and snacks and taken photographs of young mothers and their children, which I returned to them as 4 x 8 prints. I knew that poverty and personal struggles were widespread and that self-esteem was low. To witness it being knocked down even further by a feeling that they were at fault was something I could not abide. While I could tolerate poor project design and wasted project resources, new harm to vulnerable people—feelings of shame, guilt, inadequacy—was another matter.

My interim report, and a brief discussion with a Council member, detailed my concerns and described the potential harm from what was looking more and more likely to be complete project failure. I called for concerted attention to the child care gap and stronger local coordination with other education resources and people in the community.

I also called George to say that I would not submit my report directly to the funder because I didn't want to embarrass or foreclose the Chief's options with the foundation. Even though I was an external evaluator, I didn't want to exercise undue influence over the future of the project, as the Toronto consultants were doing. This, I felt, would be another form of settler re-colonization. What if I was wrong about the direction and problems of the project?

A few weeks later I received a polite letter from Chief Matthew announcing a council decision to completely rework the project, including the role of evaluation. They were starting over, he said, and asked me to wrap up any outstanding business. It meant that I would be out of work, but I didn't argue with him. I was never invited back.

Reconciliation and belonging

Being cut off from the community affected me deeply. I asked myself, what had I missed? What could I have done differently? I lingered on my Facebook account for a time, following the posts of people I had come to know. I struggled to hold on to the good in both experiences, one that had produced an outcome on housing welcomed by Indigenous leadership and the other uncovering a situation of incompetence and abuse of power I couldn't ignore. I didn't want the negativity of one to completely displace the positivity of the other. After a few months, however, I lost hope that there might be some rapprochement with George and Chief Matthew.

During the COVID-19 years that followed I wanted to call George and ask him what became of the project. Did they hire a completely new team or simply continue without me? We had parted amicably, with him simply lamenting that it was too bad his dream team hadn't worked out.

I didn't call. I knew that I had been respectful and that I had done what I thought was true and necessary. As the sadness faded, I also realized that my relationship with the community and the people I came to know did not need to be validated by the outcomes of my work. What was demanded of me, and is at the heart of reconciliation, is to have the courage to join Indigenous projects and be "in relation" with Indigenous worlds and people. To put it more simply, all that is needed is to stand with people and to love unconditionally.

On my last visit to Eagle Sound, before receiving the letter of dismissal, Chief Matthew asked me if I had ever seen a polar bear in the wild. I hadn't, even though the previous year I had contributed to a feasibility study for a project to bring polar bear tourism to the community. It was a long-standing dream of the Chief, and a recurring idea for local economic development. Eagle Sound has many natural and cultural assets to build from.

My assessment of the infrastructure (lodging and access to food) needed to accommodate dozens of well-heeled tourists was not encouraging, and some hunters I interviewed were not supportive of the idea. They knew that any conflict between people and a polar bear would inevitably end with the bear dead. Between these two problems, I couldn't conclude that polar bear tourism was a sound idea, although my views got buried in more favourable assessments by other consultants.

The day before I was slated to leave was late fall, with snow on the ground but no ice yet on Hudson Bay. Bears were wandering the coast, I'd been told, waiting for very cold temperatures to freeze the salt water and give them access to seals, their main source of food. Chief Matthew loaned me an all-terrain vehicle (ATV) and asked John, a young man in the office, to take me out for a look.

John had recently returned to Eagle Sound after a stint in the army and then time living on the street in Toronto. He had dried out from addictions and returned home to continue his healing. We had already bonded over photography, prompted by seeing on Facebook a video he had made of the Northern Lights. It was spectacular and technically professional.

I had invited him to contribute to the evaluation work I was doing for the education project by interviewing and video-taping young mothers talking about their experiences. He had agreed, but not yet started by the time my involvement ended abruptly.

On my last day, he piloted his snowmobile along the snow-covered coastal trail while I followed on the ATV. When the snow got deeper, I parked and climbed on behind him. He wanted to cross a small stream that had not frozen over completely and knew that the ATV

John on his snow machine.

could not pass. With a smooth turn to build up speed, he piloted safely across until we came to another unfrozen river too wide to breach.

When we dismounted again, we saw polar bear prints in the snow. They were twice the size of my heavy gloves and paralleled with tracks he identified as wolf and mink.

We turned back, stopping briefly while I climbed back on the ATV and looked out across a narrow strip of open water and a jumble of ice and rock on the far side. There, walking along the opposite shore, was a polar bear. It stopped at the sound of our machines, stood on a rock outcrop and shifted its head back and forth trying to see what was making the noise. After what seemed to me like a pause of recognition, it dropped to all fours and continued up the coast.

John laughed. "I'm supposed to be the bear spotter here," he said. I knew, however, that he was home and I was not. Both he and the polar bear were the ones waiting for the ice to come.

16

The Ten Ox Herding Pictures

For a dozen years, between 2011 and the current date, I have been on a path of action and self-discovery in my own neighbourhood and city. It centres on my love of trees, a common form of nostalgia in this age of steel.

Every fall I walk through a nearby degraded woodland with a bag of acorns and a steel pole to drive a hole in the ground and drop in a seed, channelling Jean Giono's allegorical story *The Man Who Planted Trees*. I have a tree nursery in my back yard and distribute saplings to any that want them. Among neighbours, we map the trees in the neighbourhood, recording what we have and what we are losing in the way of urban tree canopy. Together, we organize community walks to visit and celebrate the ancient trees on our streets and in the woods nearby. On a de-paved street, we plant and care for a forest of saplings and a pollinator garden, doing what we can to bring beauty and nature into the city.

A heritage burr oak, Ottawa, Canada. Photo by Chris Osler.

There is also struggle. Development industry greed tries to turn every urban space into profit, without regard for the future of neighbourhoods stripped of living things. Gaps and limitations in municipal policies are big enough to drive a logging truck through. City staff, often passionate and knowledgeable, are worn down or worn out by the mantra of risk aversion, theirs and that of political leaders.

In response, we call out violations and rail against political leadership in the city. We mobilize people to demand action on the twin climate and affordable housing emergencies, and engage each other in thinking through the policies needed to build a liveable, inclusive and sustainable city.

For years, Debra gave as much of herself to the cause as I did, adding the fire in her belly that gives our actions added emotional force and momentum.

My journey into municipal politics and local activism did not proceed in a straight line. Nor did it follow the logic of my work-life as an anthropologist, researcher and facilitator. I did not set out deliberately and methodically to trace a path to greater understanding of municipal problems and better policies. Mostly, I reacted to abuses and local harms, letting my intuition and experience guide me from one response to another. Sometimes I felt like an insect fluttering helplessly on a light bulb. At other times, I moved like a shark smelling blood.

The experience has been a spiral of successes and failures, full of optimism but also tainted with frustration, struggle and even despair. The themes of participatory action research developed throughout this memoir are present here as well: What goals do we pay attention to and from whose point of view? How do we engage with people to co-construct a better future?

Many of the situations affecting my partners and friends in India, Honduras and Cameroon—racism, abuses of power, violence—are also here in my own backyard. So too is human connection to nature, others and the interior life. Hope is everywhere.

I tell this part of my story through the metaphor of the *Ten Ox Herding Pictures*, a twelfth century series of folk images accompanied by poems or commentary that depict the Zen path of self-development and self-realization. The ox herder is on a quest to find the essential self, a process represented by taming the ox—the mind. Poems on the different stages from Master Kusan's book *The Way of Korean Zen* accompany the account.

My quest started with a protest.

1. Searching for the ox

High mountains, deep waters, and a dense jungle of grass—

However much you try, the way to proceed remains unclear!

To alleviate this sense of frustration, listen to the chirping of cicadas.

It is May 2, 2011. I'm standing on the sidewalk, camera in hand, watching as an arborist climbs a massive oak in a backyard a few blocks from my own. Two men approach and stand on either side of me, each twice my weight and half my age. One man says, "We are here to make sure you don't go onto Mr. X's property while the tree is being cut down." My assurances don't seem to be enough. They don't move from their posts except to reposition themselves as close to me as they can. I move along the sidewalk to take pictures of the tree and the work of the arborist.

Two police cars arrive. Officers step out to talk with Mr. X as he sits behind tinted windows in his truck nearby. One officer climbs the crumbling steps of the house that will soon come down to make

Police checking the tree cutting permit on the door.

way for a new building. He reads the tree cutting permit posted to the door and returns to the sidewalk to tell me to stay back.

As he turns to talk into the walkie-talkie on his lapel, I approach the truck. Mr. X, a property developer, is known to a school teacher in the neighbourhood who taught his daughter. She told me he is connected to the Montreal Mafia. During a teacher-parent interview he made an offer she couldn't refuse that reminded her of a Mafia Don. Another neighbour told me that he had been photographed at the funeral of a major Mafia figure in Montreal. "Be careful," he said, "he is dangerous."

Down comes the tinted glass window to reveal his face, young but already burdened with deep furrows between his eyebrows. I tell him I have no intention of interfering with the felling of the tree and that calling the police was unnecessary. "You've cost me a lot of money," he says.

The Committee of Adjustment (CoA), a quasi-judicial tribunal appointed by City Council, had initially ruled against his plan for a massive house—three stories with roof-top patios and multiple decks. It did not fit in with the character of other houses on the street and would, according to the Chair of the committee, "have unacceptable adverse impacts on green canopy."

Debra and I had brought to the hearing a round piece of cardboard cut to show the diameter and shape of the massive tree the applicant proposed to fell for the project. We argued that the tree, a burr oak, is worth protecting because it is a community landmark and elder of the eastern forests of North America. The trunk, measuring over a metre in diameter near the base, was a sapling in 1867, Canada's birthday. It is exceptional due to its age, size and good condition.

The committee agreed, and rejected the building proposal. We celebrated. Then Debra asked me to install a motion-detecting camera on the garage to monitor for sabotage of our car, just in case Mr. X wanted revenge.

Now I feel lost, standing before the same tree festooned with ropes and an arborist balancing a chainsaw twenty-five feet above the ground. Ottawa police are here at the behest of a man who thinks he can make offers no one can refuse. The Forestry Department has issued a tree cutting permit, following a directive from the City's lawyers. While he cannot build what he originally had in mind thanks to the CoA ruling, he cannot be denied a permit to remove a tree that is in the way. Private property rights trump collective rights, at least in a city that lives on property taxes and election campaign funds from property developers and the building industry.

"You could build a different house on the property that protects the tree," I say to Mr X. I get no reply. The tinted window goes up and the police officer asks me to move away from the truck.

A few days earlier we had mourned the pending loss, gathering forty or so adults and children in light rain to hang hearts and poems from wool strands encircling the trunk. The tree species name comes from the burr-like cap on the acorn. We searched for viable acorns in the ground litter. There were none. Debra wrote a blog post about the gathering, titled "I can't tell the tears from the rain."

I want to clone this oak from the budding branches now littering the ground as the arborist begins to dismember the giant limb by limb. The Archangel Ancient Tree Archive Debra contacted had offered to collect material from the "champion tree," to add to its own archive of the oldest, largest and most important trees on Earth. Burr oaks are in their top fifteen global priorities for genetic conservation and propagation.

The organization is in Minnesota. The tree is in Ottawa. There is no budget to bridge the gap. Now it is too late to collect specimens. The swollen buds will be dead within the hour. How am I to proceed? I'm searching, but the way is unclear.

It takes five days to dismember the Grandmother tree.

2. Seeing the footprints

A tangle of thorny bushes: the faint murmur of running water.

But here and there are footprints—Is this the right path?

If you want to pierce its nose and tie it up, do not rely on someone else's strength!

I live on Daniel Avenue in Champlain Park, unceded territory of the Algonquin Anishinaabe. The link between the street and my name raises a smile from people whenever I tell them my address. I have two jokes handy if the opportunity presents itself: I paid the City to name the street after me; When I get very old and forgetful I should still be able to find my way home.

My name is like a set of footprints. What is your name? Daniel. Where do you live? Daniel.

Getting to know my immediate surroundings and connecting to my neighbours has always been important to me for reasons rooted in childhood experiences. As the son of an air force lieutenant, I grew up bouncing from one community to the next, forced to make new friends and adapt to a new school four times in five years of high school (Ontario used to have a Grade 13). The anxiety of the first weeks of school would send me outdoors during the lunch hour to walk the streets surrounding the school while eating a sandwich and apple packed by my loving mother. Eventually, I learned to make new friends, and push beyond the limits of my natural shyness.

When our son Ryan left home to launch his life at university, both Debra and I stepped up our contributions to neighbourhood life. I joined the executive of the neighbourhood community association while Debra became the editor for the community newsletter. We did this on the side of our professional work and other personal projects for a dozen years. It provided us with a compelling reason to connect with neighbours and get to know them and the surrounding streets.

The loss of the Grandmother tree prompted us to study the history of the neighbourhood and why it was blessed with an abundance of tree canopy.

The explanation began with the street names, Daniel, Keyworth and Cowley. Together they form the name of a riverboat captain who in 1867 moved his family of eleven children into a stone house in the area. One of Daniel's sons later purchased the surrounding land and divided it into cottage lots. Much of it was covered in open forest, too rocky for agriculture and of little interest to a lumber industry focused on felling the great eastern white pine of the Ottawa Valley. He hoped to sell lots to people seeking respite from Ottawa's downtown and named three of the streets after his father.

Coincidentally, Daniel Keyworth Cowley had a connection to Samuel de Champlain, the French explorer-cartographer who led the first European foray into Algonquin territory in 1613 and after whom the neighbourhood is named. In the course of Captain Cowley's work plying the Ottawa river he acquired an astrolabe, a medieval instrument that was once used to determine latitude by taking sightings of the sun or other celestial bodies. A boy had come across it while clearing land near Cobden, Ontario. It is believed to be the lost astrolabe of Samuel de Champlain. Eventually it made its way to a collector in New York City and was then repatriated in 1989 by the Government of Canada for the Canadian Museum of History.

The subdivision project of Daniel's son did not succeed and for decades a small forest remained on part of the land. Residents recall that in 1939 they walked from their homes through "the forest" to see the open-car procession of King George VI and his wife Lady Elizabeth Bowes-Lyon (the Queen Mother) along Island Park Drive on the western edge of the community. The King and Queen had come to Canada to rally the troops for war.

A decade later, the dream of a subdivision finally took hold. Veterans and others built homes for young families and planted trees in their front yards. Decisions by some home builders left old-growth oaks in backyards or shading the street.

The historical record of the oaks of Champlain Park is even deeper. Samuel de Champlain makes no mention of oak trees but his later compatriot, Pierre Chevalier de Troyes, wrote in his 1686 journal that he "walked through an oak forest" on his way between *Akikpautik* (Pipe Bowl Falls) just upstream from today's Parliament Buildings and Deschênes Rapids (des chênes is French for "some oaks"). Because the oak was important to shipbuilding, many European kings claimed ownership of all oaks on lands they ruled. Chevalier de Troyes' main assignment from the king of France, however, was to travel to James Bay and burn down an English fur trading fort, which he did that same summer.

Oaks in Champlain Park survived the arrival of settlers in the late 1800's mainly because the river edge has very thin soil unsuitable for crops. My great, great, great grandmother, a widow arriving in Canada from Ireland in 1820 with eight sons, would have passed nearby on her way along the famed Opeongo Line to her eventual farmstead in Killaloe, Ontario. My maternal grandparents met there, married and had ten children of their own.

The footprints are everywhere, connecting me to this place.

The Anishinaabe that lived along the Ottawa River for thousands of years also had a deep relationship to the burr oak. The acorns were an important nut for everyday use, and a critical famine food. They were soaked in running water to remove the tannins and roasted to

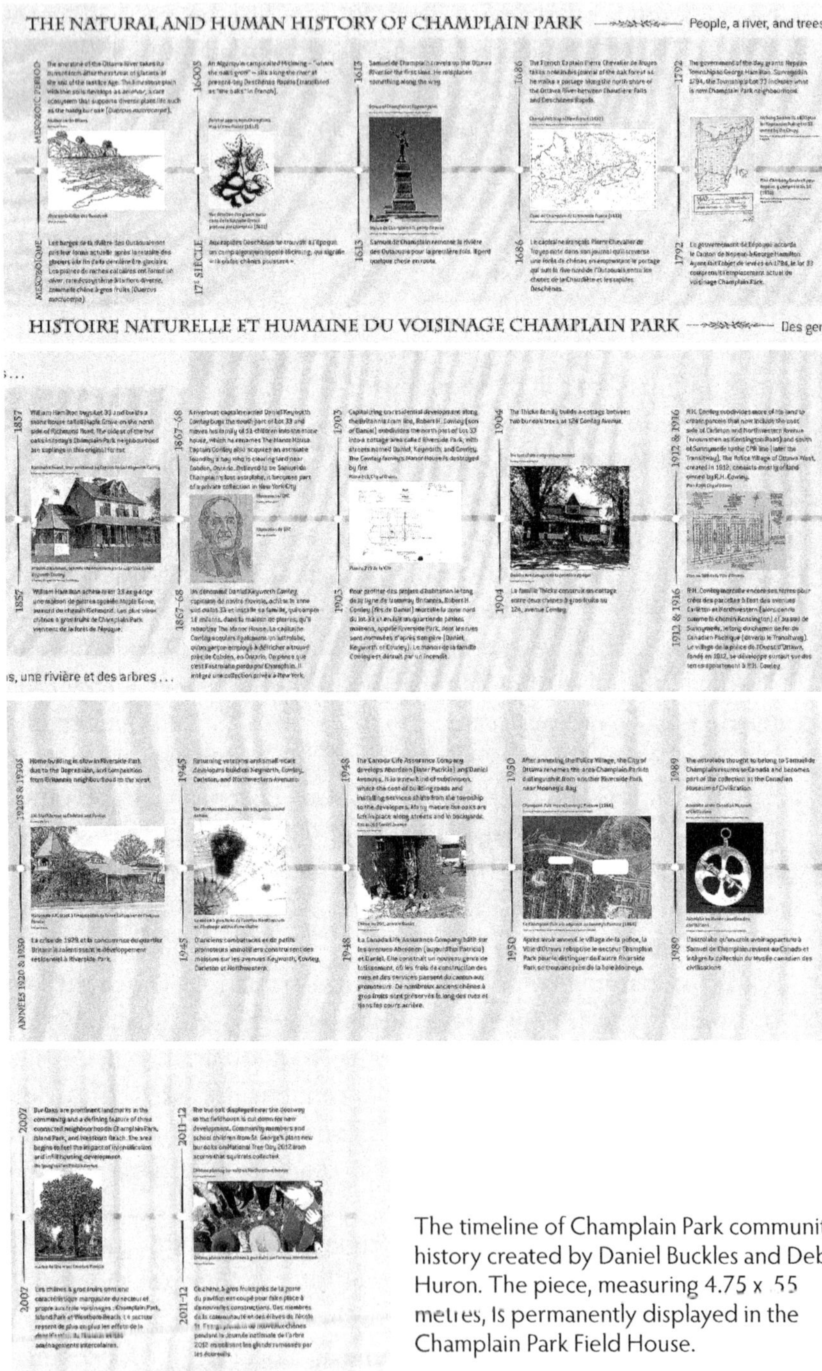

The timeline of Champlain Park community history created by Daniel Buckles and Debra Huron. The piece, measuring 4.75 x .55 metres, is permanently displayed in the Champlain Park Field House.

be eaten directly after removing the pericarp. They were also ground into flour and mixed into soups, much like the velvet bean I studied in Honduras and Mexico. The nut is protein-rich and packed with healthy fats and nutrients.

The nearby village of Aylmer, across the river from Champlain Park, marks a place the Anishinaabeg called *Michiming*, the "place where the oaks grow." This name was like a map for times of need. It is one of many details in the contemporary Indigenous claim to the unceded territory of the Algonquin Nations.

Seen across this timeline, the forest fragment set among the houses of Champlain Park is connected through direct genetic ancestry to the primeval oak forests of the Ottawa River. For some 10,000 years, since the retreat of the glaciers, an oak forest has graced this stretch. The footprints are everywhere, connecting many things to this place.

3. Seeing the ox

Among willow branches swaying in the spring breeze an oriole is singing.
How can the sparrow experience his joy in calling to his mate?
Isn't the moonlight glimmering in the forest my home?

The timeline of the burr oaks of Champlain Park taught me to appreciate and value tree genetic diversity, something I understood well for agricultural crops like maize, wheat and rice but had not considered in trees. The long-lived, forest-grown oaks, adapted to local growing conditions, are a local source of ancient genetic material for future generations of trees, something which cannot be said of nursery trees imported from afar.

Seeing the importance of conserving the forest genes hardened my resolve to protect the ancient oaks. It also made me feel joyful, transforming my and Debra's experience of our neighbourhood. We began to notice them everywhere, learning to distinguish the burr oak from other species not only by their leaves but also by their acorns and bark. In the fall, the cap covers almost all of the acorn and is festooned with soft, wiry hairs. The smaller branches have a corky quality, easy to notice even in winter.

Burr oak of Champlain Park, in winter.

The older trees have tufts of small branches growing directly from the trunk like hairs in the ears of old men. The bark is thick and rough, intended to protect the tree from wildfire. The mature burr oak is like an Ent from *Lord of the Rings*, a gentle and powerful giant with a tap root that finds its way into cracks of limestone underlying the natural features of the neighbourhood. I call it the Halloween tree because of its craggy look in comparison to the elegant red oaks, sugar maples and silver maples planted by people along our street.

Mr Holiday, an elderly man who used to live kitty-corner to our backyard, shared his observations on the relationship between squirrels and oaks in an article for the Ottawa Field Naturalist Club. He noted that squirrels sometimes nibble at the germ of the acorn, and then bury it. He speculated that they do this to prevent germination and keep the rest of the nut whole for a later meal. Fortunately for us, squirrels often forget where they buried their stash and some of the acorns sprout anyway, leading to oaks coming up in garden beds and next to the curb throughout the neighbourhood.

Noticing the trees for the forest put us on a good path after loss of the Grandmother tree, celebrating what signs remained. Neighbours joined in a friendly competition to find the largest oaks in the neighbourhood. A tree a few doors down the street from me was the clear winner, at 1.16 metres across and 3.66 metres in girth. It is so big and powerful it has caved in the garage built beside it fifty years earlier. In all, we mapped twenty-four trees older than a century in this small neighbourhood of six square blocks.

We created a blog, *The Champlain Oaks*, to share our discoveries with others. The name, coined by Dennis, a branding expert who lives down the street, reflects both the name of our neighbourhood (Champlain Park) and the long history of the trees evoked by Samuel de Champlain's name. Today I would have suggested *Michiming* as the moniker, to make the even older connection and acknowledge the Anishinaabe.

Our excitement with the remaining oaks prompted me to ask Mr. X for permission to enter his property to rescue a cross section of the Grandmother tree from the remaining stump. I thought we could use it as a teaching tool. "Sure," he said, "but first you need to sign a letter saying you will never oppose my housing projects again."

Instead, I arranged for a Carleton University history professor to call him. She wanted an artifact to use as a centre piece in an exhibit called *Six Moments in an Urban Forest* chronicling how trees have been viewed, used and abused in the City of Ottawa. The exhibit was planned for the Bytown Museum, a stone's throw from Parliament Hill and next to the last lock of the Rideau Canal built by Irish arriving in Canada a generation after my own ancestors. The professor succeeded in getting permission without selling her soul.

A carpenter friend in the neighbourhood cut the cross section, just in case Mr. X got wind that I was behind the arrangement. He grew up in British Columbia where, in the 1980s, some environmentalists drove spikes and other metal objects deep into mammoth trees to prevent loggers from taking them down. It became a federal felony in the United States because of the risk and remains a controversial tactic in the environmental movement.

Tree house on Island Park Drive, Ottawa.

We talked about spiking the oak before it was felled, but decided it would be dangerous for the arborist.

Sparks flew part way through the metre-wide stump as the saw bit into a piece of chain link fence buried deep inside the tree. We later determined it was from the 1930s when the large federal property next door was an active pasture in need of fencing to keep cattle contained. The tree had fully engulfed a section of fence into its body, turning the wood around it a Payne's Grey. Several chain links, exposed once the cross-section was cut, became a talking point in the Bytown Museum exhibit.

The Ottawa Forests and Greenspace Advisory Committee (OFGAC) asked Debra and me to host OFGAC's first guided walk that year, 2011, to see the Champlain Oaks. We stopped under one of them, towering over the street next to mine. "This is the party tree," I explained, "where people gather every year in the summer for a street party." Down the street we stopped at another mammoth tree, tucked into a niche in the house wall created to accommodate it. The design was a

A heritage burr oak bursts it's britches as it grows. Photo: Debra Huron.

bet, I'd been told, between the builder and a friend who didn't think it was possible to raise the house without first bringing down the tree.

Stories like this popped up everywhere in the neighbourhood, where trees act as community landmarks and house identifiers, waypoints to something of value.

Forests Ontario, a provincial body based in Toronto, took an interest in the Champlain Oaks and our drive to bring a heritage tree program to the City of Ottawa. They decided to organize their annual conference at the Experimental Farm in Ottawa, inviting city officials and staff in the hope they would be moved by heritage tree bylaws and programs from other Ontario cities. My telling of the Champlain Oaks story was a featured presentation. Many conference participants toured the oaks of Champlain Park on the last day.

Some years later, Debra and I registered seven of the twenty-three remaining pre-settlement burr oaks in Champlain Park with the Forests Ontario heritage tree program. The organization's CEO came from Toronto to Ottawa to deliver the heritage certification to property owners. Kay and Steve, the elders of the Kot family, served lemonade to the crowd gathered in their front yard under the shade of one of the largest remaining burr oaks. These are still the only trees in Ottawa with heritage status, an accomplishment the Ottawa Field Naturalist Club acknowledged through their annual Conservation Award. A framed certificate hangs prominently on our kitchen wall.

"Trees as witnesses to history." Installation at Champlain Park, Ottawa.

The local councillor, impressed with the burr oak story, offered to sponsor an installation celebrating the relationships between people and trees in Champlain Park. Debra and I created a timeline of photos and text and worked with the City to create a permanent installation at the field house in the community park. Inside is a long panel with the timeline (see page 300). Outside, a plexiglass and aluminium display case holds the cross-section of the trunk from Mr. X and the Bytown Museum exhibit. Dated tree rings, mapped by a specialist at Carleton University, trace the history of the tree, the neighbourhood and the nation, from a sapling in 1856 to the end of its life in 2011.

The inauguration of the installation took place on a cool day in early May. Neighbours gathered. The councillor came and thanked everyone for their contributions. The big attraction, however, was the arrival of five descendants of Daniel Keyworth Cowley, the river boat captain. A neighbour with an interest in genealogy had tracked them down in Bristol, Quebec, a village across the Ottawa River.

Seeing and celebrating the Champlain Oaks brought to life the web of relationships in my own backyard—my neighbours, past generations, historical and present-day Indigenous lives, birds of many kinds, the squirrels that gorge on acorns in the fall and maple buds in the early spring, the rabbits that inhabit the cedar bushes, and the fox and the turkey that pass through my backyard to forage. This, I came to understand, is what it means to belong in an urban forest.

4. Catching the ox

Advancing with difficulty; the ox's nose is pierced.

But this fiery nature is hard to control.

Dragged here and there, you stray through cloud-covered forests.

Trees brought me into the realm of municipal activism.

There was lots to shout about. Kitchissippi, the ward within which Champlain Park is located, caught fire around 2011 as a hot spot for urban infill housing. A steady stream of tear-downs and rebuilds continues to this day, with mature trees falling by the dozen in every neighbourhood. A local tree activist described the situation as a tree extinction event (extirpation, which means localized extinction, would be the more accurate biological term).

Debra and I, moved by our experience with the burr oaks in our neighbourhood, launched a wider initiative—Big Trees of Kitchissippi—to provide a voice for the outrage, lobby for improvement and enforcement of tree by-laws and make trees a municipal election issue.

I was by then known as the "neighbourhood tree guy," taking calls and emails from people across the city desperate to save trees on their street or in a neighbouring back yard.

The range and frequency of problems was shocking. Urban developers routinely damaged public and private trees with construction machinery. Trees on the property line lost half their roots to excavation. Trees were removed or severely damaged in the course of connecting a new water main. Plans submitted for a building permit did not require mapping of trees on the property, making objections based on the tree bylaw difficult to document and enforce.

The "oops" strategy—cut down, then apologize—was a standard practice among urban developers, to the dismay of residents who had come to know and love the trees around them. Even when fines were levied for the more egregious violations, the few hundred dollars involved was a minor cost for doing business in a real estate market with rapidly rising land values.

I was still doing consultancies in Mali, the U.K. and northern Ontario, but took breaks from the sedentary work of report writing to jump on my bike and inspect the damage. I sent photographs and email complaints to the Forestry Department, using the City's 311 hotline to create a paper trail. I learned to look, take a few photographs, and leave the site rather than engage with the construction workers or heavy equipment operators. They sometimes threatened to knock my head off. Not all of my neighbours approved either, privately describing me as "the tree police."

I was outraged at the impunity with which trees were being discarded. The city manager at the time said that tree protection was still in an "education phase." The forestry officer for our ward, a man who loved trees as much as we did, was overwhelmed with complaints from irate residents yet powerless to do anything but occasionally issue warnings.

In 2015 there were one hundred requests made for the removal of large trees in Kitchissippi Ward alone. Most were being replaced with exotic shrubs or, sometimes, artificial turf. Clearly, the education was not going well.

Tree on a neighbouring property, devastated by an excavation, Carleton Avenue, Ottawa, Canada.

One Friday afternoon, at one end of our street next to the public school, a contractor cut fifty percent of the roots of a large black walnut. The trunk was fully within the property of the school, providing shade to a play area used by the kindergarten class. The excavation destabilized the tree to such an extent that removing it became an emergency expense for the school board.

The City charged the contractor and the house owner with violation of the tree bylaw, a first-time test case against a private citizen. Debra sat in the court when it was brought forward, planning to report on the outcome. Much to everyone's surprise, the judge dismissed the case because the City had failed to establish that the property in question was in the City of Ottawa. The articling student sent by the City to argue the case had missed this important detail in his opening remarks, an error I'm sure he will never make again.

A year later another black walnut on a property line on Daniel Avenue suffered a similar fate. This time I jumped into the fray, leaping off my bike when I saw the arborist with a chainsaw. I stood under the tree, hoping my presence would stop the cutting until a bylaw officer could be brought to the scene and halt the work. Cell phone to my ear, I stared up at the arborist draped in the upper branches.

He was unfazed and continued cutting. I relented after a while, realizing that no bylaw officer was coming. My fifteen minutes of fame were for naught, although a more reasoned interview I gave later resulted in a widely read article in the *Ottawa Citizen*, the city's main daily.

Debra had her own networks and strategies. She wrote profusely for community newspapers, using her journalism training to combine news on tree loss with good news stories about community events, community history and resident profiles. She made regular story pitches to mainstream media, finding some willing to write about one City of Ottawa gaffe or another.

Saving trees makes for easy journalism even though the underlying issue hits hard at developer influence at city hall. Too much criticism threatens the bottom line of private media companies funded through business advertising from the real estate and development industries. Still, she wrote or inspired dozens of articles in local media.

We knew we were on to something when the negative publicity around tree loss began to generate new developer tactics. The most common one was to promise to leave a tree on the property even though the excavation and gradual death of the tree would inevitably cause a problem for the future homeowner. Large trees could take years to slowly die and by then the developer is long gone.

Calling out these and other developer tactics was satisfying—we are on to you Mr X—but entirely ineffective. Few were charged and fewer still handed a meaningful fine. Still, our public reporting on the onslaught and urban developer impunity tapped into a swell of emotion felt by many residents. The media attention gave people permission to express concerns that had only been acknowledged privately. They began to realize that trees on streets and in backyards manage storm water, shade buildings to reduce energy use, improve air quality and remove and store carbon safely. Trees, they learned, even add directly to human lifespans, provided they grow where people can feel their positive effect in their daily lives.

"Save the trees" became a widely heard rallying cry in Kitchissippi, and more generally in Ottawa. Like all things in the media, however, the voice of the trees hovered like notes in the air, like the sweet voice of Mario Lanza singing the poem *Trees* written in 1914 by Joyce Kilmer. Timeless, until it is gone.

In 2014 we caught the attention of Jeff Leiper, a candidate for city council on the campaign trail. He was a former president of the nearby Hintonburg Community Association and understood how to run a grassroots campaign focused on issues important to residents. The ward, with neighbourhood names such as Westboro, Westboro Village and Westboro Beach, had become known as "the wild west" because of haphazard and intense condo tower development. A low-rise, post-war collection of residential neighbourhoods was being transformed by random infill with high rise towers, "monster" homes normally found on country estates and doubles thrown up on a single lot like shoe boxes. Trees were decimated and driveways and concrete poured so liberally it left no space for new trees to take root. Many residents were livid, something Jeff tapped into through his first election platform. He won the seat and made tree protection one of three pillars for his first term of council. None of us realized that the intractable nature of the challenge would stump us all. It was not enough to catch the ox and pierce its nose. We also had to tend to it.

5. Tending the ox

Fearing that it may fall into a steep and perilous path,

You hold it tight with whip and bridle, and with the strength of both legs firmly hold your ground.

Once past this critical moment, the ox comes following you.

Municipal governments everywhere seem to receive more than their fair share of vitriol. The reason may be that people experience the government policies they love to hate on the street where they live. Potholes, confusing recycling guidelines, a monster house with a rooftop patio staring down at you, and, most of all, property taxes, are personal in ways that federal foreign policy and provincial environmental policy are not.

Hyper-locality also makes it difficult to distinguish between local politicians and the bureaucracy they direct. Both are "the City," to be loved or criticized as one, depending on your experience on the street. Many even think that city staff, a bureaucracy with its own rules of conduct, are at the direct service of people holding political office, even though the two functions are distinct under law.

Big Trees of Kitchissippi was not a docile group, in large part due to Debra's fiery character. The shared experience of others in the group, all women except myself, converged around the same themes: poor enforcement of municipal tree bylaws and political resistance to protecting green space and the urban tree canopy whenever it bumped up against developer commercial interests.

The stage was set in 2015 for Big Trees of Kitchissippi to make these points during the launch of City consultations on a new Urban Forest Management Plan. The event took place during National Tree Week in the historic Horticultural Building at Landsdowne Park, a sixteen-hectare facility owned by the City of Ottawa with retail, residential and entertainment facilities, including the city's 1888 exhibition grounds.

The launch, attended by more than a hundred people, included presentations on urban forests and table displays by neighbourhood groups and environmental organizations.

Tree Fest, an initiative from Ottawa South, had its inaugural celebration there. It was a large format photography exhibit featuring trees and stories from across the city. One was a stunning photograph of the winner of the Champlain Oak biggest tree contest (image at the top of this chapter).

Debra attended the event as a tree, dressed from foot to shoulder in crepe fabric held in a round shape with hula hoops. A floppy hat and sleeves adorned with cut-out oak leaves completed the ensemble. She and eight other women from our group carried placards with messages for the Mayor, who was expected at the event. Her sign read "Stop Killing the Trees," and included drops of red paint just in case the message was not clear.

When the Mayor approached the group near the entrance to the hall, he introduced himself to Debra. He then leaned in, looking intently at the wooden stake in her hands. "That stake is made of wood," he said. "Ironic isn't it."

Debra's retort was equally pointed. "At least it is not the kind of plastic your council refuses to recycle." The two stared briefly at each other with what she later described as "hairy eyeballs."

I had my opportunity shortly afterwards when the Mayor came to our table and asked about the Champlain Oaks. We had met a year before at a tree planting event in Champlain Park organized by the City's communications department. A notoriously thin-skinned politician, he bristled when I said the City was not doing enough to protect healthy, mature trees in neighbourhoods. He then set his gaze on the far wall, looking for a more sympathetic reception somewhere else in the hall.

Consultation on the Urban Forest Management Plan (UFMP) tapped into a longing among residents to do something about tree loss in Ottawa. Turnout was high from across the city and feedback on the draft plan copious. City senior management and more city councillors began to take notice of public demands. Even the Mayor, an urban man who could not handle a spade, did not deny the depth of feeling residents had about the trees on their streets and backyards.

Forestry staff were delighted, for their own reasons. Forestry issues, and forestry staff, were on the lowest rungs in the municipal hierarchy, far below the rank and policy attention given to infrastructure, parking infractions, buildings and planning for growth. Much like clip art of trees on architectural drawings, City foresters and arborists were the last group considered internally.

A senior forestry planner told us later that the attention trees were receiving as a result of citizen activism, in Kitchissippi and other wards in Ottawa's urban core, was making a difference to their profile in the City bureaucracy. It gave them added gravitas, something I was happy to hear and support so long as it translated into steady change on the ground.

Progress, however, was deathly slow, and the impact on policy of public input minimal. Very few things changed in the UFMP by the time the consultation was over—the first draft of the plan presented by consultants was almost identical to the final approved by Council in 2017. It was a cookie-cutter plan, repeatable for virtually any municipality in Ontario. It was also grossly under resourced, serving more as a wish list than a concerted plan of action.

A subsequent review of municipal tree bylaws produced a better outcome. Big Trees of Kitchissippi lobbied hard for changes to the bylaw, convening meetings and facilitating discussions among numerous members of a city-wide network of Community Associations for Environmental Sustainability (CAFES). We pointed to what was wrong with the current bylaw and made specific demands for clearer and more meaningful policy language and bigger budgets for enforcement. We also presented a united front, compiling formal signatures of endorsement from more than twenty different neighbourhood associations across the city, all demanding improvements and greater political, financial and legal support to enforcement. This may have smoothed the way for City staff, who brought forward important changes to the bylaw and better internal procedures for infill development in the urban core.

Council approved. We were cautiously optimistic that the revised bylaw and a shift in City tree-culture could make a difference. Tending the ox seemed like a worthwhile endeavour.

6. Riding the ox back home

Sitting astride the ox, the noble person happily returns.
The sounds of his flute mingle with the crimson sky:
He has discovered the garden of joy.
Who else could know about this endlessly pleasurable taste?

People's participation in making public policy often centres on setting the goals and assessing the options, based on evidence generated and presented by specialists. Citizen science takes the idea of engagement further. Enthusiasts become researchers, contributing to the collection and organization of observations in nature and society.

The practice has roots in the Age of Discovery and the science of cartography. It was also formed by the experience of seventeenth century gardeners of the Royal Society who were not scientists but rather lay experts in their fields. John James Audubon, the famous ornithologist of the Romantic era, inspired the National Audubon Society and its attention to combining science with education and grassroots advocacy to achieve a conservation mission. Jacques and I reviewed this history for a chapter in a book on participatory action research. At the time, I was doing citizen science in my own backyard.

During a coffee break at a City consultation on the urban forest management plan, I chatted with a recently retired forestry professor from the University of Toronto, one of the consultants on the plan. He described a protocol he and a colleague had created to engage community groups in mapping the trees in their neighbourhoods. It has a lovely title: *Neighbourwoods*.

Citizen science is usually aligned with management and conservation objectives. *Neighourwoods*, for example, involves describing every tree bigger than a pop can in diameter on certain criteria, from species name, height and crown width to branch structure, girdling roots and indicators of tree health. The purpose is to help communities plan tree succession, keep the forest diverse and coordinate interventions to deal with tree pests and diseases.

I had already mobilized neighbours to map the remaining presettlement Champlain Oaks and one hundred other large neighbourhood trees. Our mapping, however, was political in its objectives. Trees more than fifty centimetres in diameter at breast height was the minimum threshold used at the time by the City of Ottawa to determine whether or not a tree permit was required for removal. I wanted to be sure that we had tabs on every tree above this threshold as a check against urban developers ignoring the bylaw. Mapping was a line of defence, not an exercise in citizen science *per se*.

Still, I could see the potential for community stewardship of trees and dove into a *Neighbourwoods* tree mapping effort in the spring of 2016 with several neighbours. We mapped 342 trees and poured the data into a state-of-the-art, peer-reviewed tree benefits calculator developed by the USDA Forestry Service (i-Tree). It demonstrates the annual flow of financial benefits from trees due to storm water

"Lost Trees of Ottawa" app, Ottawa, Canada.

management, energy saved through shading, air quality improved and carbon dioxide removed and stored. All of these effects have well documented financial benefits, adjusted according to tree species, diameter, height and canopy health.

Debra turned the result into two infographics, one to help neighbours appreciate the financial value of the urban forest where they live and the other to guide people interested in planting a new tree on their property. It showed neighbours the need to diversify through succession planting, beyond the dominant mix of sugar maples, silver maples and burr oaks that the inventory showed make up most of the urban forest in Champlain Park.

As an educational device, the mapping and the infographics were a hit, informing neighbours and mobilizing tree activists in other neighbourhoods. *Neighbourwoods* initiatives emerged in several other parts of the city. I fear for their survival, however. The City departments that should be encouraging and coordinating with community groups, and making use of the data, have completely ignored the efforts and the outcomes. Citizen science aspires to link technical experts and scientists with the lay public, but what happens when there is only one hand clapping?

Frustrated by City indifference, I turned to counter-mapping politics in the lead up to the 2018 municipal election by focusing on the "Lost Trees of Ottawa." A friend, a Palestinian working in Ottawa for one of North America's largest providers of geographic information systems, built an app for mapping lost trees across the city. It was simple: place an icon on the spot where a favourite tree had been lost due to human or natural causes and upload a photograph and text of a personal memory of the tree. The data could be viewed through filters such as ward boundaries and year.

I wanted the platform to provide a venue for expressing emotions but also for engaging with municipal candidates for City Council in discussions on what to do about the declining urban forest in their ward. My hope was that the hard numbers of trees lost combined with personal meaning would feed into local politics, acting on events in real time and space. The City's own monitoring of tree loss was absent, forcing the public to step up to fill the gap.

The concept caught people's attention, stimulated in part by the impact on trees of an intense windstorm in the Ottawa region. However, after a flurry of entries, use fell away. I did not have the institutional base needed to manage a sustained promotional effort or the resources and energy to translate the findings into an organized election campaign. Lost trees may also have been too negative an idea for citizen engagement. I felt alone. I was riding the ox, but, try as I might, it was not coming willingly.

7. Forgetting the ox, the ox herder rests alone

Bright Moon and cool wind: what a splendid home!

Sitting all alone, the ox has gone away.

Even if you doze until sunrise, what use would be a whip and bridle?

The Centre Block on Parliament Hill contains the iconic Peace Tower with its clock face and Canadian flag at the top. It houses the Memorial Chamber, a vaulted room dedicated to Canada's war dead. A very large book, the Book of Remembrance, sits open on a glass covered table in the centre of the room with the names of every Canadian soldier that died during the First World War. At 11:00 a.m. daily a page is turned to display a new set of names. Seven other books list Canadians killed in other conflicts, from the 1884 Nile Expedition through to the 2001-14 war in Afghanistan.

I took my father to the Memorial Chamber when he was ninety years old to witness the turning of the page that revealed the name of his uncle, Robert James Buckles. At age eighteen, my father's namesake died storming Vimy Ridge in France, the battle credited with separating Canada from the shadow of the British empire. My father went on to serve in the Second World War as a Spitfire pilot. Shot down on a mission over the French countryside, he spent nineteen months in a Prisoner of War camp before being liberated by the Russians at the end of the war.

In April 2019, I returned to the Centre Block with Debra. We were there to petition a committee of parliamentarians to halt plans to cut down the last mature tree on Parliament Hill. A white elm stood like a sentinel at the east end of the building, prominent in the live feed from the Parliament Hill webcam that shares the view of the capital every Remembrance Day with the nation and the world. It had witnessed a hundred years of Canada Day celebrations and political comings and goings, and even survived the arrival in 1931 of the elm diseases that took so many others.

Debra and I had been tipped off by a specialist hired to assess the health of the tree. It was going to be cut down, he told us, to make way for staging of a multi-million dollar renovation of Centre Block and a new, underground visitors centre. His diagnosis was that the tree was healthy and could live for many more years, if only the machines and construction equipment were stored somewhere else.

Robert Buckles and a soldier in the Memorial Chamber, Ottawa.

We called on Owen Clarkin, an expert on rare and endangered trees of the Ottawa Valley, and Paul Johanis, the Chair of the Greenspace Alliance of Canada's Capital, to join us in the Centenary Elm Campaign.

To start, I prepared a nomination for heritage status under the same Forests Ontario program registering the Champlain Oaks, digging up photos of the tree from 1914 onwards, including a picture of Pierre Elliot Trudeau being interviewed in 1968 at the Eternal Flame on Parliament Hill with the tree in the background. Debra worked fervently to interest the media in the story. Paul gave detailed and forceful interviews in flawless English and French, published in multiple outlets: Five stories by CBC Ottawa, an extensive article in the National Post, several in the Ottawa Citizen and The Sun, plus articles in various specialized media outlets such as Ottawa Matters and the Capital Current.

Debra also used her knowledge of parliamentary affairs from when she worked on the Hill as the communications liaison for a New Democrat member of the House of Commons. She asked Paul Dewar, the MP for Ottawa Centre, to raise the fate of the last elm standing on Parliament Hill during Question Period. He declined—questions are a rare and valuable asset for a backbench politician—but brought our concerns to the attention of the chair of a House of Commons committee overseeing the Centre Block renovation. An emergency meeting was called to hear our testimony.

Paul, a former Assistant Chief Statistician of Canada, provided the gravitas and steady hand the moment needed before the committee. Debra and I sat nearby, within easy hearing of the MPs sitting around the committee table, three Liberals on one side and two Conservatives and a New Democrat on the other.

Membership in House of Commons Committees reflects the share of seats in Parliament, giving the ruling Liberals a nominal majority. On this particular day, however, the Liberals were short a member. After Paul spoke, the New Democrat brought forward a motion calling for a moratorium on cutting the tree until June so that the responsible department could do a more complete assessment of tree heath and reconsider alternatives.

While the motion was being discussed, I noticed the Liberal member sitting closest to me pull out his phone, dial and urgently say, "Better get down here. The Chair is about to call for a vote." With moments to spare, another Liberal Member of Parliament appeared in the committee room, and, without having heard any of the testimony, voted with his colleagues to defeat the motion. It was a victory of party politics and the human-built environment over nature.

For me, a neophyte in matters of parliamentary procedures, the crassness of the vote was a shock. Appeals to reason, and even legitimate differences in opinion and perspective on things of value, received no attention when sealing the fate of the elm. It was to be swept aside in what was a battlefield operating in another realm, underground like the visitor's centre the renovations were meant to accommodate.

Parliament Hill showing the Centennial Elm (above) one day, and the denuded trunk the next (below).

The expression "toeing the party line" was more evident, and barren, than I had ever imagined.

Every morning the following week we checked the live feed from the Parliament Hill webcam. On April 13, 2019 a crane arrived, visible on our computer screen at home. Debra and I rushed down to the site, joined later by Owen, to do what we could: Stand witness with a video camera as the tree was dismembered, branch by branch. Towards the end, all that was left was a main stem and a single canopy spray of branches. With one final cut the tree was decapitated, the remaining canopy caught in the air by the crane and lowered slowly to the ground.

An arborist moved in, cut fine branches from the top and placed them in separate bags. He was preparing one hundred cuttings to ship to the University of Guelph where they could be grafted to elm root stock, preserving the Centenary Elm's unique genes. The idea had come from Owen, who told us about the Elm Recovery Project, a University of Guelph program to assist the recovery of white elm from the fungal disease. According to the university website, the project is a "dating service for lonely elms," bringing disease-tolerant elms to the arboretum for crossing with others.

Five trees from these cuttings are now rooted and cared for at Guelph University waiting for the day when they can be returned to Ottawa and planted on Parliament Hill. The elm will not be forgotten.

8. The ox and the ox herder are both forgotten

Since space has collapsed, how can obstacles remain?

Could a snowflake survive inside a burning flame?

You cheerfully come and go: How could you not always laugh?

In February 2019, the City of Ottawa launched plans to create a new official plan, a municipal policy framework that guides where people will live, how they will get around and to what extent and how they will care for each other and for nature in the city. It is the most consequential policy of a municipal government in Canada, setting the tone and direction for all more specific policies, programs and projects pursued locally.

When I read the plan's initial vision statement, projected on a wide screen in the City Council Chamber, I could only shake my head in disbelief. It promised "to make Ottawa the most liveable, mid-sized, globally oriented city in North America."

Beyond the gobbledygook, a torrent of objections immediately filled my mind. "Livable for whom?" The homeless, low wage workers, people with disabilities, new Canadians, Indigenous people, the elderly and many other situations of disadvantage, marginalization or vulnerability were buried under the facade of an inanimate and homogeneous "city."

The global orientation held up world markets as the lodestar. The dream for Ottawa, it seemed, was to become a vassal city, subservient to the flow of goods and services to Toronto, New York and London. The regional economy and the thousands of people up and down the Ottawa valley and across the Ottawa River in Quebec were nowhere to be seen.

The comparative and competitive framework—"the most" this or that in North America—seemed juvenile to me. Is the future of our city to be framed as a high school rivalry?

My reaction to the vision for the Ottawa Official Plan may have been unkind, considering how difficult it is to craft a single statement that works for everyone. I understood the writing challenge. Still, I was irate, and resolved to push back.

What followed was a deep dive into the weeds of policies impacting a thousand dimensions of city life, and a novel experiment in citizen engagement involving dozens of grassroots organizations concerned about urban environmental responsibilities, social justice and the livability of neighbourhoods. It coalesced under the umbrella of a new coalition, the Peoples Official Plan (POP). Leadership from different people, each contributing at different times and in different ways, created an authentic collaborative environment and rich analysis of the details of City of Ottawa plans and alternative proposals. By the time the "offical" Official Plan was adopted by City Council in October, 2022, the Peoples Official Plan had built up a body of work and broad set of relationships unique in the history of municipal activism in Ottawa.

Several moments in the genesis of the coalition stand out for me.

The first was a conversation with Paul of the Greenspace Alliance shortly after the February launch at City Hall. "This new Official Plan," he said, "must be Ottawa's climate plan."

The assertion was prescient. A month later, in March 2019, City Council passed a resolution declaring a climate emergency in Ottawa. Municipalities across the country and around the world were doing the same on the heels of the Paris climate accord and extreme weather in Canada and elsewhere. This was followed a few months later by the declaration by the City of a housing and homelessness emergency.

In neither case, however, were words backed up with strong policies and budgets. Nor did the Mayor and City Councillors provide direction to staff to fashion the new official plan, arguably the most important policy for any city, as a direct response to these twin emergencies. The most significant opportunity in a generation to reset the direction of city building was being wasted on platitudes and policies supporting the *status quo*. Paul and I agreed that a robust response was needed.

A second key moment was more directly related to my professional interests. I had shoehorned myself into a stakeholder group the City convened with organizations representing low income households, people with disabilities, seniors and other marginalized, racialized or vulnerable communities. My purpose, representing the Greenspace Alliance where I sat as a board member, was to bring the theme of equitable access to green space and tree canopy into Ottawa's Official Plan. Joining the group was also necessary because the City had not included any environmental organizations among their consulted stakeholders.

They called us "the Ambassadors Group," a name that immediately signalled the group's function: to act as ambassadors for the City by faithfully communicating the City's plans and core messages. City staff knew how difficult it is to reach people unlikely to attend public meetings and hoped the organizations in the room would do them the favour. A woman representing the Ottawa Council on Aging responded to the terms of reference with a message of her own. "It sounds," she said, "like you want us to do your work for you."

One of the first slides the convenor showed us at the meeting was a "word cloud" she said she had used earlier to make a pitch to her bosses and to councillors for approval of the budget for the Ambassadors Group consultations. The most prominent word in the cloud was P.R. (short for public relations), in font three times the size of everything else.

It became clear in a flash that the underlying purpose of the group was to make the City look good. No meetings directly with City planners were proposed. No problem-solving sessions were planned to collect information from marginalized groups about their lived experiences with transportation, housing or green spaces. Critically, the organizations that could have done the consultations were not offered the mandate and resources to do so. The Ambassadors Group was a P.R. exercise and a one-way communication channel, pure and simple.

A metaphor for the approach to consultation came to me shortly afterwards: a wagon wheel with the City as the hub, defining the problem, extracting the information it wanted from the spokes and limiting direct contact among the various spokes affected by plans. Specific and general publics were isolated from each other and engaged simply to feed information into the hub, where it could be sorted and filtered in the dark. A member of the POP coalition much later described the City's approach to public consultation as "a policy of containment."

The underlying assumption of the City's consultation process, an approach common to public engagement everywhere, is that the public body is simply a collection of individuals, each pursuing their individual interests. In this view of society, the role of government and the bureaucracy is to impose order on the chaos of multiple voices and balance points of view. Adopted policies are then routinely heralded as "compromises," even when they contradict other established policies or reinforce bias in favour of developer economic interests.

My work with groups of people around the world has tried to challenge this perspective with a more social understanding of the relationship between the individual and society. Human beings are social animals first, gifted with the capacity to communicate and engage in dialogue with each other. Reason, emotion and imagination combine to create novel thinking and clarify options through the crucible of connection to others and a sense of belonging in a society.

How can governments or any other representative entity develop a common human plan or program if they fail to recognize and engage with collectivities? Connections need to be made between the spokes of the wheel and between all spokes and the hub for collective desires and goals to emerge.

My concerns gave rise to the name of the coalition, the Peoples Official Plan (POP). I wanted to express the idea of multiple peoples engaging with each other not just as individuals but also as organized communities of interests grounded in common places and common experiences. This was different from a populist perspective on "the people" and "a people's plan," which perpetuates the problems of a representative style of political organization and governance. What was needed, I thought, was a coming together of organized grassroots groups with their own internal governance procedures, speaking for themselves, not as proxies for others.

The inaugural meeting of POP got off the ground in a good way. People gathered at the Champlain Park Field House on a cold, wet night in the early spring of 2019. One participant arrived by bike from a distant ward, signalling a commitment to "walk the talk" of active transportation in city planning.

Paul spoke representing the Greenspace Alliance as did Robb from Ecology Ottawa while I chaired the meeting as a member of CAFES. A dozen other organizations were present, each with their own voice and perspective. The dialogue among spokes in the wheel had begun.

A third key moment in the genesis of POP took place at Bayview Yards, a City of Ottawa facility along the Ottawa River. A recorded speech from Dianne Saxe, the former Environment Commissioner for the Province of Ontario, helped launched a two day workshop of some 120 people from organizations across the city. We had gathered to develop strategic directions for various dimensions of city life: the density of housing in the built up parts of the city, walkability and active transportation, access to greenspace, management of our own waste, the challenges of food insecurity, homelessness and marginalization, as well as thinking about biodiversity loss and governance of the city.

Saxe spoke about the urban boundary, driving home the importance of the policy with the phrase "Land use is Ontario's tar sands." Urban sprawl, she argued, was just as consequential to the Canadian carbon footprint as the whole of Alberta's dirty oil. Other presenters, including a cadre of university students, drove home the urgency of the situation.

Participants rose to the occasion, creating a richly detailed picture of a collective vision for Ottawa, captured over the course of an evening and full day in a "living tapestry" by the graphic facilitator Jennifer

Shepherd. I designed the process to help participants do their best thinking, supported by a careful selection of aids to facilitation: tables covered by heavy paper to write on, modelling clay to sculpt objects of attention, strategic instructions for note takers, a piggy bank to collect donations. And a nice lunch. My colleague Jacques facilitated, generously and expertly carrying this load so I could participate as a stakeholder.

The most consequential outcome of the Bayview workshop was that it provided a model for a deliberative and action-oriented approach to public engagement. Over the following years, POP animators organized other workshops and convened regular smaller meetings, bringing together people and organizations with social justice, environmental and neighbourhood concerns. Together, we analyzed draft City policies, formulated detailed critiques with alternative policy language and sent coordinated delegations to present at City Council meetings and other City organized public events. These were combined with public rallies, letter writing campaigns, public-facing summary statements and meetings with staff and councillors. Magdalene Carson,

Where will our food come from if we pave over farmland?
Image by Magdalene Carson.

the designer of this book, produced numerous graphic images to visualize the issues at hand and support public advocacy.

I did a lot of writing for the group, including twelve opinion pieces published in the *Ottawa Citizen*, the main daily newspaper. My next-door neighbour, a leading columnist for the paper, joked with me that I was publishing more than he was.

When presenting the final draft of the City of Ottawa Official Plan for review and approval by the Mayor and City Council, the City's chief planner said "there has been an unprecedented level of public engagement on the draft New Official Plan, far surpassing anything we had projected and what occurred during the last Official Plan update." While numerous small and larger civil society groups contributed in multiple ways to this outcome, the Peoples Official Plan was at the centre of the movement, informing, amplifying and galvanizing the will of many collectivities.

9. Returning to the original place

My very own treasure is recovered: all those efforts spent in vain!
It would have been better to be blind, deaf, and dumb.
The mountains and water are just as they are!
So is the bird among the flowers.

Giving my everything to the Peoples Official Plan brought me home in a new way, beyond my neighborhood but closer than the international settings of my professional life. It rooted me in matters affecting my immediate surroundings and nurtured a sense of belonging to a territory and a community of people united in common cause. I felt part of a social movement bigger than all of us, yet grounded in local action. POP, with its attention to people and place, embodied the "glocal" mind set needed to address the climate, biodiversity and justice issues of our species.

When I surfaced from the final hectic weeks, after almost three years of effort, the pandemic, an illegal occupation of downtown Ottawa and a once-in-a-lifetime windstorm had swept through the city, leaving trauma and devastation in their wake. Sadly, efforts to "hold the line" on urban expansion, led valiantly by Ecology Ottawa on behalf of POP, had failed. Ottawa City Council, under Mayor Watson, approved the largest expansion of the urban boundary in two decades, caving to urban developer financial interests. Developer

Still image from the musical video "Doug Ford's Favourite Things."

influence in the Mayor's office, and unwillingness to break with the *status quo*, opened up more rural and agricultural lands for new, car-dependent subdivisions than any previous municipal government. Reason combined with massive public mobilization had done little to change the course of local carbon history.

Ottawa's new Official Plan, with its large carbon footprint, fell prey a year later to an even more cynical political move, this time by the Conservative Provincial Government of Doug Ford. Without any debate or option for appeal, the province announced in November 2022 that the City of Ottawa Official Plan would include 500 additional hectares of urban sprawl, over and above what had already been included. Urban developers, the owners of the additional land, were delighted.

The autocratic fiat was a disconcerting exercise of raw political power, and part of a broader set of provincial policies that have provoked significant opposition. Only time will tell what becomes of the struggle against Bill 23, developer incursions into the Toronto Greenbelt and the chaos in rural Ontario released by a blind and deaf provincial government beholden to the forces of developer greed.

My contribution to the Ottawa-based opposition to Bill 23, and to Christmas cheer in 2022, was to produce a satirical music video on the likely impacts of the bill. I wrote lyrics set to the tune of the

Hammerstein and Rodgers song *My Favourite Things* from *The Sound of Music*, brought to life musically by Paul's vocal talents. While not exactly a viral success, it drew 430 views in a few days and was a great emotional release for me and others. We had no choice but to laugh and carry on, like birds among the flowers.

10. Entering the marketplace with helping hands

Ragged and bare-footed, you approach the market and the streets.
Even covered in dust, why would the laughter cease?
The bees and buttterflies are happy because flowers have bloomed on a withered tree.

Struggles never end, which means they also need to be paced and balanced with what gives joy and meaning to life. I found my oasis in trees and in helping people in the city think and organize differently.

An op-ed I published in the *Ottawa Citizen*, "How closing Ottawa bus lanes can open a green corridor" proposed that Ottawa close a downtown street once clogged with cars and buses made redundant by a new light rail transit line. Fewer vehicles were needed on a major downtown street. "Rip it up!" I said.

The idea of turning a downtown street into a linear park with big, mature trees, dedicated cycle lanes and places to sit and walk is now under serious consideration. Following the 2022 occupation of downtown Ottawa by anti-vaccine extremists posing as truckers, talk turned to dramatically rethinking Wellington Street as it passes in front of Canada's Parliament. Never again, said the thousands of downtown residents that lived through relentless honking of air horns from big rigs, closed businesses and weeks of intimidation, harassment and hateful conduct by the occupiers. Consultations are underway to make the street closure to traffic a reality.

My inspiration for the opinion piece came from a less traumatic experience several years earlier. In the summer of 2019, my neighbours in Champlain Park had come out to literally cart away 400 small squares of pavement from Pontiac Street. The community and Jeff Leiper, the City Councillor for Kitchissippi Ward, had lobbied to close a one-hundred-metre-long section of the under-utilized street and turn it into a new green space. It now connects the neighbourhood park and residential area to the Ottawa River, allowing people

Neighbours de-paving Pontiac Avenue, Ottawa.

to pass unimpeded and storm water to soak into the ground instead of running off through storm sewers.

It became evident immediately after the de-paving that other actions were needed to make the most of the public space and to improve its overall aesthetic appeal. Broken fences, dead trees and abandoned gravel parking areas along the roadway that had gone unnoticed or were tolerated prior to closure of the street marred the new experience. This prompted neighbours and me—Catherine, Kris, John and others—to dig holes, build terraces and establish planting beds for several hundred trees and a native pollinator garden along the de-paved former street.

The Miyawaki method of tree planting—high density and high diversity trees and shrubs—allowed us to seed a native forest ecosystem one hundred metres long on a former gravel parking strip. A gardening technique called Hügelkultur—planting in small piles of rotting wood, leaves and soil—created conditions in shallow rocky soils for tiny saplings to take root in open patches of the neighbourhood woodlands.

In a terrace, we planted "near native" species from northeastern North America, anticipating the forest species mix likely to thrive here in a warmer climate. Ecologists call the strategy "assisted migration." Fruit-bearing plants were added, including wild strawberries,

Monarch butterfly on white turtlehead. Photo by Catherine Shearer.

highbush cranberries, american hazelnuts and a McIntosh apple tree. I selected the McIntosh because this world-famous apple variety was first noticed as a unique cultivar on a farm just beyond the Ottawa city limits.

We also began to flag and protect rare native trees like the rock elm coming up on their own in the nearby woodlands—resurgent nature aided by helping hands.

What was once a paved street is now an expression of another possible world, hosting native bees, butterflies and birds. It calms and nurtures the people that walk there. While the trees are tiny and their long term fate uncertain, the experience of connection blooms on the apple tree.

EPILOGUE

< Yellow birches and lilies, Temagami..

Epilogue

Death is in my future. Of that I can be certain. But what of the desires, projects and dreams I have dedicated so much of my life to? Given the current state of affairs—climate breakdown, surveillance capitalism, the rise of autocracies, runaway A.I.—what responses in me can prompt possible futures compatible with what I imagine the world could be?

The act of reflecting and writing on my life, like the quest of the ox herder to find the essential self, has helped me identify three steps on the path.

The first is to tap into the power that comes from connection to self, that which guides and provides the spark needed to encounter the defeats and celebrate the joys. Human life offers so many paths to self that there can be no excuse for not taking one, two or many more. The pleasures of the body, silent meditation before a blank wall, gardening, reading, making a musical instrument or a child's chair, drying seed under moonlight, poetry, walking on stilts, our breath, our fears, our sense of awe; these are all available to us like tantric secrets, practices that help us experience the fullness of life and connection to our own inner peace. The gift of connection to self is the raw material and the electric charge that gives direction and meaning to who we are, what we do and how we learn about the world.

Belonging in an attentive relationship to the self helps us connect to infinite possibilities. The opposite is also true. Failing to connect fully to the inner life cuts us off from the joy and diversity of human experience. The balance is simple: taking "time in" connects us to the present moment and makes it possible to discover the world through our senses, from the inside out.

The second step, and call to action, is to connect to the community of others, including those strange to us or suffering in ways we do not. For more than four decades I have been moved by the realization that we cannot live for ourselves alone, a simple truth that arrived in my youthful hands on a postcard from a friend. I've carried this idea in my head, heart and hands ever since, examining it and extending it through my own personal and professional choices. I've tried to enlarge my heart, to feel more compassion and to do what I can with and for others.

This is the work of Karma Yoga, the yoga of action on the gifts of self and the principle of solidarity. My core task has been to honour and develop the gifts I was born and raised with: steadfastness; positivity; integrity of word and deed. Other gifts I discovered and nurtured along the way have brought me firmly into relationship with others: a capacity to bring people together around causes and activities; the courage to join the projects of others rather than insist on my own; the calm and confidence to stand before a crowd and listen. I came to trust these gifts and to use them to develop genuine connections with people and places, whether near or far, over time or for a brief period.

My practice of solidarity, often clumsy even after all these years, is how I belong to and seek to contribute to community. It has been a constant in my journey from art to anthropology to a form of research grounded in people and positive action on the social justice issues that confront us today. The blessings and struggles of connecting to others, and, inevitably, losing that connection through distance, changing circumstances or death, is, I believe, how we find our own way.

The third step on my path, and most compelling act of imagination, is to connect with nature as though it was my own body, which it is. When I was a young man, living in the Yukon and then developing a thesis in Canadian Studies focused on deconstructing Dürer's etching of The Garden of Eden, I felt the disconnect of our society from nature. Hiking, canoeing, skiing and witnessing examples of self-provisioning from the land brought me into the orbit of the sensual world and the experience of being in and of nature. The truth of this material existence is always available to me, even as I walk to the bus stop.

A later connection to the practice of agriculture, rather than the flora and fauna of wild places, opened my mind to the realization that if we are to survive and thrive as a human community, we need to connect to the life world in fundamentally new ways. The work of farmers of Bangladesh, India, Mexico, Honduras and elsewhere, and insights into their practices from Farhad, Farida, Satheesh and other teachers, helped to show me another way to relate to the earth and to other human beings. This is not some abstract proposition or New Age spirituality but rather a concrete political demand.

My outlook on life is basically positive and hopeful, but my politics are angry and a bit old fashioned. Like many on the political left, I'm committed to calling out fascist practices, laissez-faire capitalism and the extreme concentration of private wealth and power. Occupiers, deniers and defenders of sexism, racism and violence are, in my politics, to be resisted directly and relentlessly.

I also have no patience for those that say "go slow" in the face of injustice and an unprecedented ecological crisis. Greta Thunberg and Martin Luther King are my heroes in this regard. King, in his 1963 "I Have a Dream" speech said, "We are now faced with the fact that tomorrow is today. We are confronted with the fierce urgency of now. In the unfolding conundrum of life and history, there is such a thing as being too late." While he was speaking to the urgency of racial equality, the same admonishment applies today to a Western political culture of *status quo* and self-interested timidity that continues to lead us off the cliff.

The gravity of our situation is partly hidden by the misinformation that circulates regarding the causes and consequences of the current state of affairs. Of graver concern, however, are the many, many layers of *miseducation* regarding what we have become as a global society. The climate and biodiversity disaster, the gluttony of consumer society, the legacies of colonialism, bullshit jobs, commodity fetishism, the concentration of property and wealth—forces that define our material conditions and threaten all life at the same time—are not seriously examined and questioned. It is even hard to say what the problem is without sounding terribly out of date or overly earnest, and yet the answer could not be clearer: three centuries of capitalism have completely overwhelmed our senses and our desires, shaping us through advertising and manufactured consent to our own slavery. These impersonal and manic forces block the way to anything remotely sustainable and just.

Meanwhile, the State acts as a handmaiden to the power of wealth and the mindless logic of profit voraciously feeding on people and the Earth. Western governments hide behind the illusion of individual freedoms in societies rife with inequities and systemic injustices, making transformative collective action nearly impossible, and empowerment an epic struggle. They also crow about their own moral superiority, all the while supporting authoritarian regimes that serve their interests. Plainly put, we do not yet live in a free and fully human society where truly new paths can be charted. How we respond to this situation is the task before us.

These old tropes, strung together in black and white on a page, ring true to me but do not tell the whole story. Fire the truth in the pen! The story I tell in this memoir is not a manifesto on the politics needed to lift us out of the historical conundrum. That ability is not one of my gifts. The memoir is simply an account of a journey with countless setbacks and countless gains in understanding, often forgotten or ignored by me in the struggle with the ox. Genuine efforts to connect worlds are recalled here and expressed through my art as honestly as I can and with a plea to save ourselves from being extinguished as a collectivity before we can even take flight.

I sit before an early morning fire at Temagami, the family cottage that is more home to me than any place else in the world. Instead of dwelling in feelings of fear, anger and sadness over the future of the earth and the human species, I decide to take the canoe out into the lake. I head for the birch stand across from the cabin kitchen. I'm on a mission to adjust the chicken wire my father installed years ago to protect the trees at the shoreline from harvest by beavers. My mother and my grandmother both loved the view from the cottage kitchen, and my father sought to keep it alive long after both had passed away.

I decide to look for chaga, a fungus with medicinal properties that grows on paper birch and yellow birch trees. Leaving the canoe at the shore, I walk deep into a birch grove, scanning for the black outer layer of the fungus. I see some, but too high up the tree to reach. The birch stand extends farther, but I'm on the edge of becoming unsure about the precise way back to the canoe.

Instinctively, I turn my face to the sun, feeling the direction of light through the leaves. A loon on the lake calls, a high pitch shifting to a low pitch and then into a silence that seems to linger in the air. I walk back towards the shore and come across a chaga growth tucked into a notch between two branching stems.

The words repeat silently in my mind, "This is what is given to me. Thank you. This is what is given to me. Thank you." Satisfied, I consider how much chaga to take for my purpose.

Wind in the cedars, Temagami, Canada.

Acknowledgements

The choices I have made over the course of my life—my becoming, being and belonging—are not entirely of my own making. They have been shaped by countless people, the ideas we discussed, the situations we observed together, the actions taken and the paths not followed. Friends have been mentors, people wiser than I in some way with whom I have had lengthy and multifaceted relationships. Young people calling for climate justice or freedom from oppression have also inspired me with their courage to stand up and be counted. To all of these courageous beings, some identified in these pages and others simply held lovingly in my thoughts, I give my heartfelt thanks.

I launched the memoir project and announced my retirement from a professional life with a virtual sixty-fifth birthday party in November, 2020, attended over the course of the day by family and friends from around the world. I realized then that I was in something of a sweet spot in my life, with professional and personal contacts still in place going back to my youth.

I started not with writing, but rather by curating a collection of my paintings and photographs from over the years. The images, posted to a temporary website, provided an entry point into virtual conversations with friends and colleagues on our lives together, accomplishments and lessons learned. Shared memories, fact-checking events long past and reflections on how and why we evolved professionally and personally, helped me ground the exercise in heart felt stories rather than abstract ideas and project themes.

My friend and colleague Jacques gently coached me into being the centre of my own story, and ambitious about what I had to say. The courage to think, a Socratic insight, but also to cultivate understanding and compassion, are qualities Jacques has shown me throughout our long association, making this book as much a dialogue with him as an account of my own.

Eleanor Millard, a longtime Yukon friend and an accomplished writer in her own right, helped me find my narrative voice. She also spent countless hours reading and correcting errors. This helped create the foundation that kept me going despite many doubts along the way.

Erwin Dreessen was the first to read the complete manuscript in one go, from start to finish, and caution against puffery creeping into my stories. Emma Bider, a young anthropologist with her own passion for trees, read later versions of the manuscript with a critical eye and attention to detail. Both of these readers played pivotal roles in helping me improve the manuscript and, hopefully, avoid me completely embarrassing myself. I am very grateful to both.

Other readers provided consequential feedback and tips on various details and impressions of the book that helped me think more deeply about what I was trying to accomplish. The questions and reactions to draft text helped me shape the narrative and presentation. My sincere thanks, in chronological order, to Charles Hodgson, Graydon Carter, Derek Byerlee, Grant Dowdell, John Lodder, Richard Marquardt, Yvan Breton, Shahid Zia, Wardie Leppan, Farhad Mahzar, Farida Akhter, Luisa Pare, Bernard Triomphe, Melinda Smale, Mauricio Bellon, Pat Roy Mooney, Paul Johanis, Steve Buckles and Donna Patrick. To all of these people, I give thanks.

Magdalene Carson of New Leaf Publication Design, with her finely tuned aesthetic and attention to detail, made it possible to present the printed and electronic book far more beautifully and elegantly than I had thought possible. For this I am very grateful.

I would also like to acknowledge my brothers Steve and Casey, who, as siblings, have shaped me more than they realize. I couldn't be prouder and happier to have them in my life. This is true too of my two sons, Daniel and Ryan, and of my growing relationship with Ryan's wife Anabelle and her extended family.

My wife, Debra, is my lodestar, truest friend and love of my life. Thank you. Migwitch.

All images in this book are my own, except for a few gifted by friends and noted accordingly. My thanks for their generosity.

Printed in Great Britain
by Amazon

49344541R00205